The Stranger Artist

Praise for *The Stranger Artist*

'Utterly compelling. Vivid and unflinching. Beautifully written. An exceptional and intimate portrait of artistic collaboration informed by a deep knowledge of place, people and culture, this is the story of how Indigenous art emerges in the Kimberley, inseparable from the Country itself, and the embers of history. *The Stranger Artist* captures the texture of everyday life in the Kimberley in a way no other book has done before.'

Mark McKenna, author of *An Eye for Eternity: The Life of Manning Clark* and *Looking for Blackfellas' Point*

'Sprague's hauntingly beautiful descriptions of country, his deep understanding of two cultures in collision, and his sumptuous descriptions of the act of painting, mark this work as a literary gem.'

Judges' comments, 2021 Prime Minister's Literary Award

'Lucid, moving, and bears the mark of first-hand experience. This book is destined to become an invaluable accounting of a ground-breaking art group that was also an audacious political gesture.'

Robyn Ferrell, *The Canberra Times*

'The rise and fall of Tony Oliver and the Jirrawun artists is one of the more flamboyant and maverick episodes in the story of Australian Indigenous Art. In his forensic exploration of the partnership that promised a new model for the production and sale of Aboriginal art, and the central relationship between art impresario Oliver and the Gija master painter Paddy Bedford, Quentin Sprague has written a grand cross-cultural tale of genius, co-dependency, brotherhood, mythmaking and hubris.'

Kim Mahood, author of *Wandering With Intent* and *Position Doubtful*

'The absorbing origin story of an Aboriginal painting movement like no other. Quentin Sprague draws us into a world of heat, busted LandCruisers and community decay with a lyrical portrait of tragic hope where art and cultural exchange come to life.'

Ashleigh Wilson, author of *Brett Whiteley: Art, Life and the Other Thing* and *On Artists*

The Stranger Artist

Life at the edge of Kimberley painting

QUENTIN SPRAGUE

Hardie Grant
BOOKS

This edition published in 2023 by Hardie Grant Books,
an imprint of Hardie Grant Publishing
First published in 2020

Hardie Grant Books (Melbourne)
Building 1, 658 Church Street
Richmond, Victoria 3121

Hardie Grant Books (London)
5th & 6th Floors
52–54 Southwark Street
London SE1 1UN

hardiegrant.com/au/books

A catalogue record for this book is available from the National Library of Australia

The Stranger Artist
ISBN 978 1 74379 932 1

10 9 8 7 6 5 4 3 2 1

Cover design by Pfisterer + Freeman
Front and back cover photography by Simon Georgeff
Inside cover photography by Alana Hunt
Internal design by Mietta Yans
Typeset in Sina Nova 11/15pt by Cannon Typesetting
Printed in Australia by Griffin Press, an Accredited
ISO AS/NZS 14001 Environmental Management System printer.

We move as if we had no shadows and were
unperturbed by that appalling fact.
Roberto Bolaño

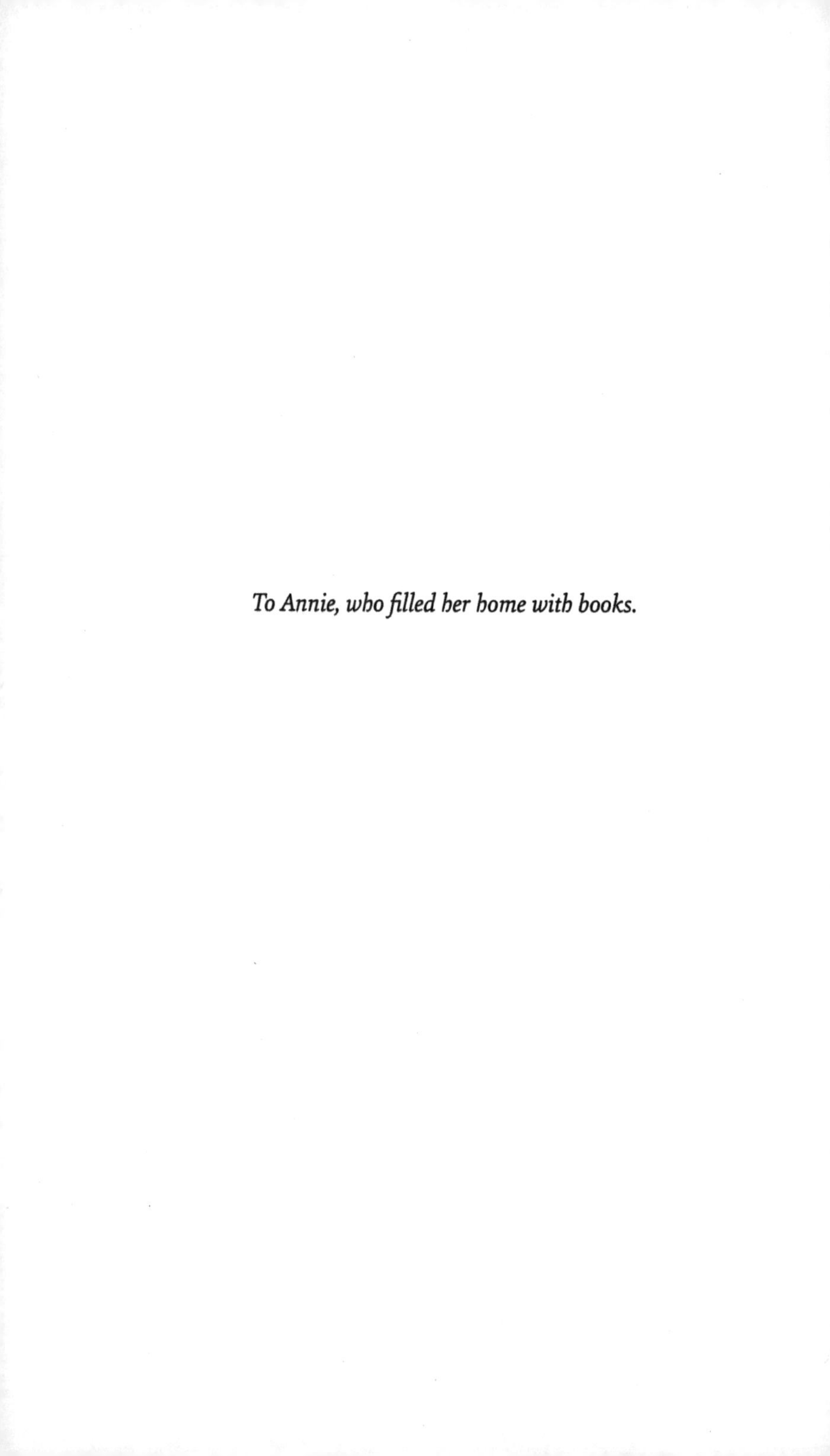

To Annie, who filled her home with books.

Contents

Aboriginal and Torres Strait Islander readers are advised that this book contains images and written depictions of people who have passed away.

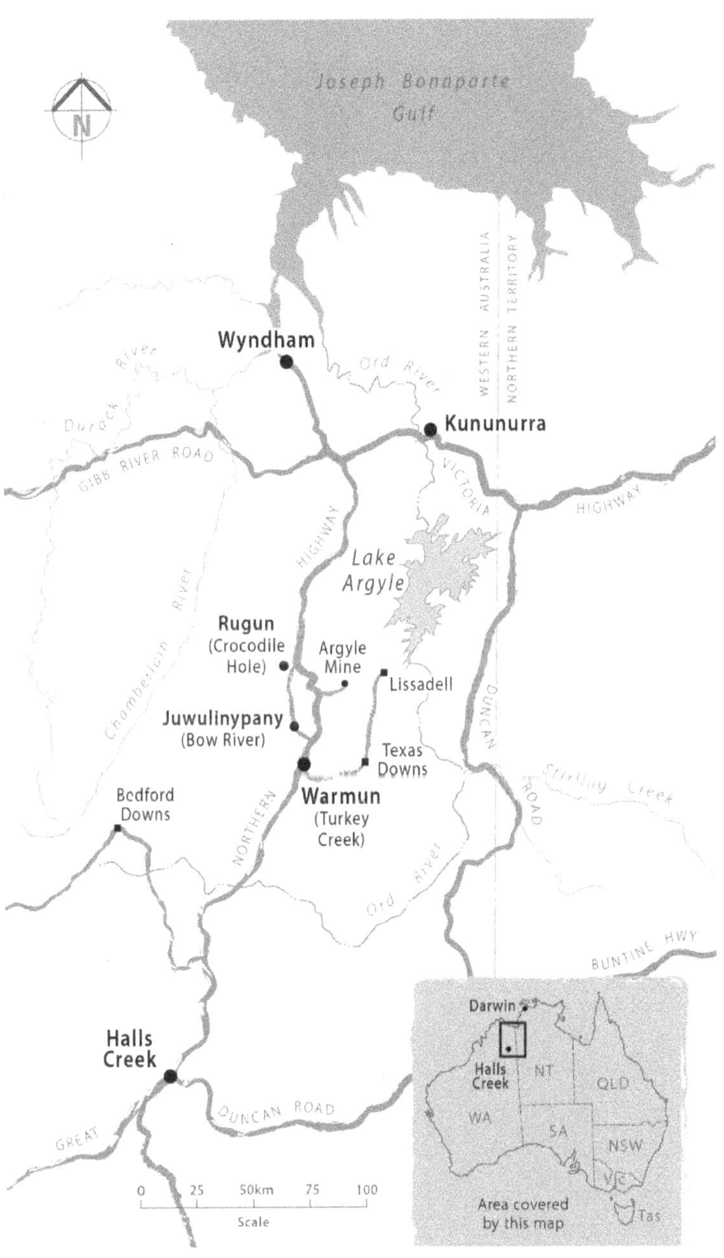
N
Joseph Bonaparte Gulf
WESTERN AUSTRALIA
NORTHERN TERRITORY
Wyndham
Ord River
Kununurra
Durack River
GIBB RIVER ROAD
VICTORIA
HIGHWAY
HIGHWAY
Lake Argyle
Chamberlain River
Rugun (Crocodile Hole)
Argyle Mine
Lissadell
Juwulinypany (Bow River)
Texas Downs
Warmun (Turkey Creek)
DUNCAN ROAD
Stirling Creek
Bedford Downs
NORTHERN
Ord River
BUNTINE HWY
Halls Creek
DUNCAN ROAD
GREAT
0 25 50km 75 100
Scale
Darwin
Halls Creek
NT
QLD
WA
SA
NSW
Vic
Tas
Area covered by this map

Prologue: Vietnam

At first, Tony Oliver would never remember the dreams in full. They were strange, impressionistic sequences: the faces of those he had known, the old people who had taken him in and guided him, the young ones he'd so often seen buried.

Black faces, all of them. He'd lived in the Kimberley for nearly a decade and couldn't count the funerals he'd attended.

He would wake tired, his sheets tangled about him, sweating.

That morning he woke waiting for his great friend Paddy Bedford to die.

•

He had said goodbye to Paddy only two weeks earlier, just before departing to visit his girlfriend Le Chi in Vietnam. By the end he hated the Kimberley as much as he loved it, but he knew he couldn't truly leave until after Paddy's death. It would be unthinkable; he and Paddy enjoyed a closeness he found hard to articulate.

Painting lay at the centre of their friendship, and always had. Soon after the two had first met in the community of Warmun, Paddy had become famous for his roughly elegant canvases, for the sweeping lines and ellipses he traced there, for the fields of muddy white that, in the crowded world of Aboriginal art, were so uniquely his. Many among the art world had come to know him as 'PB', which is how the ex-stockman signed his paintings, but few knew his stoic presence in real terms, nor his quick laugh and distinctive humour. Few knew his life story, how the hardness of it sat in such contrast to his generosity of spirit.

Few knew him as well as Tony.

He had been there, watching Paddy as near every painting the old man made took shape. 'It's like we were tied together, climbing the mountain,'

Tony would say years later, attempting to capture the feeling. Consciously or not, he would be paraphrasing Georges Braque's words explaining what it felt like to invent cubism with Pablo Picasso.

Recently, Paddy had been almost marooned by failing health, too frail to get around much at all. There had been misguided talk that doing some painting might be 'good therapy' for him, but it wasn't. A male nurse had brought him out to the studio Tony had set up at Wyndham, but by that stage watching Paddy try to paint was heartbreaking. With the nurse in the background, the intimacy of the studio was gone. Tony couldn't assist, couldn't steady Paddy's reaching arm. The old man made a mess of it, his once perfect hand perfect no more.

The day they said goodbye, Paddy arrived at the Wyndham studio again, but this time any talk of painting had vanished: everyone, it seemed, understood. The nurse knew to give the two men space – not much, maybe half an hour – and Tony simply pushed Old Man in his silver wheelchair around the studio, past the new paintings by his friend and countryman, Rammey Ramsey, past the big windows at the end that looked out across the spear grass.

Although Paddy was far from shy, Tony had known him to most often speak quietly, sometimes little more than a rasping whisper. To hear him, one would have to lean close. Sometimes Paddy would reach out a hand, place it firmly on his interlocutor's shoulder, and draw them closer still. It was likely he did this because he was partially deaf and wanted to hear more clearly, but just as often he did it to share small intimacies.

Once, he drew the art dealer Dallas Gold in close and said in his sandpaper voice, 'I love you', as if it were the simplest thing in the world, as if old Aboriginal men told white people this all the time.

Now, with Tony, he wanted to know if his money was right.

He asked this quietly, but his concern was clear – his health had stopped him from painting and he had found it harder and harder to visit the studio. He was worried. Previously, he'd been taken to the Kununurra bank on a regular basis so he could check his balance, something he would do with habitual flair, sometimes wearing his button-down shirt over nothing but a pair of bright satin boxers, his walking stick clasped in his hand. Old Man was largely illiterate, and possessed only working numeracy, but in his final years, the news was always good – painting had made him a wealthy man.

Towards the end, Tony had extricated himself from the money side of things near completely, but that day he knew Paddy was simply seeking reassurance. He told him that his money was fine, that he would be well looked after.

Then Paddy wanted to show him his new purchase: the white LandCruiser the nurse had driven him out in, down the gun-barrel-straight highway from Kununurra.

He was so proud of it.

Cars had always brought the two of them together. Paddy loved them: there was no greater measure of wealth in the Kimberley than a new LandCruiser. Family could pile in and an old man like Paddy would be driven wherever he wanted to go. The previous year, Tony had gone as far as renting an open-topped red Cadillac and chauffeur to drive Old Man to his retrospective at the Museum of Contemporary Art in Sydney. Tony, who had walked down from the hotel early, was already standing at the entrance as the sleek vehicle arrived: he watched as it crept along the side of the museum and pulled up at the front, back-dropped by the harbour.

The whole scene played as a kind of riff on the art world's vanities – the Cadillac, Paddy immaculately dressed in his three-piece Henry Bucks suit, Rammey Ramsey similarly attired in the seat next to him, both cool behind black sunglasses. But for Tony it was also deadly serious. Back in the Kimberley, in the rundown fibro house outside Wyndham that he called home, he had recently begun a rough collage directly on the kitchen wall. This was partly to keep himself occupied during the long hours he spent alone, but it was also a map of influence, one that charted the kinds of references that he'd always been alert to in the work he'd undertaken with Paddy and the others.

He'd pinned a photograph of the jazz great Dizzy Gillespie next to one of Paddy dressed to the nines during a city visit: Gillespie in his suit and shades, his silver trumpet clasped to his chest; Paddy with his immaculate black felt hat and his neatly knotted tie. Nearby he'd added reproductions of paintings: Bedford's work alongside Tony's enduring favourites, the American Philip Guston, the New Zealander Colin McCahon.

Equivalences.

Shuffle all those pictures together and Tony's work with Bedford began to make sense: like the Cadillac they were icons, all of them, played for maximum effect across the colour line.

At the museum, Paddy was helped into his wheelchair and pushed up the ramp towards the entrance hall. People were still talking among themselves but, as it became clear the artist had arrived, a quiet began to spread.

For Tony the theatre of it was irresistible. It always had been. That's what got him. He knew that symbolism was as important in Bedford's Kimberley life as it was in the white art world. Images were power; they proved knowledge. But they could be recalcitrant and contradictory as well. What better way to signal the old man's success to a crowd of whites than a red Cadillac, this ridiculous vehicle once the domain of American rock 'n' roll stars and oil barons? Tony knew that Paddy understood the symbolism too: none of the whites in the Kimberley – the gardiya, whose lineage extended to the settlers who had taken Bedford's ancestral country by force and killed his people – possessed anything nearly as grand.

Inside, the retrospective unfurled across two floors of the museum's galleries. The first gallery looked especially stunning: it was hung with recent works like *Mad Gap*, with its corner of ochre red and its blushed ground, and *Motor Car Yard – Blanket Lizard Dreaming*, with its central black void like a bolt of velvet against the white wall. The curator, Russell Storer, had offset them beautifully: on the same gallery's far wall a selection of PB's much sought-after works on paper hung in a neat grid, their bright colours anarchic against the sombre tones of nearby canvases. As Tony walked through for the first time, he couldn't help but see it as a measure of the success that he'd helped Paddy achieve, proof that his time in the Kimberley had paid off. But although the experience would form one of the pinnacles of Tony's Kimberley life, doubts had already begun to plague him.

Later, he will question whether he succeeded in his undertaking with Paddy or not, whether the play of icons that came to define their work together had been his alone, or Paddy's too. It was true that Paddy died a millionaire, that in his final years he had wanted for nothing, including the kind of medical care largely unavailable to his countrymen and women. But towards the end, even as Paddy's retrospective was met with widespread acclaim, Tony could never quite ignore how distant all that was from the blunt fact of Kimberley life. Nothing had changed since he'd first arrived; he would wonder if he was once really naive enough to think it would.

It was easy to despair, and he did.

When the two of them said goodbye that day at Wyndham he said, 'Take care, Old Man,' and returned to the studio alone as Paddy was driven away in his new car.

•

Waiting for the call to come was hard.

He sat in the hotel in Vietnam, in the mountains above the coast, where it was cold and the mist lay heavy in the mornings. *So far from the Kimberley*, he thought. Le Chi went sightseeing, but he waited behind.

When his phone rang he received the news quietly, and hung up as the inevitable wave of numbness washed over him. It was a feeling coloured partly by regret: he should have been there holding Old Man's hand as he died; it would have made the shape of their story more complete.

There was also relief, and the sharp spark of guilt that followed. If he was honest with himself he knew that among the small group of artists he'd worked with in the Kimberley, it was Paddy who had kept him there. For all that place had offered him, it had also intensified the darkness he'd always carried. Now he knew he could leave. He had waited until the end and felt now that his conscience would at least partially be clear. He found he couldn't cry, so he sat there alone and began to drink. That particular Kimberley habit would take years to kick.

Later, once he'd slept again, Tony sat with Le Chi in a taxi as it slowly wound its way down the mountain. The houses there were made of lengths of timber, their thatched roofs were arched. They were long and raised off the ground on stilts: in the mist they appeared otherworldly.

Local K'Ho people lined the roadside in procession, quietly ascending against the taxi's descent. It was a religious holiday: the people were dressed in brightly embroidered cloth; there were garlands of flowers and clusters of smoking incense. Young women clutched perfect babies to their chests.

A knot of anxiety began to form slowly in Tony's stomach. He now had a funeral to help organise. This one would have to be a big production. It would need to honour Paddy as both a famous painter and a manambarrany, a senior Lawman. Family would come from across the greater Kimberley, art collectors and other supporters from around the country.

How many people? Five hundred? A thousand?

The grave would have to be dug at Bow River, in the cemetery that almost seven years earlier Tony had helped reopen for the burial of Paddy's brother-in-law, Timmy Timms. It was hard to believe it was seven years since the death of the old Bow River boss had brought a mass of people to the tiny community.

Now it was Paddy's turn.

Old Man.

As the mountains gave way to the tablelands below, Tony steeled himself for the weeks to come.

Warmun / Turkey Creek

1.

Picture a vehicle moving at speed through a landscape, the near-empty highway a straight black line before it.

The vehicle is a red Toyota LandCruiser and is registered to the Gija painter Freddie Timms; the landscape is one of stark red ranges, of dry earth scattered evenly by clumps of spinifex and sprays of young cane grass. It is only sparsely treed: gums, spindly acacias, the beautifully malformed boabs that seem spaced at impossibly regular intervals. Later in the year, by the time the low fires of the dry season have moved through, the flanks of the ranges will be stripped clean, and the crumbling, ore-rich bones of the place exposed. In the heat of the day, it will appear as if the country is breathing with almost malevolent energy. But now it's far softer: after the regular rains of the wet, the earth is veiled by a wash of bright green.

Tony Oliver, an ex art dealer from Melbourne, is sitting in the cabin next to Freddie. Although Tony's gallery has been closed for a number of years, and his own practice as a painter has never quite found form, art remains his passion. Tony has not been in the Kimberley long, but already the possibilities seem endless. He and Freddie are starting a painting group together, one that will unfold independently of government funding and will hinge on the distinctive work of artists like Freddie. But Tony's relationship to Freddie is far from transactional. They are also friends driven by a shared desire to try and make something together with what skills they have.

Beyond the windscreen the landscape flings past.

•

Their day has begun early, they have risen with the dawn in Kununurra, and driven out of town and across the bridge at the dam while the sun still hangs low on the horizon.

Over the years they will drive this highway together countless times; each journey will blur into the next. They might stop at the tiny settlement of Doon Doon so Freddie can visit family – perhaps to drop off some money, or collect a rough cut of recently butchered beef – or they might continue past. From there the highway begins to curve smoothly through a series of shallow valleys. The ranges give way to hills and, here and there, strange sentinel-like rock forms. Freddie, who often appears taciturn and brooding in the presence of whites but already knows Tony well enough to trust him, might point to them, and in his clipped, slightly severe manner, recount the names and stories of these places. Tony's learning, but he still sees only with Western eyes.

That rock, for instance, which rises almost vertically from a surrounding hill, is known as Pompey's Pillar by European settlers. Gija call it Neminuwarlin. It was there that an Aboriginal outlaw called Major once hid from a punitive party of police constables, trackers and station workers intent on his capture or death. This story is one of Freddie's favourites: his grandmother and her older sister were among Major's entourage. A lifetime later Freddie rode that country as a stockman and, through his grandmother, carried Major's story with him.

As they pass Neminuwarlin, surely Freddie gestures towards the site. Surely he makes mention of the paintings he has already made of Major's story (Tony knows them well). For Tony, the pieces of his friend's world fall more securely into place.

The signs for the pastoral stations begin around this point. One, which reads 'Lissadell', arrives on the highway's western side.

Freddie has known Lissadell since his youth – at ten years of age he was taken there to live after a childhood in the bush. His father was sent to Bungarun, the leprosarium far to the west, near Derby, and died soon after. Freddie was raised alongside the station manager's children: as they grew, they learnt to speak Gija, just as Freddie learnt English.

These are the kinds of stories that Freddie has for the places they pass: how the manager's daughter later cooked for him after long days of station labour, how he'd sit in the homestead kitchen for his meals, how this was a sign of the esteem in which he was held.

By the time he left for the outstation of Frog Hollow in 1987, Freddie had risen to the rank of head stockman. By then he was the last Aboriginal worker at Lissadell: it was just him and a handful of white jackaroos.

In step with the turn-off to Lissadell comes another story.

Since the 1980s the station's entrance has been shared by Rio Tinto's Argyle diamond mine, which by the time Tony and Freddie pass in 1998 has become the largest producer of natural diamonds in the world. Look up above the highway and a neatly tiered gap in the ridge line draws slowly into focus. The Gija who drive this stretch daily – coming and going between Kununurra and Warmun in a procession of overloaded vehicles in various stages of disrepair – have, over the last decade and a half, watched that gap open in staggered increments.

In his first years in the Kimberley, Tony will hear the story for that place in many variations: how the Ngarranggarni women hunted Daiwul, the barramundi ancestor, in the creek there, pushing tangled clumps of spinifex through the shallow waters as a net; how the barramundi leapt not only over the women, but over nearby Mount Pitt too, and then became stuck between two hills. Her attempts to struggle free scattered her glittering scales (or was it her eggs?) that in turn brought forth the miners and their trucks. As they dug in search of the pink diamonds that would soon be world famous, they set in motion all kinds of trouble in the Gija spiritual realm.

Along that same stretch of highway, Freddie and Tony pass the dirt turn-offs to Crocodile Hole and Bow River: the first just before the mine, the second after. 'Rugun', Freddie might say, or 'Juwulinypany', offering Tony the Gija name for each of the tiny outstations where Tony will soon live, one after the other.

The two men won't stop that day – the road into each outstation is long and rough – but will instead continue towards the roadhouse at Turkey Creek, where, on the other side of the highway, the community of Warmun lies sprawled beneath a Kangaroo Dreaming site.

There, at a rundown house in bottom camp, a friend of Freddie's called Chocolate Thomas is already waiting.

2.

Some two years before, Tony had arrived early at a house in Ivanhoe, a suburb in Melbourne's north-east.

It was a simple place, only partially furnished, and owned by an entrepreneur turned art dealer called Peter Harrison who had recently closed a fledgling tech business and opened a gallery called Kimberley Art.

Harrison's venture was straightforward: he was flying Freddie down to Melbourne to prepare a new suite of paintings that Harrison would then sell. He had worked directly with Freddie before and this time was paying Tony to act as both studio assistant and minder. It would take ten days, Harrison had said, and, because Tony needed the money and was already familiar with Freddie's work from Kimberley Art's stockroom, he'd readily agreed to do it.

Inside, one room had already been set aside as a studio in anticipation of Freddie's arrival: there was a stack of blank canvases there, along with paint in various colours. Tony waited there and when Harrison arrived with Freddie, fresh from the airport, he introduced them and then left them there together.

Tony had been unsure what to expect, but he now sized Freddie up. The Gija man was tall and, although he was quiet, he seemed self-assured. He was also handsome. At barely fifty, Freddie was as healthy then as Tony would ever see him. His clothes appeared meticulously chosen: boots, jeans, a black stock hat, a deep blue RM Williams shirt, the colour of which would sear itself in Tony's memory. Freddie's belt even had an elaborate silver buckle on it.

All this was worn with absolute ease and although it was a decade since Freddie had worked in the cattle industry, it was clear that his clothes spoke of that time. *A real stockman*, Tony thought. Tony would soon learn that near everything about Freddie was passed through this lens, even his practice as an artist. All his distinctively spare work showed country that spread across the stations he'd once worked on: Lissadell, Old Greenvale, Bow River. The canvases stacked in the studio would soon be named for those places and others like them. In the coming days, Freddie would paint them all from memory as Tony watched: the hills and waterholes, the river-ways and roads that bound that country together.

Although shy in those first moments, Freddie hid it well. He wore a stoic-seeming expression composed of a careful scowl and slightly pursed lips – it would be days until Tony saw him smile. Tony was nervous too, not sure where to begin. Harrison had left the fridge stocked with beer, so they had each taken a can and sat there at the kitchen table, drinking.

Tony would recall an antique clock on the wall, ticking away above them. As he tried his best to draw Freddie out in conversation, the clock marked the many silences with excruciating precision.

•

Freddie was already an old hand as far as the painting business was concerned.

In those years the Aboriginal art market was booming: over the previous decade and a half, attention had spread quickly from the distinctive and optically vibrant canvases of the Western Desert, replete with their roundels and fields of dotting, to work from other areas: the bark paintings of Arnhem Land and the large, all-over 'abstractions' from the Utopia region in the Central Desert. Against that backdrop what had quickly been dubbed the East Kimberley painting movement had carved its own niche – another regional style that marked yet another chapter in what then seemed a constantly unfurling narrative.

As far as the white art world was concerned, the 'inventor' of East Kimberley art was a man of Gija and Wangkajanga descent called Rover Thomas, or Joolama as he was also known by his countrymen and women. Rover still lived in Warmun, the largest of the Gija communities, but by the time Tony and Freddie met he was at the tail end of what had been a short but storied painting career. Like Freddie, he had once been a stockman and at the pastoral industry's height had driven cattle from the desert to the Kimberley but, following a series of prophetic dreams, he had eventually become a celebrated artist.

That's what had started it all: dreams. It was almost too perfect.

The story went something like this: Rover had fallen asleep one night in 1975, not long after an accident on the highway near Warmun had fatally injured his kinship mother-in-law. Near death, she had been airlifted to the Wyndham Hospital and had flown above the vast patchwork of Gija country before succumbing to her injuries mid-flight.

Her spirit continued its passage, moving as a shadow across the landscape. She was accompanied by a changing cast of other spirits: at one point they stood together on a rocky outcrop at the edge of Kununurra and watched in the distance as a rainbow serpent in the guise of Cyclone Tracy destroyed Darwin, far to the north-east. She returned to Rover in his dreams to show him the path her spirit had traced, the vast catalogue of ancestral narratives that had unfolded below. She gave him the songs and images for those places and, when he woke, Rover made of them something new.

Much was held in that vision and, as his sequence of dreams played out, Rover transposed them into a dance cycle that focused on his mother-in-law's journey. It wasn't until 1979 that the resulting performance – by then known as the *Guirr-Guirr* – took hold in Warmun, but when it did it held fast: it was soon performed widely. The songs had by then been arranged as verses; the images were translated into paintings, the first of them created by others under Rover's careful direction.

Those first works were simple, but for that reason they were all the more striking. They showed the iconic Kimberley landscape as short sequences of planar symbols, isolated on single-colour backgrounds and outlined in white dots. For paint, the artists used locally sourced ochre, ground up and mixed with water. Glue would later be used as a binder, but at first it was spinifex gum, even kangaroo blood. Within the *Guirr-Guirr*, the paintings were intended as little more than props: objects to be deployed as part of the performance's narrative cycle: a visual accompaniment to the pattern laid out by the songs.

They were revealed at key moments, held aloft by dancers: *this* place, the paintings intoned, *this* ancestral being.

Similar images could be seen in caves throughout the region – Tony would later be shown a handful of them, glowing like icons on dusty rock faces – where the simplicity of them made immediate sense: they had to be seen in the half-light and understood readily. In the firelight of ceremony, things were essentially the same: simplified images moved faster through the darkness, lodged more readily in the minds of viewers.

To those who would one day look back on the movement's beginnings it would seem a foregone conclusion that such paintings had so quickly become items of desire for white collectors. They were as beautiful as they were pragmatic. Materially, they embodied the place where they had been made with near-brutal precision. In those years Warmun was still new, much of it still under construction: a new pocket of housing, a health clinic, a community store; all this was being built as the early paintings of the movement were being realised. It is no surprise that the early works made use of whatever detritus could be found around the community's dusty streets, or salvaged from the local dump: an irregular offcut of particle board, or a repurposed plywood packing crate. These were the substrates that carried the first paintings. They were later deemed 'masterpieces' in the white art world, but the material they were made on would always reflect their origins.

As he worked with Freddie in Ivanhoe, Tony soon learnt that, for this reason, it didn't matter what a painting had been made on – canvas or not – to Freddie it was always a 'board'.

'I'll start a new board now,' Freddie would say by way of direction and Tony would set up another canvas. He would prime it with a base coat colour and then mix Freddie's paint to the right consistency.

Then Freddie would begin.

He'd start with a thin brush dipped in black, carving the canvas into sections with an arcing line, or mapping out a series of near-perfect ellipses. Tony would watch as a resolved composition was laid down in minutes.

'How many boards have we done now?' Freddie might ask after a few days in the studio had elapsed and Tony would count the finished works, one by one.

Boards.

Simply by way of naming, the history of the movement was always close.

•

Rover himself didn't begin painting until 1982, but when he did he soon became known as the movement's figurehead. As a painter he had a way with space; like Freddie after him, he could construct a near flawless composition with a few judiciously chosen lines.

But he also had the character for fame: he clearly enjoyed moving in the white world. When he represented Australia at the Venice Biennale in 1990, he was mobbed by art world enthusiasts as he moved through the Giardini: everyone wanted a piece of the Aboriginal painter from Australia. Rover, an amiable character with a ready smile, welcomed the attention as if it were nothing.

Tony had first seen Rover's paintings in the late 1980s, at Deutscher Fine Art in Melbourne's Fitzroy. At first he was simply enthused, but by the time he attended Rover's 1994 survey at the National Gallery of Australia he was a convert. For Tony, Rover's practice was one of near sublime beauty. There were fields of open colour cut through by lines of ragged dotting; the surfaces were dusty and tactile, in themselves a gentle revelation. He read the accompanying narratives – the Dreaming stories or histories that each of the works depicted – but, like so many Westerners, he readily saw in Rover's work the eloquence of the best late-American modernism, which he then loved. The paintings tugged at his existing passions, but directed him elsewhere; he found them hard to shake.

A local economy was soon sparked alongside the fledgling movement – it grew in step with the broader market. By the time Tony and Freddie met in Melbourne in 1996 art dealers were clamouring not only for Rover's work, which was seen as a finite resource now the much-celebrated artist was rumoured to be unwell, but for anything by the small group of artists who had quickly risen around him: Queenie McKenzie, George Mung Mung, Jack Britten and whoever else was poised to follow. As long as the collectors kept buying, the dealers and other speculators, it seemed, kept arriving.

Freddie was a generation younger than the others and was enterprising. Not only was he willing to travel, but he was able, at some level, to negotiate the many demands of the painting business. He had known Rover for much of his life and had watched closely as the older man's star had risen.

The two had travelled to Melbourne, where Freddie had worked as Rover's offsider for a controversial art middleman in the Dandenong Ranges. Once Tony and Freddie had built a level of trust, Tony would ask about those painting sessions and Freddie would offer tantalising details: how it had been cold up there in the hills; how they had laboured on large-scale works; how trucks had arrived and the canvases were stacked inside and driven away.

Although in later years it would often be claimed that Freddie had been exploited in Melbourne, that his trips there had brought him unwittingly into the Aboriginal art industry's more shadowy byways, the truth was more complex. Stories of Aboriginal artists being led astray by white profiteers played well, but Tony would come to understand Freddie as a kind of adventurer: his forays to the city were marked by new experience, by stories he could take back to country.

It was also clear that he'd looked at what was then available to him and weighed his options. Back in the Kimberley, Freddie had painted for the independent art business that then operated in Warmun, as well as for the community art centre in Kununurra, but found each wanting. Gija had a name for the kind of income one could make that way: 'finger-money', so called because it was too little to even reach your pocket. Freddie had chosen to travel with Rover just as he'd later chosen to work with Peter Harrison: each experience had been worth it, regardless of whether or not he'd ultimately been paid finger-money there as well.

Part of this simply came down to an exposure to new ideas and materials. More recently Harrison had brought Freddie down to stay with an artist called John Bursill in rural Victoria, at a place called Diamond Creek. Bursill was a fellow painter and had introduced Freddie to colour, then nearly unheard of among East Kimberley artists. Freddie had taken to it well. His recent paintings were bright: fields of yellow, red and magenta, threaded through by winding black pathways. They didn't possess the calm authority of a good work by Rover Thomas, but they were unmistakably Freddie's.

It was this body of work that Freddie continued in Ivanhoe: bright, arresting images constructed of interlocking organic shapes.

One new board followed another.

At times Freddie would push a tendril of road or river into an open expanse of colour and Tony would be reminded of the renowned mid-century Catalan painter Joan Miró.

That's what painting was: a chamber of echoes.

3.

At the beginning of his career as an art dealer Tony quickly became known for two things: being almost impossibly young and having what was known as a 'good eye'. In the art world, this latter quality is a much discussed but poorly understood asset: it refers not only to simple discernment – to good taste and an accurate feeling for the whims of fashion – but to the ability to see an artwork and 'read' it with some accuracy.

Tony's love was painting and he could readily visit a painter's studio, view works there, and hone in on the best of them. This was rarely the largest, or the one that might hang perfectly above a client's couch, or even the most conventionally successful. Invariably, it was the work that proved the breakthrough, the one the artist had struggled with. A work like that might not be resolved, but it suggested what was to come, how the artist might from this point move forwards. For that alone it was valuable.

He had opened his first gallery when he was only twenty-two, still in his final year of a painting degree at the Preston Institute of Technology. It was 1981 and the Australian art world was markedly provincial. He leased a series of interconnected rooms – one large, the others smaller – above an antiques shop in Gertrude Street, Fitzroy that had until recently been a Macedonian nightclub. The area was still more than a decade away from its eventual gentrification: street drinkers hung out there; there were housing commission towers just across the road. He reclad the walls, painted them white and named the gallery Reconnaissance. He sat there late at night in the newly illuminated space planning an ambitious program.

Some who knew him in the early days would recall him as an outsider – to one friend he was 'always so idiosyncratic in everything he did, even then ... always a little bit lonely' – but his commitment to art pulled him through. There was an appealing subtlety to the way he spoke about the work he represented, something that put him at odds with the tide of postmodernist theory then rising through the art scene. By contrast there was something old-fashioned about Tony's belief in the human potential of art, especially painting, almost as if the great modernist romantic tradition – seeded in Europe, then transported across the Atlantic where it found late form in American abstraction – had for him never ended.

Reconnaissance soon became known for considered exhibitions by up-and-coming figures, a number of whom would go on to forge long-term careers. Younger artists visited and dreamt of showing there. Although it was a commercial enterprise, the surrounding milieu was scattered liberally with aspiring poets and performance artists. This combined with Tony's youthfulness to lend the venture an anarchic touch: to some, it seemed almost punk. But if the gallery made a lasting mark, it was due less to Tony's work with the local scene and more to his far-reaching focus. Soon after opening, he took the first of what would become many trips to New York and returned with exhibitions of the artists he met there.

The gallery was the subject of an article in *The National Times* just eighteen months after it opened. Tony had only recently returned from his first visit to New York, and the accompanying photograph captured him standing in front of a painting by the American Richard Bosman, a second wave pop artist whose show he'd secured there. His arms are crossed; he stares at the camera with his mouth firmly set. A collar and tie peek out from the top of a rough-knit wool sweater. By now, he's already set the local scene briefly abuzz by exhibiting a suite of prints by Andy Warhol, and although Bosman will never reach Warhol's heights, he is at this moment a rising star in the New York art world.

Tony explains to his interviewer that he's spent much of the gallery's first months living on a dollar a day: 'Marlboros every couple of days, a burek for breakfast'. He says he allows for no luxuries, that he owns only three sets of clothes he keeps clean enough to get by. He paraphrases the American painter Jackson Pollock as a means to criticise the very notion of Australian art, which he finds promising, but limited. He tells the interviewer he sleeps in a tiny room beside his office, where he often sits up at night, alone, wondering if it's all worth it. His ambition usually convinces him that it is.

'Love of art has wrecked my personal life,' he says.

For one so young, it's an impressive performance.

•

The first New York trip had been productive, but it was on Tony's second visit, when he walked into McKee Gallery – a well-respected space on East 57th Street – that he made the most lasting of his New York connections.

The gallery's director, David McKee, shared Tony's belief in the kind of experience art engendered: he represented a range of acclaimed artists, among them the recently deceased Philip Guston, a searching and forceful painter who was among the few of his generation who truly saw what painting might be in the aftermath of abstract expressionism. Tony had adored Guston's work since he'd first encountered it at art school and had sought out McKee Gallery for that reason. A friendship developed: over the following decade, as Tony continued to fly back and forth across the Pacific, it was through McKee's support that he secured his best exhibitions.

Tony would be remembered by some as a haphazard businessman more at home in the studio than the office, but by the time he had opened and closed his second gallery – an eponymously named space that he immaculately fitted out in Melbourne's Clifton Hill – his program had made an impact. Along with the early shows by Warhol and Bosman that had graced the walls of Reconnaissance, he had exhibited prints by Roy Lichtenstein and had consigned from McKee a group of luminous works on paper by Guston: a crowning achievement for an Australian gallery. In Clifton Hill he'd similarly interspersed a range of local artists with a handful of Americans, key among them the critically acclaimed McKee Gallery artist Harvey Quaytman, whose geometric paintings were known to be subtle and precise in equal measure.

But no matter how enthusiastically the exhibitions were received, the gallery business was tenuous: Tony had invested heavily in fitting out the Clifton Hill space, and when he lost the lease at short notice it hit hard. What would prove to be his final show as a dealer came in 1992: an exhibition of the New Yorker Jake Berthot at a project space in Sydney. He left Melbourne soon afterwards, near penniless, and at the encouragement of a friend moved to the coastal New South Wales city of Wollongong, and eventually into a rental property pressed between the Illawarra escarpment and the sea.

It was there, subsisting on welfare, that he first attempted to rekindle his original passion and began to make his own paintings. He was chased by depression that would at times confine him to bed for days. Such darkness had already come to pattern his life, but it now threatened to overwhelm him. Painting demanded long hours alone, grappling with uncertainty, and at times it only made things worse. He fell into a self-lacerating routine of destroying everything almost as soon as he made it. Only a few works would survive, scattered between friends and supporters who made minor purchases or ended up with gifts.

He painted one on a small square of cardboard packaging, the text of which remained just visible beneath the painted surface. It's abstract: a warm red cradles a blue rectangle; a wash of magenta veils much of the right-hand side. Another from the same period was dashed off on a rough sheet of wood veneer. Loose black lines cut through fields of brushed white; a doubled half ellipse rises near the centre of the composition. Tony ripped the veneer from the wall of his house, and at the time thought of it, with its ragged, uneven edges, as a kind of suburban bark painting.

This second work is from 1992 – four years before Tony and Freddie first meet – but like others from the same period it effortlessly reaches forward to the Kimberley and touches the paintings Tony will one day help realise there.

4.

It didn't take long for Freddie to invite Tony to the Kimberley. Tony's life was still provisional, at times maddeningly so, and he was more than open to the suggestion – they had two studio sessions together in Melbourne, after which he booked a ticket to Darwin and then on to Kununurra.

His visit hinged on the kind of haphazard arrangement that he would soon understand as integral to Gija life. He and Freddie had spoken on the phone before his departure and agreed to meet outside the BP service station at the town's edge, but when he arrived it appeared Freddie had forgotten. Tony sat on the grass median strip each morning for two days until Freddie finally drove past in his flash-looking red Toyota LandCruiser. Peter Harrison had bought Freddie the vehicle as payment for his most recent painting trip and had shipped it north.

Now, it was overflowing with a retinue of family; Freddie – clearly surprised to see his Melbourne friend – looked momentarily guilty.

Ah! Tony!

Freddie disappeared quickly with an assurance he would be back, and when he returned, the LandCruiser had emptied. Tony jumped in, and from that moment Freddie's time was his.

•

First, Freddie took Tony to Frog Hollow, the outstation just past Warmun where Freddie then lived with his second wife, Berryline Mung. It was a tiny place, little more than a scatter of houses set out among trees above a bend in a creek.

Along with a group of family, they had then gone to a favourite camping spot of Freddie's on Lissadell Station. They piled together into the LandCruiser, threw in mattresses and swags, and held on as Freddie steered the vehicle down the highway, and then along a series of increasingly rough dirt roads.

The country opened up vast around them, a feeling Tony would soon know well.

They eventually parked next to a fallen tree, and Freddie lit a fire among the dry wood at its base. It burnt all night as the Kimberley stars turned slowly above.

Those moments were magic: Tony felt accepted among his new friends, loved how they conversed together in Kriol and Gija. He lay there on his swag listening, taking it all in. He would later recount that it was this night, as he sat with Freddie's family under the stars, that

Freddie first raised the idea of the two of them working together to start a painting group.

It was also on this trip, during a visit to the Argyle Dam at the top of the Ord River, that the subject of Freddie's painting earnings was first raised in detail.

Freddie had pulled up at the lookout and shown Tony the view.

Beneath the water lay Miriwoong country, Freddie explained, referring to the language group whose ancestral lands clustered near Kununurra. All the sacred sites there were now held in stasis, unceremoniously removed from the cycle of Law that was intended to keep that country strong. Argyle Downs Station lay there too: the first of the region's pastoral leases drowned to make irrigation a reality. The old homestead had been saved, though. It had been taken apart, stone by stone, and reassembled on higher ground. It was now a tourist attraction, part of what drew the mobs of retired travellers who crowded the lake's shore with their caravans and air-conditioned four-wheel drives.

Freddie often returned to Argyle Downs in his paintings: sometimes he showed it beneath the dam; other times, as it once was. As with so many of the places he painted, he'd ridden that country over and over again before the dam was constructed; in a painting he could still mark the original site of the homestead with precision. Tony had watched him do that in the Ivanhoe studio. Now he was here, looking out across that same country, long flooded: the peaks of high hills had become islands, the water that spread between them was vast.

The way Freddie told it, the money he received in return for his work could be okay – maybe a few thousand dollars in cash, perhaps even as much as ten or eleven, but he claimed that his most recent trip had resulted in a pittance: an envelope containing just $300. There was surely truth to this, but Tony also knew that in addition to expenses like accommodation, food and travel, Freddie had received the LandCruiser too. What ultimately concerned him was that Freddie was essentially being paid a wage to paint, rather than a percentage of each painting's value: a system that made it near-impossible for Freddie to understand how much his work was worth.

Although the practice was then common in the world of Aboriginal art, it was otherwise almost unheard of: at his own gallery, for instance, Tony had never directly commissioned work for cash payment. Even what he knew of government-funded community art centres – the much celebrated lifeblood of the entire movement – made little sense to him: after paying a commission to the gallery dealer *and* a further cut to the art centre, the artist was left with only thirty or forty per cent of the commercial value of their work. It seemed a tiny amount, especially when it was the white dealer who was receiving the lion's share.

At his galleries he'd followed the well-established method of receiving bodies of work on consignment, taking a forty per cent commission on each sale, and then returning the rest directly to the artist. It was this model that he explained to Freddie that day as they sat at Argyle Dam and looked across the water. He also made a proposition: if Freddie came to paint with him in Wollongong, he would arrange a proper gallery exhibition so Freddie could see the consignment practice in action.

That's how Freddie's brief but productive arrangement with Watters Gallery in Sydney came to be. Tony had known its co-director, Frank Watters, for years: at first by reputation (as a young dealer, he had always been slightly awed by the older man), and later as a friend and supporter. In Wollongong, Frank had helped him on a small exhibition he put together for the Ivan Dougherty Gallery at the University of New South Wales, and had soon invited him to spend weekends at his country retreat, a rustic mud-brick house in the bush near the small town of Cassilis. Frank, a slim-framed man whose skullcap beanie and round-lensed glasses were near iconic in the Sydney art scene, had an early feel for the avant-garde and, although the leading edge of contemporary art had long been redrawn by other galleries, Watters remained an institution. Even if the gallery had shown Aboriginal art before, its focus remained far broader. This was the context Tony wanted Freddie's work to be seen in.

Freddie travelled to Wollongong and painted with Tony in his rental house. Tony ordered the best acrylic paint he could find, choosing much the same palette Freddie had used in Melbourne: the bright colours – the purples, the yellows, the fields of red – were a far cry from much of the work Freddie would become known for, but it was a good start. As they worked, Tony continued to explain to Freddie how the consignment system worked. He had already secured the show with Watters and could now use that as an example. Watters would take thirty-three per cent, slightly less than most dealers: a standard practice for the gallery. Freddie would, in addition, reimburse them for expenses: his airfare from the Kimberley to Sydney and back again, the cost of canvases, paint and other supplies. Tony, who was still on welfare, had negotiated his own small cut from the gallery's commission.

They made less work than Freddie had made in Melbourne – Tony wanted quality, not volume – and when it was finished, Frank Watters was enthusiastic. Freddie titled each of the paintings for sites they depicted, among them Violet Valley, Red Butt, March Fly Creek. They were priced between $3000 and $12,000: not too much, but enough to flag to collectors that Freddie was worth paying attention to.

The gallery delivered well on their end of the arrangement: the show grossed just over $100,000. Less gallery commission and expenses, Freddie walked away with close to $60,000. Compared to his experiences in Melbourne it was, as Freddie later put it with characteristic restraint, 'a lot better'.

•

The money made a difference, of course, but what cemented Freddie and Tony's friendship had come the year before.

It had occurred in Melbourne, during one of those long, slow afternoons that are carried by happenstance late into the night. The city was in the throes of the annual Melbourne Cup carnival; Tony knew that Freddie liked horses and offered to take him to the big race, thinking they might simply lose some money together and then get drunk.

But for Freddie the races were deadly serious: the annual race meets in the Kimberley town of Wyndham had been a regular feature of his youth, and he knew the energy and rhythm of the racetrack well. On arrival at Flemington Racecourse, he and Tony went to the mounting yard and watched as the course clerk led the horses around, one by one. When a small chestnut gelding appeared, Freddie immediately picked it as the winner. His reason was simple: whereas the majority of the others had seemed unsettled among the distractions of the day, this horse was notably calm. Tony shook his head at the logic of it: it was exactly the kind of observation a career stockman like Freddie would make.

The horse's name was Saintly and at Flemington that year he won the Cup by an easy margin. Tony had followed Freddie's lead and put money on the horse: not a lot, but enough to add a brightness to proceedings and put a grin on each of their faces. Afterwards, they sat drinking at the track until the surrounding scene took on the slightly darker edge that can often cut through events like that, once excitement sours into daytime drunkenness and the many losses of the day sink in.

Tony had said, 'Do you want to get out of here?' and Freddie had said yes, that there was money to be spent.

In the city they visited a saddler, where Freddie bought a saddle to take back to Frog Hollow and give to his son Shaun, whom he adored. They then went to Lygon Street, one of Tony's old haunts, and ate and drank at a restaurant table on the pavement outside. The image of Freddie sitting there with his stock hat cocked on his head and the burnished leather form of the saddle draped over the chair next to him was pure gold: Tony would remember it always.

In later years, when the practices of some operators in the Aboriginal art industry were drawn into question, it was with that kind of memory in mind that Tony would sometimes attempt to complicate such judgement. Sure, it was hard to justify a business model that saw the artist underpaid – he had encouraged Freddie to push against exactly that – but it was also true that if he'd never travelled to Melbourne to paint, Freddie's world would have remained coloured by his immediate environment alone. Without someone like Peter Harrison, Tony and Freddie would never have met, and none of what followed would have been possible.

5.

On his initial visit to Warmun Tony was horrified by the place. It was during his first trip to the Kimberley in 1997, when he'd camped with Freddie and his family at Lissadell Station. He'd stayed the previous night at the Turkey Creek roadhouse and in the morning crossed the highway and walked into the community.

He was, of course, drawn by the promise of art. Rover Thomas's success had already placed Warmun at the epicentre of East Kimberley painting; Tony's visit was in that light not unusual. But although it was common for tourists to drive in on their way to Purnululu National Park, or for independent art dealers to make their way to the community unannounced, it was almost unheard of for an unknown white to appear on foot.

Much of the infrastructure Tony passed was rundown and blasted-looking, almost as if an apocalyptic event had moved through and this was the aftermath. Young Aboriginal men watched his passage in silence from the shadowy verandas of wrecked houses. Tony moved through Warmun's dusty streets that morning with a sense of gathering dread: he felt like an intruder, and realised he probably was.

Even after he'd been in the Kimberley for several years, a visit to Warmun would fill him with that same feeling. It wasn't that it looked worse than the smaller outstations he would soon become familiar with – they too were places of obvious poverty – but more that Warmun, a metropolis by comparison to those thin scatters of tin houses in the bush, felt harder, less welcoming. As with too many of the Aboriginal settlements that dotted the northern reaches of the country, the title 'community' seemed at best a kind of wishful thinking; at worst, it could appear a means to veil the reality of Aboriginal life from outsiders who were likely never to visit. 'Community' did nothing to capture the bleaker qualities of such places: the young men hunched and seemingly aimless in the heat of the day; the women and men one would see with ravaged faces; the way so many of the local whites carried themselves with a sense of arrogant paternalism.

Nothing prepared someone fresh from the city for the reality of that. Tony's mind was left spinning; he couldn't quite make sense of what he was seeing. At one level, he never would. But even if the full picture remained elusive, history imparted a certain context: as he slowly learnt Warmun's origins he wasn't surprised to find it had been established as a refugee camp in all but name, that its very existence spoke of the dispossession that had wrested the Gija so violently from the surrounding country.

First, the cattle stations had been established, and the old ways that had sustained Aboriginal people for generations were fatally altered, and then broken. Many of the Elders who now called Warmun home had been raised as indentured labour in the pastoral industry: their lives had been inextricably bound to those whites who had taken the Gija's ancestral country by force barely a generation before. Stories of murder and massacre threaded through their oral histories, but by the mid-twentieth century a life of uneasy reciprocity had been established. Aboriginal family groups had by then gathered at each of the stations and while the men and women worked, their old people and children had a permanent camp and access to rations.

Although the stations embodied brutal change, life there had followed a pattern that made some kind of sense. As each year's wet season made regular work impossible, the people would be released from their duties, and they would walk back to their ancestral places and gather for ceremony. Children would learn how to sustain themselves in country; youths would undergo initiation. On the stations the Gija were paid with nothing but rations – bags of flour and sugar and salt, sticks of tobacco – but in coming decades they would look back on those days with an unmistakable nostalgia.

This wouldn't be because station life had somehow been idyllic, or even fair – at its height, the era was a period of violence and authoritarian control by any reasonable measure – but simply because Aboriginal people's separation from country would soon be far more pronounced.

•

In the late 1960s, the Federal Pastoral Award was enforced in the northern cattle industry, which meant for the first time that station owners were required by law to pay their Aboriginal workers. They instead opted to let the vast majority go: in an industry that had in large part been driven by free labour, there was little else to do. The development came in step with other changes – the use of helicopters for mustering, for instance – but when a disastrously timed drop in global beef prices soon followed it left the pastoral economy in freefall.

Nor was welfare available to unemployed Aboriginal workers who remained on the stations. In the Kimberley, where many pastoralists were either unwilling or unable to continue supporting the family groups who had come to depend on them, this meant the families were forced to move to regional centres like Wyndham, Halls Creek and Kununurra where makeshift camps could be constructed on Crown Reserve Land. The edges of those towns soon became home to clusters of humpies and hastily built tin shacks. Warmun was intended not so much to replace what people had once had on the stations, but to funnel them away from such camps.

The site that was chosen for the future community was a place already known by settlers as Turkey Creek. It too had a history: Gija and Miriwoong people had always met there for large seasonal gatherings, but it wasn't until the discovery of gold led to the construction of Halls Creek to the south in the late 1880s that it became a place of any importance for whites. Pat Durack of Argyle Downs bestowed its European name in 1887: he travelled through the area and shot a turkey there. Wyndham, first established the year before, lay to the north and boomed with the Halls Creek gold rush. When it was found that the quickest route between the two towns led through Turkey Creek it quickly became a staging post for travellers who arrived on horseback or foot, and later by camel and donkey.

There was briefly a hotel there, as well as a butchery; it was soon earmarked for a telegraph station, and when that was constructed in 1897, a postmaster, telegraph operator and lineman were all installed there. This was a period of intense upheaval in the immediate region. The pastoralists were still then carving up the surrounding land, imposing new boundaries across the many ancestral pathways and intersecting language groups that already lay there. As the European occupation of Gija country took an ever more secure hold, conflict increased. Cattle-killing rose in frequency; whites rode the stations gripped by a fear that made either pre-emptive or punitive violence all the more easy to justify. Stockmen riding the boundary lines of newly established pastoral leases were known to carry revolvers in their belts, and .32 rifles within easy reach under their saddles. There were stories of murder by gun and poison, of violence breaking out over access to country, even access to Aboriginal women.

It was technically illegal for settlers to take independent action, but in the absence of any real legal consequence there was little to deter the more mercenary among the settler world. As it had been elsewhere, 'frontier justice' was tacitly approved by the authorities: this was simply how the colony expanded its boundaries. Francis Connor, the East Kimberley's first member of the Legislative Assembly, outlined the stakes of the conflict in an 1893 speech: although he predicted that the 'dispersal' of Aboriginal people might not be broadly popular, the issue, for him at least, was clear. It was, he said, 'simply a question of whether the natives are to have this country, or the whites'.

Even when the tide of opinion began to shift, it remained unlikely that perpetrators would be punished for murdering Aboriginal people. In 1901 PC James Campbell Thomson made the mistake of investigating reports that stockman Thomas McLaughlin from Texas Downs Station had shot and burnt two Aboriginal men 30 miles to Turkey Creek's east. Thomson visited the site of the fire and saw human remains among the ashes but when he tried to bring McLaughlin to justice the region's well-oiled culture of silence ground into action. McLaughlin ran Thomson off Texas Downs at gunpoint; thinly veiled threats followed. This practice was pronounced enough to have a name: in a world where police were expected to enforce pastoral expansion at any cost, Thomson was 'blackballed' – ostracised – by the settler community.

It was in this same year that a police station was established at Turkey Creek, in the same building as the telegraph station. By this time a small group of Aboriginal people were already congregating around the tiny settlement, drawn by the promise of rations, which the postmaster had established for the old, the infirm and the very young. Others benefitted too: they augmented their bush diet with European food received in exchange for labour or other transactions. The new police presence also saw an aggressive surge in the arrests of Aboriginal people. It followed an established colonial method in which adult men were most often the target; as they were either killed or gaoled, women and children were then left vulnerable, and thus more amenable to moving onto the stations and providing the basis of an indentured workforce. Prisoners from the greater region began to be funnelled through Turkey Creek on their way to the

Wyndham gaol. Following the passage of the 1905 Aborigines Act, police there also became responsible for identifying and removing mixed-race Aboriginal people from the stations.

By now, battered humpies had spread out below the telegraph station, which had been built high on the hill and raised on concrete pillars so it could look out across the immediate area. Behind its windows sat the white administrators of colonial expansion.

•

Among the whites who then lived at Turkey Creek was Mick Rhatigan, a man who had already built a formidable reputation in the wider region as a police constable. He arrived in the settlement in the 1890s with his wife Kate to take up the position of telegraph lineman.

In a place where it was not unheard of for policemen to be disciplined for not shooting Aboriginal people during punitive dispersal expeditions, Rhatigan was spoken of approvingly as 'uncompromising'. From his earliest days he was known as a brutal enforcer: a perfect shot with a rifle who had already been responsible, in the language of the day, for 'cleaning up the blacks' along the Osmond River. Only two years before moving to Turkey Creek, Rhatigan, along with Sergeant Jack Wheatley, had been implicated in one of the most vicious recorded massacres in the region's history: twenty men, women and children killed in response to cattle-spearing on Ivanhoe Station. Two weeks later Rhatigan and Wheatley's party arrested twenty-five women, thirty children and twelve men, chained them neck-to-neck and marched them for the remainder of their patrol: a meandering 400 kilometres that eventually took them to Wyndham, where fourteen so-called 'prisoners' were gaoled.

When the postmaster departed Turkey Creek in 1903, Rhatigan took over rationing duties. The old people would line up and he would hand out the flour, sugar and tobacco. The role clearly did little to soften him: more than a decade later, in 1915, Rhatigan was implicated in another massacre, this time at a place called Mistake Creek. The region's culture had by then shifted, but true change was only incremental: Rhatigan was arrested, but any charges were soon dropped and he returned to work. He would live another five years in Gija country until his death in 1920.

None of this history was secret. The Gija knew where the murders and massacres had occurred. Tony would soon come to understand that they knew those places in the kind of inchoate, bodily way that anyone would know the sites in which their father was shot to death, or their grandmother burnt, or their infant siblings bludgeoned with a stick as a means for the whites to save their ever-finite ammunition ('expended 40 rounds of Winchester ammunition' a constable's report from those early years might dutifully record, carefully accounting for every precious shot). Accompanied by Gija, Tony would see the massacre ground at Bedford Downs, where people were poisoned and burnt; the boab tree at Mistake Creek where a group of Gija were cornered in a shallow valley and shot; the cave across the sandy river bed at Chinaman's Garden where an old man had hidden while the remains of his murdered family members were disposed of below. He would learn that such sites exuded a kind of power equal in intensity to the many places across the Kimberley at which ancestral presences can still be felt, that colonial atrocities entered that same space, were carried by the same traditions of oral history from one generation to the next.

In the company of people who knew those stories, Tony would feel something of the terrible hold such sites could still enact upon the victims' descendants. It's not just culture that ties Aboriginal people to place, he would realise, but history too.

Only then would his initial response to Warmun become clearer. What shocked him was not how people lived, but the weight of the history that hung over them as they struggled to find traction in the colonial world.

6.

When award wages were enforced in the 1960s, the wave of Aboriginal workers and their families leaving the stations surged over the years that followed. The scatter of semi-permanent tin humpies at Turkey Creek soon expanded. The people squatting there were permitted to draw water from the bore and tank next to what was now the post office alone; the police had relocated to Halls Creek in 1950. Kate Rhatigan had lived there for seventeen years after her husband's death and was remembered as a kind woman who had raised Gija children as her own, but Rhatigan's kin had by now long gone.

In the late 1970s, Warmun entered the more familiar, bureaucratic phase which had long rusted into place by the time of Tony's first visit in 1997. It was officially named, and officially recognised, as a 'permanent community' for the purposes of Department of Aboriginal Affairs funding; a grant was soon secured to construct the first of the houses there: simple tin-clad structures. Another bore was sunk and a communal vehicle purchased. As one decade carried into the next, the familiar infrastructure of a remote Aboriginal community was erected: a small store, a health clinic, a school run by Catholic nuns. Soon there was a mechanic's workshop and an old people's home; later came an organisation that administered funding to the outstations that would spring up over the coming decade. The post office, which was the community's oldest building, was set aside as housing for white advisers.

Government funding to the community emphasised private sector commercial activity, but although the local skill base was still firmly rooted in the pastoral industry, the surrounding area was far too small to establish a working station. Nor did local skills necessarily run to the management and development of a pastoral business. With the exception of community liaison and trainee positions, Warmun was soon largely run by whites. Small-scale projects intended to sustain independent income were established in the early years – a market garden and a chicken run among them – but little took hold. Children drifted in and out of school; Elders moved to the old people's home. For much of the younger generation of men and women a pattern was soon set in motion. They shuttled between Warmun and the Kimberley's far-flung network of towns, many among them gripped tight by a toxic mix of grog and welfare.

All kinds of whites found their way into the community. Many were altruistic – simply seeking to help establish the place, to keep it running – but others were far more self-interested. If Tony hadn't yet heard the common northern dictum to describe them – mercenaries, misfits and missionaries – he soon would. It rang true, but the neat demarcation between the terms overlooked their often tangled nature: Tony would understand in coming years that it was not uncommon to encounter a long-term interloper who somehow embodied all three.

•

On that first day, the sun was already hot as Tony made his way down what served as Warmun's main street, past the school and the store, and the offices of the Balangarri Aboriginal Corporation. The road dipped before him over a causeway that cut across a dry creek bed and then curved up a short, steep hill. There were white painted boulders placed at seemingly random intervals along the road's edge.

As he approached the old police station, he knew nothing of its history. It was notable for the simple fact that its construction was so markedly different to the houses and administrative buildings that lay dotted beneath it. Even though it was raised from the ground on its wide concrete pillars, it somehow managed, with its enclosed veranda and small windows, to appear squat, even mildly menacing.

The building was now the home of a local business called Narrangunny Art Traders – the reason for Tony's visit. It was one of a number of loosely interconnected places at which artists like Rover Thomas and Queenie McKenzie still painted. Many of the most striking works Tony had seen at Kimberley Art in Melbourne had carried the Narrangunny Art Traders imprimatur – not only those by Rover and Queenie, but works by lesser-known figures like George Mung Mung and Jack Britten.

The enterprise was little more than a painting wholesaler, and only superficially related to the network of community-based government-funded art centres that already supported remote art in other regions of northern and central Australia. It was run by a white couple called Maxine Taylor and Terrence Brooks, who was known as 'Serge'. The two were long-time bush residents who had taken the reins at the Turkey Creek roadhouse in 1995. It was there they first began to commission paintings and offer them for sale to passing tourists. By then, Peter Harrison at Kimberley Art had already put in place a structure designed to tap the growing market for East Kimberley painting. It was a streamlined arrangement: Harrison would send art materials to an ex-policeman who worked for the Warmun community council; the former policeman would organise for canvases to be painted and then ship them south where Harrison would sell them.

In 1996, Maxine and Serge moved from the roadhouse to the old post office, where they readily took over the supply end of the chain. They quickly gained the trust of older, more 'saleable' painters like Rover in a simple and reliable fashion: Maxine was a good cook and the old people were often hungry. In the coming days, Tony would see this in action: he too was fed a good meal – perfectly cooked roast beef – and understood why the artists came back for what they called 'number one tucker'.

Tony stayed at the roadhouse for several nights, and during his visit, the couple seemed to warm to him. Serge was a laconic, straight-talking northerner of the kind Tony would soon come to know well. He had once worked in the meatworks in Wyndham and, as he and Tony talked, it became clear he'd turned to the art business for a simple reason: there was easy money to be made.

'What's this shit, this *minimal* shit, that people down south like?' he asked Tony one afternoon (or something like it).

They were inspecting a beautifully simple painting by Rover. As the renowned master had grown older he'd taken to leaving larger and larger expanses of his paintings free of anything but fields of roughly brushed ochre. Some of his works at the time were simply traced around the edges of each canvas: compositions increasingly restrained by physical limitation, by his inability, after suffering a stroke, to comfortably reach into the centre.

Serge's question was not without its insight: it was true that these works were partly popular for the fashion in which they echoed Western precedent, particularly the school of colour-field painting that had driven to acclaim figureheads of late-modernism like the American Mark Rothko. Most with even a passing interest in art knew Rothko's shimmering fields of subdued colour, and it was his name that was most often evoked for white viewers confronted by Rover's work for the first time.

If Tony didn't already know the story about Rover's visit to the National Gallery of Australia, he soon would. There, on an immaculate white wall, hung one of Rothko's iconic paintings, known interchangeably as *1957 #20* or *Black, Brown on Maroon*. It was a striking work, one of the gallery's crowning jewels: earthen-toned horizontal bands floating over a blood-red ground, all of it brushed in thin layers of oil pigment to a seductively matt finish.

'Who's that bugger that paints like me?' Rover asked the curator accompanying him, Wally Caruana.

Rover, it seemed, recognised the simple, graphic charge in Rothko's work: it was by the same means that his own images were projected into the world around them. In his own way, Serge was similarly identifying what carried so much Aboriginal painting into the white art world: it looked like Western art; the core difference of it was wrapped in familiarity.

As Serge continued to go through Rover's recent paintings, expressing his disbelief at the more minimal among them, he clearly expected Tony to share in his disdain. If anything, this man who'd once slaughtered Kimberley cattle for a living couldn't believe his luck.

Not long after, Serge took Tony to collect Rover.

Rover was by then much diminished – he would die less than a year later – but he was still responding to the demand for his paintings. On the trip back to Warmun he sat up front with Serge, while Tony looked on from the back seat. Serge passed Rover a beer, which the old painter drank warm. He then expertly flicked the empty can out of the window, only to have it violently rebound into the cabin: he hadn't wound down the glass. The three of them laughed about that, and although Tony would later sit with Rover and watch the old man trace the bones of a new composition across an otherwise blank canvas, it was this story he would recount most readily: the old painter, the rebounding beer can, the highway flinging past.

But although Serge and Maxine treated Tony well during his brief visit, he could never quite ascertain the outline of their business model. He would always associate them with a story that he would soon hear through Freddie, who had often painted for the couple but didn't trust them. The story was that when Maxine paid the artists, she would do so from the window of the old police station, hanging out and scattering notes over the yard below.

She'd call out like a crow: 'Waak, waak, waak' and the painters, many of them among the most respected Elders of the Gija world, would have to peck around in the dirt there, gathering up whatever money she had deemed their labour to be worth.

As Warmun's history became clearer to Tony, the absolute perversity of this scene was unavoidable: Maxine paying the old painters in the same spot where the killer Mick Rhatigan had once doled out rations.

•

There were a group of artists at Narrangunny Art Traders who were obviously regulars: on the first morning of Tony's visit they were spread out around the old post office, working cross-legged on the ground.

Jack Britten was there, a solid, severe-looking man bent over a distinctive painting of the Bungle Bungle Ranges. Beside him was another old man, then known in the art world only by his first name, Birribi, which he signed 'Beerbee'. He was working on a painting of hills, simple and unadorned.

Others were there too, but it was Hector Jandany who stood out.

He was still then often called Hector Chundaloo, and Tony recognised him immediately from a photograph he'd seen in a National Gallery of Victoria catalogue. It had been published to coincide with a 1993 survey of Kimberley art titled 'Images of Power' and showed Hector standing with a group of fellow Warmun artists: Britten, Queenie McKenzie and a beautiful old man called Henry Wambini to whom Freddie had already introduced Tony at Frog Hollow.

In the photograph the others appear resigned to the intrusion, but Hector is a natural. He takes the camera's gaze and makes with it something beautiful: his body seems to twist up through the frame; he leans in close to Wambini, but loosely gestures in the other direction. The effect is coy, slightly wry, more than a touch flamboyant. His eyes are hidden behind circular-lensed sunglasses, a near-perfect counterpoint to his patterned short-sleeved shirt and striped pants.

The photograph flagged Hector as an eccentric among his countrymen, and now, as they met, Tony wasn't disappointed. Hector was wearing a dressing-gown over his clothes, a flourish that Tony soon learnt the artist favoured. In a place where the older men almost exclusively wore battered wide-brimmed stock hats, Hector preferred terry-towelling fishing hats with a tiny brim. Sometimes they would be dog-chewed and frayed, but on Hector even the most far gone would appear somehow princely.

It was Hector who welcomed Tony as he approached the painters for the first time, and then went about telling him what he needed to hear to feel comfortable in a place so foreign. It was a role in which Hector had long excelled – this practice of taking whites under his wing and explaining to them the local world – and Tony soon became his newest project.

Without fanfare, it was Hector who would soon offer him a skin name, Jungurra. With that, he identified Tony as his brother: 'Ngaji' in Gija.

7.

Later, as Tony recalled those early years in country, when his head had been swimming with new ideas, it would be Hector's voice he would often hear. Sometimes, he could still feel the old man's firm hand clasping his shoulder or his leg as the two of them talked.

When Tony returned to the Kimberley for another visit, several months after his first, he found himself on the veranda of Hector's house in Warmun's 'bottom camp'. He camped there in a swag, and each evening Hector would set out to educate him about the local world. Sometimes Hector would corral a group of young Gija men into listening, but just as often it would simply be the two of them.

The old man was a generous guide. Often he began or ended at points of contact, moments where Gija ideas passed, however imperfectly, into the world brought about by the settlers.

'That Ngarranggarni,' Hector might say, gesturing vaguely across the ranges that lay visible over the community's low rooftops. 'He man, that Ngarranggarni. He like a Jesus: might be him Jesus.'

The Ngarranggarni was the animating spirit of Gija country: that's what Hector explained to Tony in his famously digressive, elliptical fashion. It was the Law that Gija were bound by, but it also seemed to be like time itself: the space in which the ancestral present lived on with all that had ever happened, or would happen. Even what was happening around them as the two men spoke there on the veranda was somehow part of it.

'Gardiya' was another word that Hector quickly introduced. This was the Gija name for white people, and the old man spoke it often. 'Kartiya' it was spelt further south, in the desert, and when Tony learnt this he imagined the word spreading between language groups, adapting ever so slightly to new tongues as it announced the coming of the settlers. Gardiya was a subject that Hector constantly parsed. It described a world of hidden motivations: an enduring, unsolvable mystery defined by way of difference alone.

Individual gardiya could be figures of ridicule or fear. '*That* gardiya,' Hector might say, referring to a specific figure from the past or present, someone whose world had collided with his own and created a tangle of crossed intentions that required scrutiny.

That gardiya at the Balangarri Corporation was always talking about money.

That other gardiya was good; that one couldn't be trusted.

Back in the station days, *that* gardiya had chained Hector's grandmother to a tree while she was pregnant with his mother, and beaten her.

Often, it could be used far more generally: 'You gardiya' would simply mean Tony and his kind. 'Gardiya' alone was broader still: it could be deployed as a means to capture the whole carapace of European law that had enacted so much change over the old man's lifetime.

This was the real issue that Hector kept returning to: gardiya had imposed laws that had nothing to do with the Ngarranggarni, yet Gija were compelled to follow them. Gija had experienced gardiya law as destructive rather than generative: it wanted to take everything into its belly, to smother it all.

As they sat there in the evening, the lowering light pushing the shadows long, proof of the brutal effectiveness of gardiya law lay all around. The very community, whose fortunes rose and fell with faraway acts of government, spoke of its power.

Tony would never master the intricacies of Gija language, but listening to Hector he soon began to build an understanding of Kimberley Kriol.

'Bat, bat, bat,' Hector would say mid-story, pushing the word out in quick succession.

This was a marker of time passing, a narrative quickening that linked continuity without having to dwell on unnecessary detail.

'La', used often, was another linking word: something like 'at', or 'on', or 'to'. Understanding it depended on context, which in turn depended on how closely Tony was following Hector's circuitous ruminations.

'Mefella' was a group in which Hector was counting himself; 'meself' was he alone. As he spoke he would often point or gesture, his hand tracing clipped arabesques in the air before him.

Some words were holdovers from the station times, when Hector had first learnt English as a child. These could be old-fashioned. 'Killer' was beef, and came from the days in which a single beast was selected from a mob of cattle and dispatched to eat: a 'killer'. Words could equally betray their childhood origins: Hector referred to his late mother as 'Mummy'. She had been raised by Kate Rhatigan when Warmun was still Turkey Creek. His mother's mother, the one who'd been beaten, was 'Granny'.

'Nalija' was tea, which was served in huge enamelled mugs, one of the very few household possessions that were jealously guarded. In the early days it was often Tony's job to steep the handful of teabags in a pot of hot water. Once he had, he and Hector would sit side by side with the heavily sweetened brew cradled before them.

In those moments Hector would repeat one assertion again and again. It went something like this: 'If gardiya and blackfella got together, they might be learning one another, teaching one another.'

It was an idea Hector was uniquely qualified to discuss: he had dedicated much of his life to this space between gardiya and Gija, this interface that, for him, promised the only solution to the mess that had been made of the Gija world.

In recent decades, a similar idea had risen across Aboriginal Australia. Like others, Hector called it Two Way.

It was a simple philosophy. Hector was a devout Catholic who had not only readily accepted the Church's teachings, but identified in them the pattern he already knew from the Ngarranggarni. Like so many Aboriginal people subject to the Church's intrusions, he felt Catholic doctrine only sought to explain the same animating force that plotted out the lives of his people and always had done.

In 1979, just after Warmun had come into official existence, Hector played a central role in establishing the local school, which they had called Ngalangangpum, a name that meant, quite simply, 'mothers and children'. An attempt to develop a mixed curriculum there had first carried forth the idea of Two Way. Before this, Gija children had travelled to Halls Creek, Kununurra or Wyndham for school, but senior figures like Hector were concerned by the lack of Gija content, by the way in which children would return to Warmun with no language but English. They wanted greater control over what the younger generation were taught.

Catholic nuns of the Josephite order were recruited from Kununurra to deliver the non-Gija lessons, but in the absence of any real infrastructure the school was at first an informal place. Initial lessons took place under a bough shelter the community had constructed for the purpose; later they moved to the shade of a large white-trunked eucalyptus, before a more permanent building was secured.

Each morning, Elders like Hector would arrive early, and before the European lessons in reading and writing and arithmetic commenced, they would teach Gija words and songs. Hector was among those who used painting as a teaching tool. As with the other artists in the community who were just then working towards the invention of East Kimberley art, Hector would transcribe his images onto whatever was at hand: a sheet of cardboard, perhaps, or a plywood offcut.

When the teaching was done, these images were hung in the classroom. Hector made no distinction in terms of content; he would paint both Catholic and Gija icons: each served a purpose in ceremonies that although distinct, were also not. He once depicted himself in a painting as Jesus, struggling under the weight of the cross as he moved through an unmistakably Kimberley landscape. When the priest arrived from Halls Creek to deliver regular sermons to the community, it would often be Hector who stood there and offered a Gija translation for those who gathered. He was known to make ready comparisons as he went: the story of Easter and the resurrection of Christ he would present in Gija terms: 'reincarnation' rather than 'resurrection'. It was a simple thing, but, as

Tony now learnt, that's what Two Way was: a search for those points of connection that might help elaborate an exchange on something at least approaching equal terms. This idea that Tony was already building towards with Freddie – this painting collective – needed to develop across the same ground: that's what Hector's discussions would circle back to.

Two Way, he would say again and again, that's how it needed to work.

8.

Now, in the red LandCruiser with Freddie, Tony was heading for Chocolate Thomas's house. It was Freddie who had suggested the visit: he and Chocolate were old friends and had once worked together on Old Greenvale Station. Freddie's intention was simple: he was taking Tony to see Chocolate's paintings in the hope Chocolate might join the painting group.

Tony had already met Chocolate – he'd recently travelled to Old Greenvale with Chocolate and Freddie – and knew him as a friendly man who spoke, like many Gija, with a declaratory abruptness. His name came from his station days, but although it seemed a perfect emblem of the casual racism Gija had been born into, the truth, as Tony had already learnt, was different. As a child, Chocolate had crept into the station cook's pantry and gorged himself on the supply of cooking chocolate: his resulting nickname had stuck fast. Now he was one of the few Gija employees at the diamond mine, a position that had clearly brought him some level of wealth: he often drove a near-new Toyota and wore fresh-looking shirts.

Tony and Freddie pulled up and, after an enthusiastic greeting, Chocolate ushered his visitors across his barren front yard. Even in a community full of rundown, broken infrastructure, the house would stick in Tony's memory. It was a mess: 'diabolical', he'd later claim. Dust and grime caked the place; foam mattresses lay about the dirt yard in various states of decay. Inside, the windows were covered with cloth; it was dark, the air heavy with burnt cooking grease. As his eyes adjusted to the gloom, Tony made out paintbrushes and tins of dried ochre paint among the debris.

Chocolate brought out his paintings, and the visit grew awkward. Tony read them in an instant and his heart sank: they were standard examples of East Kimberley art, far from special. But in the clutter of the kitchen, Tony made out another stack of painted boards.

Even in the gloom they showed promise. He stooped down and picked one up.

'Are these yours, Chocolate?' Tony would recall asking.

Chocolate explained that they weren't, that they were by an old man called Goowoomji, or Paddy Bedford, who was staying with Chocolate's family.

'He's out the front now,' Chocolate said.

One work was painted on what appeared to have recently been a cupboard door, the white Laminex surface of which now served as a blank ground for a hill painted roughly in black and red ochre. A long range-like form extended across the top of the composition. It was smudged and dirty but there was a lightness to it, a clarity. There was also a similar painting on cardboard, this time a muddy red: what appeared to be another horizontal sequence of hills. There was a second work on a cupboard door, marked by a distinctive series of vertical lines.

The largest painting was on a sheet of plywood almost a metre across. It had a black ground over-painted with a sequence of red forms, each of them outlined in white dotting. In one corner there was an organic, starburst-like shape: what appeared to be a dotted flower, but which probably wasn't.

Tony felt a rush of excitement.

The works struck him as anarchic in the best of ways: dashed off, but somehow completely resolved. He was reminded of the early, prized works that had defined the contours of the entire East Kimberley movement, the rough ochre paintings on boards prepared for Rover Thomas's *Guirr-Guirr* by artists like Paddy Jaminji. He'd seen work from that period at Kimberley Art in Melbourne, and knew it well.

Chocolate explained that Bedford had painted the boards as a simple teaching device, a means to show Chocolate what to paint in preparation for Freddie and Tony's visit. This idea drew Tony immediately: the disconnect from the market, the fact they'd been made at a step removed. He felt he could work with it.

Afterwards they had simply been discarded there in the kitchen – more refuse added to the thick drift that surrounded them. As a kind of origin story, it was near flawless.

•

Seeing the paintings returned Tony to one of the things he'd loved about his life as a dealer – that all-too-rare moment of aesthetic revelation upon which something new might be built. And although he recognised in those boards the vernacular of artists like Rover or Paddy Jaminji, the feeling of discovery took his mind elsewhere.

In New York, he had once visited Jake Berthot's studio. Berthot, then in his fifties, was not a recognised master in the league of Philip Guston, but he was nonetheless respected as a painter's painter. His work had been shown in the Venice Biennale, and collected by New York institutions as esteemed as the Museum of Modern Art and the Whitney; Tony was preparing to exhibit it back home in Sydney in what would be his gallery's final exhibition.

David McKee, Tony's gallerist-supporter in New York, had organised the visit. He described Berthot as a kind of authentic throwback from another age; in Tony's memory McKee's words were something like, 'a reincarnated version of an eighteenth-century backwoodsman'. It made sense: Berthot was tall and ruggedly handsome. As soon as Tony met him, he felt comfortable in the older man's presence. But he wasn't relaxed: as he sat in the studio he recognised he was in the company of someone whose reservoir of knowledge was far deeper than his own. Tony weighed carefully everything he said, especially when it came to painting.

Berthot was then working on his 'lozenge' paintings – abstract canvases in which sombre-coloured brush marks teased out central lozenge shapes – and he showed Tony examples. Although out of step with current trends, it was clear they were the real deal. Tony had seen them in reproduction and assumed that in the flesh they would be thickly painted, rugged like Berthot himself, but although they were physical, in places Berthot had employed soft washes of oil paint. The lightness of that was surprising. There seemed to be a lesson in it, one about balance and counterpoint.

The lozenge paintings were great, but it was another work that stood out. Tony had seen it on the studio wall when he first walked in and it had caught his eye. Berthot said he had been looking at it for weeks beforehand, trying to figure out how to finish it: only the night before had he brusquely covered its surface with a rough web of calligraphic black marks.

Tony was entranced by the painting. Berthot, surely sensing his visitor's excitement, explained that it was called *At Noontide*, after a chapter in Nietzsche's philosophical work of fiction, *Thus Spoke Zarathustra*. At the height of the day, Zarathustra falls asleep beside a gnarled tree and dreams for what seems an eternity, only to wake and discover the sun has not moved at all.

•

In Warmun, Tony stepped from the darkness of Chocolate's kitchen to find Paddy Bedford waiting on the veranda with Freddie.

He would recall the old man was dressed in a short-sleeved shirt, once white but now grime-covered, untucked over loose-fitting pants. He didn't quite yet have a beard, but it appeared days since the whiskers had been cut from his face. He had on a wide-brimmed stock hat, but no shoes, just his bare feet in the dust.

Tony tells him that the works he's just seen are 'masterpieces', explains to him what Freddie and he are doing. He invites the old man to join them in Kununurra, and within days that's exactly what he does. When he one day looks back over the nine years that follow, it will seem to Tony that from that point onwards they were always together.

Pindan Avenue

1.

'That old man's going to be the next Rover.'

That's what Tony told Simon Georgeff, a young man from Melbourne who was letting him stay at his rented house in Kununurra. Tony and Freddie had just returned from meeting Paddy in Warmun and Tony's excitement was clear.

It wouldn't be the last time he made the comparison, nor would Simon be alone in hearing it. In fact, Tony evoked Rover's name enough in the early years for it to begin to appear as much a challenge to himself as a measure of Paddy's talent. When he stopped making the statement it was simply because it was no longer necessary: under his management, Paddy would rise almost impossibly fast.

Simon's house was on Pindan Avenue, and was a peaked-roofed, fibro-clad construction in keeping with the region's simple architecture. It sat in the middle of a large and unkempt suburban block, raised slightly off the ground. There was a tiny veranda at the front; two steps led up from the dusty yard. Inside there was little more than a kitchen, a bathroom and two bedrooms. The owner had left one room locked: he'd stacked an assortment of belongings inside. What little he'd left in the rest of the house served as Simon's meagre furniture: there was a reclining chair in the front room beside an old piano; a table in the kitchen.

Although Simon, at twenty-one, was significantly younger than Tony, the two of them got on well. They'd met through one of Tony's oldest Melbourne friends, the gallerist William Mora, who at times sold paintings to Simon's father, an occasional collector. A quiet evening in Kununurra would see the two sitting on the front veranda as they shared a bottle of black sambuca between them. For some reason that was their drink of choice, and as they systematically worked through a bottle, Tony would tell stories.

There were the trips to New York, the money that had passed through his hands as a dealer, the famous artists he'd met along the way. He vividly described a visit he'd taken to Andy Warhol's studio, and told of how he was introduced to a group of the New York graffiti artists who, in the 1980s, had briefly stormed the art world. He even almost met the most famous of them, Jean-Michel Basquiat, but had to catch a plane home. To Simon, an aspiring writer who had grown up between Melbourne and the west coast of the United States, all of that seemed worldly: a life of incident and intrigue of the kind he imagined for himself. The fact it seemed so far from the relative privilege of his own world only added to the appeal.

Over the past eighteen months Simon had made his own inroads into Kununurra. After dropping out of a university degree in Melbourne, he'd ended up in the Kimberley almost by chance. At first he worked for a local Aboriginal art dealer – an ex-manager of the local community art centre, Waringarri Aboriginal Arts, who had cut out on his own – before taking a role as interim manager of Marralum, a drug and alcohol rehabilitation program on a nearby community. He had sat out there through the wet season, watching as storms rolled across the landscape. In the months before Tony's arrival, he had been spending his time with the teenagers and young men he'd met there. They were Miriwoong and Gajirrabeng, the language groups on whose country Kununurra now lay, and had opened for him a window on to town life: smoking weed in the reserve, drinking moselle in the park, wandering drunk beneath the stars. Simon had embraced it all. He even had a joey kangaroo that he kept as a pet and which he'd often carry about town in a backpack.

Before Tony's arrival Simon's house was one among a shifting network that his young friends wandered between. They would stash smoking paraphernalia there, fearful of the ever-present eyes of the local police, and turn up unannounced to get high in the lounge room as they played American rap like Cypress Hill and NWA over Simon's stereo. There was an appealing sense of camaraderie among the group: Simon loved the toughness of them, but also the fact they could be demonstrative in a way he wasn't used to. A new friend might take him by the shoulders, look him in the eye and say, 'We're brothers. It doesn't matter about our skin.' It had sparked a sense of loyalty he would carry for years.

On arrival, Tony unwittingly changed things. For starters, he brought Gija people into the social mix. Not only were they a different language group, they were for the most part old men rather than the young men and teenagers Simon had come to know. First among them were Freddie and his high-spirited, gravel-voiced offsider Churchill Cann. Both remained bound to the station days and the pattern of Law that they still understood as the animate force of their ancestral country, a far cry from the appropriated black American culture that had captured the younger generations. Freddie and Churchill listened to classic country and western like Slim Dusty with a sense of reverence; rap was the anathema of everything they'd lived.

Freddie was a dedicated drinker, but Churchill even more so. He drank with almost comedic abandon. With him onsite, the social scene stepped up a notch. It was true that evenings could be quiet – the black sambuca, the front veranda, the long conversations – but often they spiralled. Like Simon, Tony had already enthusiastically stepped into this side of local life. During one of his earlier visits, he had spent a run of boisterous nights at the Gija town drinking camp, a semi-permanent gathering of swags and blankets in a bushy vacant lot near the centre of town. He remembered it fondly. The apparent roughness of the drinking camp veiled something more complex, even unexpectedly mannered: Tony would go on to claim he learnt as much there as he did anywhere in the Kimberley. Now, with Churchill and Freddie as their initial guides, he and Simon were soon regulars at the Animal Bar, a markedly unadorned place attached to the proudly three-starred Hotel Kununurra.

It was only a short walk – just a couple of blocks through the centre of town, past the Tuckerbox supermarket and down Konkerberry Drive. The bar's name was the kind of racially charged colloquialism that was constantly slung around the town, but Aboriginal people had clearly embraced it. They drank there almost exclusively. Inside it was all concrete floors and plastic chairs; the tables were bolted down. Glass in any form had long been banned; beer or rum and coke were served in cans, spirits in plastic cups. It was one of only a handful of places in which local Aboriginal people seemed to fully let themselves go: if one was game, a night at the Animal Bar could be ridden like a wave.

Whites, for the most part, frequented the other side of the hotel bar, which was dubbed, far more innocuously, the Green Room. Tony had drunk there too, not long after he arrived in Kununurra, but had found the experience deeply unsettling. It was a place of rancid superiority, openly racist. Rough whites sat in the shadowy interior simmering over their pints: men with thin ponytails and tattoos and darting eyes, older women who appeared scorched by the northern sun.

But the Animal Bar was different. Drinks were more expensive there than the Green Room, but if you factored in the raw humanity of the place, it was more than worth it. Stray whites were likely to be directed next door, but with Freddie and Churchill vouching for them, Tony and Simon were welcomed. They chased shots of tequila with cans of beer. To Simon it quickly became a 'wild west type place' where anything was possible: he found he could as easily fall into a sprawling all-night pool tournament as get punched in the face, or that a woman would grab him for a flailing dance, 'jealousing' her boyfriend who sat glowering across the crowded room.

All of it felt taboo, as if their presence were a transgression of the way in which the town had organised itself along clearly marked colour lines. Some of Tony and Simon's best nights were spent there, and once they were done, and could barely see straight, they would stagger out to make the short walk home. Under the night sky the town took on a certain unrestrained beauty. The moon, when it rose full, seemed to hang so heavy in the sky that it appeared reluctant to let go of the horizon at all. Here and there, other figures moved beneath the streetlights. Unwieldy clumps of bougainvillea tumbled over fences, dense with sprays of pink and white and red. Walking home charged with booze could draw forth a feeling of contentment in both men.

At first, Simon had broken into the locked bedroom and set a spare mattress for Tony amid the clutter, but the switch to the air-conditioner had proven elusive and the room was sweltering, near impossible to sleep in. Churchill's nightly ritual made it harder still: he would often arrive back at the house late and cook a meal of fried kidneys and freshly chopped chilli.

The fatty aroma would drift heavily through the whole house. Seeking respite, Tony dragged his mattress to the garden and set it out alongside a cyclone-wire fence the property shared with a childcare centre. It was quieter, cooler: he could sleep there relatively undisturbed. After a night's drinking, he would sometimes wake late, long after the sun had cleared the horizon. Next door, white mothers would already be dropping their children off for the day. The barbed glances he would receive through the fence only emboldened his resolve to go as deep as he could into the Gija world.

Churchill slept wherever he could. One morning, Tony, Simon and Freddie found him passed out in the front yard, a dead snake beside him in the dust. For a moment they thought Churchill had been bitten and was dead too. But he was only sleeping and soon awoke.

He was as perplexed by the scene as anyone.

The mystery of the snake was never solved, but the story that followed wrote itself: the snake had bitten Churchill and then succumbed to alcohol poisoning.

2.

Other artists would soon make themselves known to Tony and Freddie, and the painting group would expand organically, but initially it was Freddie who put his energy into the project: the first paintings made at Pindan Avenue were his. They were destined for a solo exhibition with William Mora in Melbourne and the deadline was tight. Tony set up a trestle table in the front yard and ordered stretched canvases and large white buckets of milled pigment from the best suppliers in Melbourne.

No colour this time, just the subdued ochre palette of the Kimberley.

Without fail, Freddie would rise early. He would begin work while the sun was still low. The table was just outside Simon's window and each morning Simon would hear the sharp hiss of a beer can being opened.

Freddie would drink it, open another, and pick up his brush.

He would work methodically until the sun was high in the sky and the heat made it impossible to continue. He would then wander off into town to spend the day with a revolving cast of family and hangers-on, arriving home in the evening to cook a steak, retreat to his swag, and prepare to do it all again the next day. In this way he painted the entire exhibition in less than two weeks.

Simon became friendly with Churchill immediately, but his relationship with Freddie was slower to progress. Freddie often appeared reticent to engage, and it was only when Simon realised his ambitions as a writer and published an article in Melbourne's *Sunday Age* that relations between the two seemed to thaw. The piece detailed Freddie and Tony's project. After talking to them both, Simon framed it in terms of social justice: theirs was a stand against the more rapacious interests of the Aboriginal art industry, a struggle for something approaching economic independence in a context where this was too often denied. Simon's article offered them a platform to argue that consignment sales were the way forward, the means by which to bring the Aboriginal art industry in line with its white counterpart.

By then, Simon had lived with Freddie long enough to know something of his character. To Freddie's evident pleasure he didn't gloss his portrait: he wrote of him as a 'raging bull', someone who could knock a door from its hinges in a drunken rage. But it was a nuanced picture too: just because Freddie was part of the Kimberley's hard-drinking culture didn't mean he understood the inequalities of the Aboriginal art market any less. Simon was careful to underscore that Freddie's work with Tony was marked by an undeniable pragmatism.

He interviewed Freddie on the veranda at Pindan Avenue and Freddie recounted how he and Tony had met in Melbourne, how they'd visited the Argyle Dam and looked across the flooded country as Freddie first discussed his earnings in Melbourne in detail. He spoke about 'Old Frank Watters' and how Watters had delivered so well with the exhibition in Sydney.

In the article, Simon carefully burnished the rough edges from Freddie's Kriol-inflected English: 'It doesn't matter where you go – Fitzroy Crossing, Derby, Broome – all those Aboriginal artists, they don't get much money. They think five hundred dollars is big money. They don't know how much their painting is worth. But I found out.'

•

Word of Freddie and Tony's intent to build something different appeared to move quickly through the Gija world. Rusty Peters, a tall and slender man aged in his early sixties, arrived at Pindan Avenue soon afterwards. Simon had already met him at an opening at William Mora's that he attended with his father: it had been Rusty who had invited him to visit the Kimberley in the first place.

Tony knew Rusty too. They had crossed paths at the drinking camp, which was presided over with some flair by Rusty's brother Rammel. During the short period Tony spent there, Rusty had at times stayed too, usually after putting in a day's work at Waringarri Aboriginal Arts. He was a striking figure, stooped from an old station accident that had left him with a rolling, painful-looking gait, a testament to poorly healed bones. His face was framed by long hair, his eyes bright and dark. Although quiet, he wasn't shy. When he spoke it was in a deep, mumbling baritone; his laugh, when it came, convulsed his thin frame.

All this Tony would come to love, but at first Rusty was an enigmatic presence. He didn't yet paint in any meaningful way – at Waringarri he was simply paid a small wage to mow the grass and pack paintings for transport – but as he folded himself into a plastic chair on the veranda at Pindan Avenue it became clear that he too was interested.

A large, wryly humorous woman called Phyllis Thomas was there soon after. She lived for the most part with her husband Big Joe at Crocodile Hole, the tiny outstation towards Warmun, and arrived much like Rusty: unannounced, but confident. She settled herself in the front yard and fixed Tony with a steady gaze. ('What now, Jungurra?' she'd often say to him with an elaborate sigh.) Goody Barrett, a warm and good-natured woman in her sixties whom Tony had first met at Hector's place in Warmun, also expressed interest. Like the other women she dressed in long floral skirts: a holdover from the Catholic-inflected conventions of the station days.

Goody and Phyllis would both prove a pleasure to work with, and would each in their own way come to shape Tony's time in country, but it was Peggy Patrick, a woman who carried herself like a queen through the surrounding milieu, who quickly became the group's matriarch.

Such a role was far from uncommon – older Aboriginal women often found themselves caring for large mobs of grandchildren and great-grandchildren – but Peggy added her own distinctive touch. She would as readily appear trailing a wayward linguist or anthropologist as she would a swarm of kids. Aged somewhere in her late sixties, she had travelled widely and now moved among whites with a striking confidence, aware of the power she wielded. The patterned bandanna she often wore knotted about her forehead added a rakish touch that suited her to a tee; earth-mother and raconteur in near-equal measure.

Simon wouldn't stay much longer in the Kimberley, but he grew to know each of the new arrivals who added to the unfolding scene at Pindan Avenue. Although he would recall them all with a certain fondness, it was Hector to whom he was drawn most strongly. Hector had appeared not long after Tony, and although he eventually began painting too, he at first simply continued the informal induction he'd set in motion for Tony in Warmun. In Kununurra, he readily embraced Simon as well: another willing pair of ears, another project.

Simon was entranced by Hector, and soon took to recording the long conversations the two of them would share. He transcribed them in thick blocks of unedited English, Kriol-heavy and near impenetrable.

On tape, Hector's voice would fade in and out as the surrounding world stirred around them: a passing car, a crow's sudden lamentation, indistinct yelling from the street.

Given the ceremony of the recorder, Simon would most often be the one to begin: 'Good morning Mr Chundaloo.'

Hector would look at him and smile.

'Hello, Mr Simon,' he'd say.

Sometimes Hector would playfully repeat the title: 'Mr, Mr, Mr Simon.'

Then he would be off.

As he laid out moments from his life he jumped backwards and forwards in time, just as he'd done with Tony when the two had first sat talking together in Warmun. He would speak of his ancestors and forebears in the same breath in which he would address his concern for the Gija youth he saw falling through the cracks in the world around them.

Only occasionally would he pause briefly, look quizzically at Simon, and make sure he was following.

'You like'im, that English? Pidgin English, Mr Simon?'

Simon had only to offer the most minimal of prompts. 'When you were a little boy, did the old men teach you Law?' he once asked as they sat together.

'Not little boy time,' Hector explained. 'Big man time, like you.'

'Magic one, all the old people, plenty magic one,' Hector said.

He explained how the old people used to look at his generation, raised either in Turkey Creek or on the stations, and tell them they appeared sick. If they wanted to be healthy they needed to walk their country, looking for bush tucker. They had to feed themselves.

Another morning, Hector began with life on the stations and how he'd first learnt to speak English.

'I'll tell you a story about when I was a young boy,' he said.

'Then – when I first go to the stock job, working the cattle, when I was teenage – I didn't know about proper speaking English language. I didn't know. And manager – gardiya – he used to belt me, make me listen, teach me how to talk English language.'

He explained that he'd mastered horse-work by the same means: the station manager hanging over him, ready to 'belt' him as he learnt to saddle a young colt and break it in. He'd climb on its back only to be bucked off time and time again.

'Hard time I had, from white people,' he said, 'hard time.'

Station labour provided Hector a near-constant theme. He told Simon of droving cattle from station to port, of how he had watched over them through the night and, if they broke away from the mob, chased them down on horseback. He spoke of pushing them as a mass across the river, of how crocodiles waited there in the deep water.

Later, he explained that he had not only become a clever horseman, but an expert farrier.

'Not too tight'im shoe la foot,' he'd say.

'If a horse got no shoe, he can't gallop. He hurt'im la foot. You must put a shoe on him: then he can run like a motorcar.'

All this work was done for next to nothing.

'I bin just working for piece of bread and slice of meat,' Hector explained to Simon more than once. 'We used to have that for tucker: breakfast or dinner like that.'

Shadows lay thick in Hector's memory, but at first he only hinted at them.

'Granny brother and cousin brother all bin get killed,' he said one morning.

'Might be gardiya bin kill'im – we don't know what – but they been put'im longa hole now, old people, you know?'

Statements like that would hang there, context unspoken, until the conversation simply followed its meandering path elsewhere.

'How do you say rain?' Simon asked later.

Hector told him, offering up the correct word in language, before immediately expanding on it by explaining how to say 'rain is falling down'.

Then he offered the word for lightning and a storm that had been brewing around them broke in torrents; the sound of heavy rain washed over the recording.

•

When Paddy arrived from Warmun it was with little fanfare. He was dropped off by family and brought with him nothing but the clothes he was wearing. Hector knew Paddy well; when Paddy set up to paint in the front yard, Hector joined him.

The two old men sat directly on the dirt, their legs crossed. Tony carefully arranged everything around them, made sure the 'studio', such as it was, ran smoothly. He moved quietly, topping up paint and refreshing brush water as he went. If the old men spoke it was usually softly; at times they would pass a joke from one to the other, but painting, for the most part, was a serious enterprise.

PB's first works at the house were bracingly simple. Tony provided him with board, rather than canvas, which he had cut to roughly the same size as the largest of the works he'd found in Warmun. The paintings that followed expanded from those raw beginnings. Paddy depicted country as loosely organic circles, bordered by black, and linked together by roughly brushed grounds. Beside Hector's paintings, which were often symmetrical and exacting, PB's appeared almost clumsy, but the tenor of his voice was clear immediately. His compositions at first jostled together almost unthinkingly: it could seem as if forms risked being pushed from the edge of a painting entirely, that only by attenuating them, or pulling them out of shape, did PB manage to fit them in.

Freddie also played with the edges of his works – the long lines of riverbeds or roads that he extended off a picture's edge readily pulled a viewer's eye beyond what was depicted on the canvas alone – but there was a quality to his paintings that could appear overly calculated, as if he knew exactly what he was doing and was leaving little to chance. Years later, Tony would argue that by this measure Freddie had been the most accomplished among the painters, and at one level it was true: there was an undeniable confidence in how Timms resolved many of his works. But what PB lacked in polish, he made up for in character. As he sat there in the dirt of the front yard, it was clear his paintings had an immediacy that was impossible to rehearse.

One work followed another: a group of bulbous forms, a tentative line, ragged outlines of white dots. In coming years PB's paintings would become more and more refined, but even as his compositions emptied towards nothing, these early qualities would carry through.

By measure of his early practice, Bedford's first work on canvas was a huge step forward. Its subject was the Emu Dreaming, and the country he painted – black and red hill-forms gathered around a prominent vertical division – was laid down as a stage for the ancestral drama that animated its surfaces.

The same place cradled the historical narrative of the Bedford Downs massacre, a story that Tony would soon learn in all its terrible detail, but at first PB left this aspect unspoken. He showed the emu ancestor untethered by frontier history: a forlorn figure stuck in a deep cleft at a place Gija called Garnannayien, a rocky peak on his father's country known to Europeans as Mount King. Paddy would later speak in detail about the mountain to the linguist Frances Kofod, about how it was a dangerous place that cried out across the landscape each time someone from that country died. An answer would come from another mountain on Texas Downs in the north-east: two sites, both fraught with spiritual danger, calling to one another across Gija land.

The emu was naively rendered, but it was nonetheless perfect: its long neck drooped downwards towards dangling feet; a mass of ranges pressed in around it. He drew it all together on a yellow ground, each form picked out by its ragged border of white dots. He explained that the bird had been journeying with Birnkirrbal, the ancestral bush turkey, who abandoned him and later established the Law of night and day across Gija country.

Paddy's painting money would later be used to charter a helicopter to the site, and from above he would see that country laid out just as he knew it, the fissure in Mount King forming its cleft of shadow in the sunlight.

•

Simon, who was continuing his practice of recording audio, soon got his hands on a video camera and began to film the old men talking. In the months that followed he and a girlfriend, Sally Law, who would visit from Melbourne, would gather together footage and edit a short, elegiac film from the material. In one scene, PB would explain what it was for him to paint.

Simon had already heard Hector talk about this in detail – for Gija of his generation, painting was the equivalent of school, one of the ways in which stories had been passed down the line: the paintings Hector had seen in caves as a young man had been integral to his Gija education. He'd even gone as far as explaining that 'If I didn't know painting, I should be dumb'.

For PB, painting carried similar weight: it was a means to assert his identity, to underscore his knowledge of place, which in turn seemed to carry a direct correlation to his authority in the Gija realm. By then, Paddy was only a year into his practice, but he already knew exactly where he stood.

'You know, my mother was a painter, and my painting is different from all the other painters,' he begins as Simon films.

His voice, which Simon knew well by then, is worn with age, but it remains lively; like Hector's, his English is declaratory, peppered with Kriol.

'I run my country, for countryside. All the names in my painting, all the country, mine. From my mother, and from my father, and for uncle, grandpa, granny: all them fellas.

'Nothing left now, only myself,' he says. 'That's what I run that painting for: for the olden times, for my grandchildren, for my mother and my father.'

And then, as if in summary: 'For country.'

Later, Simon's camera captures Paddy and Hector sitting quietly alongside a waterhole. Fresh spear grass forms a green wall behind them; kids can be heard splashing in the water just beyond the shot. The conversation has shifted to far broader concerns.

Hector sits at the front, looking downwards pensively; the tiny brim on his terry-towelling fishing hat only just shades his eyes. Paddy sits directly behind his old friend. He wears his stock hat. A sleeveless shirt, once white, is gathered by only one button at the centre of his chest. He tilts his head back and takes a drink from a two-litre bottle of bright orange soft drink.

Hector is the first to break the reverie.

'I bin running around, all around here, when I bin grow up,' he says.

'When I bin like them kids there' (he gestures beyond the frame) 'me and Goowoomji be running around. They bring Goowoomji from Violet Valley. He met up with me.'

At the mention of his Gija nickname Paddy cuts in.

'We never bin to school,' he says abruptly.

He looks down, away from the camera. He's now taken his hat from his head, uncovering his thick mass of grey curls, and has donned a pair of sunglasses with clear plastic frames. As he continues, a lit cigarette hangs precariously from his lips.

'All the old people bin taught us the proper way, you know?'

His voice rises a touch, thins out as it does.

Beside him, Hector grunts his approval: he knows the theme well.

'Well, we believed!' Paddy says. 'That's why we followed the Law from the old people.

'They go gardiya way now,' he adds, referring to the children off-camera. 'They go gardiya side now.'

Hector takes up the same thread: 'I'm very sorry for them. My way, you know?

'I don't know what's going to be happening. I keep thinking about this country: Halls Creek, Turkey Creek, Kununurra. Nothing! I can't see anyone believing in Ngarranggarni.

'Why these young people can't come up and believe?' he asks softly. 'Why?'

Later still, Hector continues along the same path alone: 'Well, all these young people be dying now,' he says.

'What's wrong? *I* should be dying, I'm an old man. In Warmun, too many young people there died in the cemetery. Even Kununurra: too many young people died in Kununurra, in that cemetery over there, back of the hill.'

He describes his habit of visiting the graves there, how he sings what he refers to as 'Aboriginal corroboree' for them. 'Dead bodies,' he says.

As the film draws to a close, Hector puts what must be a great fear bluntly: 'When we die – all the Ngarranggarni man – well, you can't see Ngarranggarni man anymore.'

His point was clear. In Hector's conception it was he and Paddy, and others like them, who were the Ngarranggarni men. They understood the Law of the place they lived, knew how it required constant maintenance in the spiritual realm.

You had to be aware of the many demands of country to thrive there. The many problems that gardiya had brought to the Gija world were only underscored by their ignorance of this fact.

Everything in that country had been granted a brain by the Ngarranggarni. Hector had already explained this on Simon's recordings. The Ngarranggarni had taught Hector how to use his own brain, he'd said. It had taught him how to talk, how to dance, even how to paint.

Even a fish had brains. The proof of this lay in the fact that it wanted to touch the fishing line in the first place, that it could get hooked.

Even the smallest fish was an offering from the Ngarranggarni. White people might throw it back, but a Ngarranggarni man like Hector knew that no matter its size you had to cook it on the fire and eat it.

That was the Law.

'When you chuck him away, the Ngarranggarni will punish you,' Hector explained. 'You'll feel sick.'

Hector clearly sensed what all the old people feared the most: without this knowledge – this pattern of thought that kept the Gija safe in the place that sustained them – the lives of the young people were already lost.

3.

Others soon joined Paddy and Hector in the dust at Pindan Avenue. In her spare moments, fleeting as they were, Peggy Patrick now took up a brush and Tony attended to the first paintings she made with the new group; a young 'understudy' of Hector's called Dougie Macale, who was in his forties, also began to paint in those early moments. Churchill continued to come and go, so too did Freddie.

Tony set up a speaker on the veranda and put on music.

He played a range of CDs, but a number hit high rotation: looking back, those front yard studio sessions were soundtracked by a set of distinctive voices, many of them Aboriginal.

There was Archie Roach's acclaimed album *Charcoal Lane* and its soft title song about street drinking around Melbourne's Fitzroy; in another track, 'Native Born', Roach sang of the famous Arrernte artist Albert Namatjira, and the Aboriginal loss of country. Classic country and western like Slim Dusty got a good run, as did Paul Kelly, the quintessential Melbourne singer-songwriter. Kelly's 1992 collaboration with Kev Carmody, 'From Little Things, Big Things Grow', even became something of a studio anthem: the song's subject – the Gurindji people's struggle for land rights at Wave Hill Station – was as well known in the Kimberley as it was elsewhere. The Gurindji had pushed against the pastoral invaders and won. Gough Whitlam, the boss for all gardiya, had stood there with Vincent Lingiari, a man whose family ties extended to Gija country, and passed the old stockman a handful of soil. He'd given the place back.

From little things, big things grow: the resonance in the title alone wasn't lost. Tony played the song over and over with absolute sincerity. As far as he was concerned, they were building something big.

Simon would later recall the sense of joy that carried through those days, the feeling of momentum that had so clearly captured the group. He would listen as Tony spoke to the artists about the white art world, repeating much of what he'd already explained to Freddie: the benefits of the consignment system seemed a near-constant theme. Freddie's success with Watters remained the touchstone. Using that example, Tony would explain money, what commissions meant, how it was better to offset short-term gain with a long-term vision.

He also began to spread the word. Not long after Paddy began to paint, Tony reached out to two art collectors he knew in Sydney, Colin and Elizabeth Laverty. He'd first met the couple through Ray Hughes, the flamboyant Sydney art dealer, and had liked them immediately. He'd still had his Melbourne gallery then and over the years that followed they'd rarely been out of touch for long. He called from Kununurra and attested to the project's promise, and then followed up with two letters. He included photographs of paintings that he and Simon took on the street at the front of the house, leaning each board or canvas against a streetlight and cropping the image as close to the edge of the work as possible.

Aren't the Paddys fantastic – he's over 80 years of age, he wrote in the first letter. Into that envelope he slipped images of those first boards of Paddy's he'd found in Warmun.

Colin and Liz were widely known as serious collectors who knew what they liked. But more than that, they were the rare kind who would support an artist over their career regardless of whether their work fell out of broad favour or not. Colin, a famously gentle man, was a doctor and medical researcher who went on to found a successful network of pathology labs. Art was an abiding interest: by the time he married Liz in 1982 he'd parlayed an early enthusiasm for colonial paintings of sporting themes into a passion for modern Australian art, especially abstraction: a large Tony Tuckson was an early collection standout, as was a black 'door' painting by the Melbourne artist Peter Booth.

Liz took to art with a passion that rivalled her husband's, and the two went about building one of the largest private collections in the country. Many of the artists whom they collected in depth Tony knew and respected. Among them was the unique and undersung landscape painter Ken Whisson, an Australian who had laboured for much of his career in a tiny live-in studio in the Italian city of Perugia. Whisson was a mainstay at Watters Gallery; following Freddie's first show there, Frank Watters had staged a two-person exhibition featuring Whisson and Freddie. It was the kind of thing that happened all too rarely in an art world where Aboriginal and non-Aboriginal art was often kept apart, but it had worked a dream: Whisson's uncertain, brushy lines offset beautifully the confidence with which Freddie cut through his works with simple arcing divisions. Many who saw that show remembered it always.

By the time Tony contacted the Lavertys from Kununurra, they had long achieved a similar bringing together of previously separate art worlds. A decade earlier, in 1988, a chance encounter with a group of canvases from the Western Desert had extended their focus to Aboriginal art. Those works, so complex and intricate in design, had convinced them to move quickly: they'd soon established themselves as the most dedicated and serious among the fast-growing ranks of Aboriginal art enthusiasts.

Visitors to their impressive Balmain home would see everything at once: groupings of fine porcelain ceramics by Gwyn Hanssen Pigott counterpointed by incised artefacts from the desert; elegant wooden assemblages by the sculptor Robert Klippel offset by the painterly canvases of Anmatyerr artist Emily Kame Kngwarreye – the so-called 'impossible modernist' who'd stormed the Australian art world in the 1990s and in her wake set the blueprint for so much of the remote painting that followed. There were photographs and drawings, woven baskets and editioned prints. International artists jostled for space among the many Australians represented. Once, when the Lavertys visited New York, Tony introduced them to his old friend David McKee, the gallerist. They returned home with two sublimely restrained abstractions by Harvey Quaytman, one of the American painters Tony had once shown in Melbourne. As distinctive as they were, Quaytman's works sat effortlessly in the collection, just like everything else.

Who better, Tony was thinking, *to own the very first of Paddy's works?*

He soon followed his first letter with the second, and included more photographs, each of them carefully numbered.

I think everything here is pretty good, he wrote. *Paddy's energy is enormous and Hector and I told him to have a rest – he's very happy painting from early morning to dusk.*

The photographs had been taken on an overcast day, and he made sure to apologise for the washed-out colours: *the richness in some of the paintings [is] lost, but these are good enough to get a general impression,* he wrote.

The yellow in PB.9 is flattened out and the red in PB.8 is much richer in reality. PB.7 is Paddy's first canvas – isn't it stunning!

Here Tony included a photo of the emu painting in progress – the image was taken from above, looking down on Paddy completing the final passages of dotted outline across the otherwise finished work.

Paddy sits directly on the ground, the corner of the canvas propped on one knee, his leg folded and tucked in towards his body. His other leg extends outwards, his bare foot resting casually in the dust, the stained cuff of his workpants rolled up well past his bony ankle. Flattened cardboard boxes are laid out beneath the canvas – a fruitless attempt to keep the working area free of dirt – while a scatter of makeshift studio paraphernalia is arrayed within easy reach: repurposed tin cans bristle with a forest of various-sized paintbrushes; a two-litre cordial bottle holds clean water.

Paddy is caught in full concentration, a slender brush clutched in his right hand. He's wearing a short-sleeved shirt, light blue. He wears no hat; his hair is a white tangle; his face, looking downwards, is lost in shadow.

The painting itself is a blast of colour and form: graphic, immediate, even wild.

Washed out or not, it looks astonishing.

•

It made perfect sense that the Lavertys would be excited to hear of the project that had drawn Tony away from the city art world: by the time he reached out to them, they were seasoned travellers in remote Australia.

Liz liked to tell people that they collected 'from the heart', that they had no education in art at all. But the assessment downplayed their influence, consciously or not: a sale to the couple was a boon for any artist, and they were treated well wherever they went.

Mostly they flew in a chartered light plane from community to community. Their friend Helen Read, an ex-nurse with a pilot's licence who had harnessed the Aboriginal art boom into an art-tourism venture, would usually be in the pilot's seat. Adventure played its part: as they went, tracts of country the couple had never seen spread out beneath them; they would land on dusty bush airstrips and be met by art centre coordinators in rundown LandCruisers. In preparation, the best artworks would have already been set aside; artists would be eagerly waiting to meet their well-heeled city visitors.

In this way the Lavertys made strong connections as far afield as Maningrida and Yirrkala in Arnhem Land, and Milikapiti on the Tiwi Islands. The art centre at Balgo, a community that lay where the Kimberley's arid far south gave way to the Tanami and the Great Sandy Desert, was a particular favourite. The couple's attraction to a place like that was partly aesthetic – Balgo painting was famously colourful and expressive – but they knew well that it was largely impossible to separate art from the relationships it brought with it. In Balgo, Liz would sit with Eubena Nampitjin, a community matriarch and acclaimed artist, and listen as the old lady quietly sang to her the circuitous songs associated with each of her luminous canvases. To Liz, that kind of thing was 'fabulous'.

Such trips had already taken them to the Kimberley a number of times. Rover featured prominently on their walls at home: they'd flown into Warmun on one of their art tours and purchased work from Serge and Maxine. They'd met the artists there, including Hector, whom they'd warmed to immediately and whose work they'd also collected. When they received Tony's letters they set to planning another visit with some excitement, but first they took his word that Bedford was worthy of their attention: they purchased the four boards sight unseen.

Paddy was still entirely unknown. In coming years, single canvases of his work would sell for as much as $300,000 on the secondary market, but the Lavertys got in early: they paid only $800 for the painting on cardboard, $1000 each for the two on cupboard doors. For the red landscape forms painted on ply against a black ground they paid just under $2000.

Tony bundled them in cardboard, wrapped them in packing tape and wrote the Lavertys' Balmain address in block letters across the front.

He sent them off, confident in the knowledge that this package would be the first among many.

4.

One day, sitting on the tiny veranda, Hector told Simon about alcohol, about how it was a weapon that gardiya had cleverly wielded against Aboriginal people.

To Hector, history's timing proved his theory. As equal wages were enforced on the stations in the late 1960s, the Aboriginal role in the pastoral industry was removed with a suddenness that bordered on violence. The right to vote, which followed soon after, brought with it the right to drink.

Welfare replaced work; as the population of communities like Warmun grew, drinking became a way of life for many. Hector had watched as towns like Halls Creek and Kununurra swelled with itinerant Aboriginal drinkers. By the 1990s alcohol-related death had soared.

Hector saw the pattern in this: 'That gardiya bin sort of "Ah! Blackfella getting money. We'll have to put him in the pub",' he explained to Simon.

'Too many trick, that gardiya, but we understand.'

Hector explained he'd spent two years on the grog but, unlike most of the other male painters, he gave it away. For him, drinking was now a rare occurrence. In the time Tony knew him, he could count on one hand the number of occasions he saw Hector drink.

When he did, his amiable character could shift. Once, early on, Tony had to pull Hector bodily from the country club – a white enclave at the centre of Kununurra – after the old man had consumed too many white wines and begun to hurl abuse at the other patrons. 'White cunts!' he yelled as he struggled with Tony at the door. As shocked as he was, Tony loved him for it.

Another time, during a visit to Darwin, Hector was less explosive, but his anger was just as clear. They were visiting Leon Stainer, an acclaimed bush printmaker who would soon work with each of the artists, and were sitting on the veranda. Again, it was white wine – if he drank, this seemed

Hector's drink of choice – and after being uncharacteristically quiet for a period, he leaned into Tony and gestured towards the street in front of them. It was a humid afternoon, but groups of pedestrians were filing past, all of them white. Hector said that if he had a rifle he would shoot every last one of them.

The only other time that Hector drank, to Tony's knowledge, was at one of the Pindan Avenue parties. They were regular occurrences: the painting sessions would extend for a few days and then something would happen – perhaps someone would arrive with money, or a payment would come through – and people would turn up until the place was bursting at the seams.

The resulting scene was invariably hectic and unruly. Simon, who felt some responsibility to keep the house in order, would try to enforce a no party rule, only to break it soon after. Revelry, joyous and loud, would extend until well past midnight, when people would either crash at the house, or wander off to continue drinking in the reserve. Sometimes, Tony would wake and there would be fifteen people sleeping on the floor.

It was on a night like this that Hector found himself a bottle of wine and a wineglass. He sat in his regular seat on the veranda, taking tiny sips and theatrically washing each around in his mouth before swallowing. 'Tasting it, Ngaji!' Tony would recall him exclaiming.

Hector was wearing his old dressing-gown and, as he performed his elaborate ritual, he asked Tony to sit on his lap, which Tony happily did.

That night Hector's anger was forgotten. He simply drank and laughed, and Tony laughed too. Around them, other Gija, drunk themselves, were expressing concern at Hector's increasing inebriation, which only made Hector laugh more.

'Uncle, Uncle,' people cried out. 'You shouldn't be drinking so much! Don't drink any more wine, Uncle!'

It was funny because they were drinking too. Everyone was, but the idea of Hector joining them was unimaginable.

Parties like that were fuelled by either beer – 'green cans' or 'red cans', depending on one's allegiance to Victoria Bitter or Emu Bitter – or cheap casks of moselle or port. The more reflective soundtrack of the painting sessions would be replaced by something more energetic, more consuming: *The Best Of Creedence Clearwater Revival* was a favourite among the Gija and would often be played on repeat at increasing volume.

From there, the night would spiral into a joyous mess: bodies coming and going; people yelling Kriol phrases that to the increasingly drunk ears of Tony and Simon would sound like a foreign language until it didn't. Tony came to regard the parties at Pindan Avenue in a similar fashion to the Animal Bar – evidence of the town's beating heart – except for the key difference that everybody knew each other. He learnt to let himself go, to simply let the unfolding character of the night carry him.

Sometimes, drunken arguments spilled over into fights; other times, it might be raucous dancing to a song that struck a chord. Everything was open and raw. Tony soon understood that this was the way that people laid themselves out for their countrymen and women to see. When the grog was flowing, there was no shame, just unbridled joy punctuated by flashes of expulsive anger, by tears and yelling and laughter. The problems that attended drinking were obvious, but there was nonetheless an undeniable immediacy to it, a sense of camaraderie of the kind Simon had already recognised with his young Miriwoong and Gajirrabeng friends. Someone might grab you by the shoulder and hold on for half an hour.

The kinship system placed everyone in relation to one another, identified them by skin name, and dictated not only what responsibilities flowed from one person to the next, but what relations were right and wrong. It also opened an avenue by which Gija women could drunkenly toy with their white guests. They were openly flirtatious with Tony and Simon, jokingly or otherwise.

'Oh, I'm your wife!' a woman might yell in Tony's ear after grabbing him for a dance around the living room. 'I'm a proper wife for you!'

In the thick of the moment it was hard to argue: the very designation of 'husband' and 'wife' seemed here a fluid, malleable concept. More often than not whether someone was the 'right' or 'wrong' match could be safely taken as shorthand for their sexual availability. Tony simply embraced it all in real time. He was on their turf, he reasoned: he quickly realised the best thing would be to welcome everything with open arms.

•

As fun as they were, the parties at Pindan Avenue took their toll. Tony could easily lose a day nursing a hangover and would despair as he felt the rhythm of the studio slipping away. The artists were affected too, especially Freddie.

Tony had been disappointed by the first paintings Freddie had done at Pindan Avenue. There was something lacking in the works, as if they'd been somehow depleted by the social demands that attended them. Freddie was often painting hungover, so it was no surprise he wasn't working to the best of his ability. Tony would watch him at the trestle table, laying out a composition, or working on infill with an open green can at his side: it could all seem lacklustre, almost meaningless.

In this way the problem of town life became clear: no matter the joy of having people around, it was impossible to escape the grog and everything that came with it. Plus there was a healthy stream of demand that followed the artists when they were easily accessible. Freddie, who had established himself faster than the others, bore the brunt. Tony learnt immediately that it was known by the harmless-sounding term 'humbug', a catch-all phrase deployed across Aboriginal Australia that referred to anything from lighthearted badgering for money or drink to more forceful expressions of kinship reciprocity. For better or for worse, it was this that bound the Gija together so tightly. At Pindan, Freddie's son 'Baldhead' Patrick was relentless if he suspected Freddie had money and was holding out. He would be at the house constantly, cajoling his father to reach into his pocket. When Freddie did, he might only have a couple of hours of peace before Patrick was back. He couldn't say no. It didn't take Tony long to understand where Freddie's initial windfall from Watters had gone.

Freddie proved he could make paintings in the face of that kind of pressure, but whether or not he could reach his full potential was another thing entirely. When more money started to come in, as Tony knew it would, he wasn't sure what would happen, nor how its effects could be managed.

In the second of his letters to the Lavertys he hinted at how difficult the project was: *very skeletal operations at present*, he wrote.

To this he added a line that would prove prescient. The old men had recently taken him to Wyndham, the long-declined port town 100 kilometres to Kununurra's west. Before the Ord River was dammed in the 1960s and Kununurra had boomed around the newly fertile agricultural land brought forth by irrigation, Wyndham had been the bustling heart of the Kimberley pastoral industry. Cattle had once been mustered across vast tracts of country, at first to be slaughtered at the meatworks, now shuttered, which had until the 1980s provided the town its economic engine. They were now shipped out en masse through the Cambridge Gulf.

Freddie, Rusty and Hector had driven Tony to the top of The Bastion, a huge hill that looked out over the town, with its central street of dilapidated timber-clad colonial buildings and its rough-as-guts pub. Beyond that, a network of five rivers threaded their way inland from the gulf. If one wanted to get a sense of how vast that country was, or feel the energy that rose from it in waves, there were few better vantage points. You could also see the small blocks of land that led into town, scattered alongside the highway, quiet and contained. It was that kind of place where Tony pictured the painting project taking root.

I need to get that property outside Wyndham, he wrote to the Lavertys. It was almost an afterthought, something he slipped in before signing off.

Towards the end of his time in the Kimberley, he would do exactly that, and relocate everything to the outskirts of that tiny rundown town. But first it was the artists who led the way: they understood the challenges of town better than anyone, and it seemed to Tony that by the time he saw the problem, they were already working on a solution. Peggy, Phyllis Thomas and Rusty began to arrive unannounced at Pindan Avenue. They would collect Tony, and maybe Hector and Paddy as well, and leave Kununurra's tight grid of streets behind to spend the night at Ivanhoe Crossing. It wasn't far, but it was far enough for the quiet of the Kimberley to press in. It was below the diversion dam, and a favoured fishing spot for Aboriginal and non-Aboriginal people alike. There were wide beaches of coarse river sand where swags could be laid out around cooking fires.

Some nights the women would sing into the darkness, and if they were there, Hector and even Paddy would join them. Sometimes there would be stories. Tony would simply listen.

It was there that Peggy and Phyllis began to speak about Crocodile Hole, which they called Rugun, and how that place – a secluded community set alongside a permanent waterhole – would offer them the quiet they needed to really make things work.

It took Tony a moment to realise it, but when he did, it became clear. The project Freddie had invited him to the Kimberley to help build was now laid out before him. Everything was in place; the artists had made themselves known. Hector had already named the group during a discussion on the veranda at Pindan Avenue.

'Jirrawun,' he'd said.

He explained the word to Tony in the simplest of terms: it meant 'one mob standing together'. It was perfect.

Rugun / Crocodile Hole

1.

Their initial visit to Crocodile Hole seemed to Tony like a diplomatic mission between Gija embassies. It was still his first year in the Kimberley, 1998, but as he drove out from Kununurra with Hector in the passenger seat beside him, the route they followed was now largely familiar: south-west towards Wyndham, then south on the highway to Warmun.

No matter how many times he'd seen it, the country that way could still catch his breath. First, the Carr Boyd Ranges strung their sedate ribbon of rocky red in the middle distance. Later, past Doon Doon, came the gentle sequence of shallow valleys that soon gave way to the ridge line where the staggered silhouette marked the diamond mine's slow progress.

It was not long afterwards that the hand-painted sign to the community appeared on the highway's verge: a rough figure of a crocodile with H-O-L-E spelt out alongside in block letters. *Welcome to Rugun Aboriginal community*, the accompanying text read, *Permission required by order Chairman*. Although he'd passed the sign on visits to Warmun, it was the first time Tony had turned off the highway and made his way over the winding dirt track. From here it was another twenty minutes or more. As they drove, the landscape opened around them.

When it finally appeared, the community was minimal, almost shockingly so. They slowly passed a smashed-in Telecom phone booth standing forlorn and useless; stray star-pickets driven into the earth at irregular intervals marked sites where unwatered trees had died; a large water tank was raised high on stilts. Vehicles lay abandoned in various stages of disrepair.

The track unravelled into a network of byways that wound past a motley collection of sheds and between a handful of dilapidated houses.

They were simple structures clad in corrugated iron: some of them looked relatively new, others old. The earth between them was red and treed sparsely with gums and spindly acacia. It was dotted here and there with the charred remnants of open fires. Beside them were large billies and cooking grates, blackened by flame. Tangled piles of thin firewood lay in small heaps, dragged in from the surrounding bush and dumped.

Hector pointed out the main house where Phyllis and Big Joe lived together with their adult son, Patrick, who was most often called Fat Man. As with a number of the other simple dwellings they'd passed, it was surrounded by a scatter of camp beds and blankets spread across the dirt ground. Abandoned watering hoses unspooled green rubber arabesques in the dust. A filthy electrical cord ran in a tangle from the house to a tree, where a small spotlight had been clamped.

At first the place appeared abandoned, but as they drove in Tony saw a group of girls cooking at a bough shed. He glimpsed the waterhole through the trees and drew to a halt. When he cut the engine silence rushed in.

Peggy and Phyllis were already there, waiting. They introduced Tony to Big Joe and then to the other permanent residents: Teapot Carroll and Little Joe, half-brothers to Big Joe and Peggy. Teapot was a wiry and quiet man in his sixties whose run-in with a freshwater crocodile had left him with a pronounced limp. He welcomed Tony in simple terms: 'We're happy you're going to be doing something here,' he said.

Little Joe, who was achingly shy, said nothing. A group of kids – grandchildren, children, nephews and nieces – milled about, thin-limbed and curious.

The community was powered only intermittently by generator and got dark quickly. That first night they gathered as a small group around campfires, sitting on mattresses, broken chairs and flour drums. A bullock had recently been slaughtered, and over a meal of ribs cooked simply over open flames they formally sketched out Jirrawun's relocation.

It was clear to Tony that much of the work had already been done, that Peggy in particular had secured the necessary permissions. His own presence that night seemed largely symbolic. Rugun was Peggy's country and, with her brother in charge, she could ensure the project would enjoy a quiet base.

In the days that followed Tony made the drive again. This time Paddy, Freddie, Rusty and the others accompanied him. They clearly recognised the change at hand: the ambition of it, the vision that was developing among their tiny collective; all of it was theirs. For now, Crocodile Hole was the project's home; it was here that Jirrawun would find form.

At first that meant a deeper engagement with place. Tony was shifting his involvement in their community; he was changing down a gear, seeking to slow the daily rhythm that had propelled the weeks and months already spent among Kununurra's unruly social milieu.

They brought with them a cache of painting materials – the brushes, the stretched linen canvases, the white buckets of powdered oxide ready for mixing – and set up their swags and mattresses outside, loosely grouped around the remnants of a tin shed once used as an independent schoolhouse. A broad concrete slab quickly came to mark the borders of an open-air studio. Tony swept out another shed and designated it a storeroom for completed paintings. It was that simple. With only the most basic of infrastructure in place they could recommence work.

A sense of renewed focus followed almost immediately.

The artists would gather early. Mostly they'd sit cross-legged on the slab, each with a work in progress lying horizontally before them. Tony followed the studio practice he had already established in town: he mixed the paint and made sure that the right amount of acrylic medium was used as binder before portioning it out in plastic takeaway containers or empty tin cans that had recently held powdered milk.

The distraction in Kununurra had been visual as much as anything, but with that backdrop now gone, the colours Tony mixed seemed somehow more intense. They rang clear against the surrounding bush. When wet, the red ochre was as bright and oily as lipstick; the black appeared as dense as velvet; the white formed a pure ground against which the yellow burnt like acid.

To this palette Tony made only a few minor variations: a pink could easily be mixed from red and white; a touch of black could be added to yellow to achieve a dull olive green. Do the same thing with red and you got ochre brown. As he moved among the artists he refreshed their brush water and thinned their paints as necessary, watching as each work progressed in stages: a structural scaffold of lines, followed by the painted infill. Finally, the filigree of white dots would be added to illuminate the finished painting's composition. Although the success of each work could be judged early by a trained eye, at Crocodile Hole Tony became convinced that this last stage was always the decisive one. A work often appeared awkward or unresolved, only for the dots to incrementally draw it into focus: it was this that pulled each together, heightening its visual effect.

As at Pindan Avenue, all this generally happened in what passed for silence in the tiny community: the ebb and flow of cicadas and bird call; the brief, sharp outburst of a fight among the camp dogs; the high laughter of children in the distance. The painters most often said nothing as they worked, especially the men, but Tony soon understood that there was a constant dialogue at play around him. Watching a painting unfold would prompt a question in his mind, only for someone to answer it before he could put it into words.

'Waterhole, that one,' Paddy might softly offer as he completed a rough circle at the centre of a new canvas and look up to notice Tony watching intently.

Tony would reach back in his mind to the studios he'd known in Melbourne and recognise a similar charge of intimacy: the feeling of being privy to a creative process as it unfolded; the sense of being welcomed inside. He had already cultivated the kind of relationship with white painters that opened this usually private space outwards, but even with those he had drawn closest to there had always been a point of resistance.

Sometimes he'd think about this in terms of the anxiety that so often attended creative practice. For the white artists he'd once worked with there were the constantly parsed questions of a painting's relative 'success': whether or not a composition was 'working'; whether a colour was too intense for the subject at hand. A thousand different decisions to agonise over. From this perspective painting was an exercise in holding one's courage along a tightrope between doubt and vision.

By contrast, the Gija were strikingly pragmatic. He watched as Paddy made even his most successful paintings seem effortless: a simple combination of lines and colour and dots reworked in endless variation.

Tony had enjoyed the excitement of attending to the first works the artists made in Kununurra, but now he was hooked.

•

Paddy's early work at Crocodile Hole only made the talent he'd shown in Kununurra clearer. Soon after their arrival he turned his attention to a site called Winperrji, or Police Rock Hole, a large waterhole between Warmun and his birthplace of Bedford Downs that marks the Dreaming place of Jalangarnany, the plains kangaroo.

Against a deep yellow background, the old man depicted the waterhole as an open black circle at the work's extreme bottom left-hand corner, its heavy outline intersecting with a painted black border. Everything else he left empty.

Again Tony couldn't help but see Rover Thomas: those late works in which Rover had pushed everything to the very edges, leaving ochre voids at the centre. He thought back to Serge and how he'd shown Tony recent work by Rover at Narrangunny Art Traders in Warmun: *What is this 'minimal' shit that punters down south like so much?*

But PB rarely stayed still for long: from one work to the next he could turn on a dime.

Soon after came a painting of McPhee Hole, a site at the northern edge of the Durack Range that lay on his father's country. In contrast to his minimal depiction of Winperrji, Paddy crowded that painting with a cacophony of form. This was Jawoorraban, a Dreaming site for the little corella – the small white parrot that flew through Paddy's country in raucous flocks.

Red and yellow forms jostled restlessly for visual space; a long finger of yellow spiralled in the top right. That shape was perfectly echoed by the way Paddy pulled the painting's dotted edge away from the closest corner, curving it inward.

•

Before they began work each morning the old men had a simple ritual: they would all sit together at the painting camp drinking tea or instant coffee, all of them either smoking or chewing plugs of rolling tobacco mixed with ash.

Tony would join them. The sharp sounds of Gija and Kimberley Kriol occasionally punctuated the rising flood of birdsong, but for the most part that was it: any conversation was usually low and mumbled, indistinct. As the sun moved, the old men would rise, pick up their chairs and follow it as one, none of them speaking a word.

Around them, the community played out its own daily rhythms. Some afternoons Fat Man, an immense figure in his late twenties, would drop past the painting camp with a handful of other young men and co-opt Tony to help shoot a bullock from the surrounding station.

They'd take an axe and knives and butcher it where it fell, opening up the carcass and spilling its bright blood across the ground. The rough cuts of meat would be unceremoniously dumped in the back of their vehicle, lugged into the community and either cooked immediately over hot coals, or stuffed into refrigerators that were only occasionally running. The kids would cut free the dead animal's sphincter with a tied-off section of intestine still attached and it would be rinsed out, blown full of air and ingeniously used as a makeshift whoopee cushion. Sometimes Tony would follow the kids to a nearby gorge and lie in the shade, watching as they jumped from a rock platform worn into a smooth depression by what he could only assume were generations of bare feet.

With the tight geometry of Kununurra's streets behind him, at Crocodile Hole the connection between the landscape and the human world took centre stage. Every nuance rang clear. On the surrounding hills the wind would move through the tall stands of spear grass, rippling it like human hair. Tony, watching, learnt he could count that distance in seconds before he felt that same wind quietly touch him too. Often, at the day's height, the air would be deathly still and the heat would lie thick upon the community, sapping all energy. The only sane response was to once again follow the example set by the old men and wait supine, body covered by a thick layer of sweat.

During those hours Paddy would retreat beneath a makeshift shelter that he favoured at the edge of the painting slab. Chicken wire had been stretched between bush-wood posts; old blankets and mattresses had been stacked on top for shade.

'Too hot?' Paddy would ask quietly, reclining there in the semi-darkness, his hat shadowing his face darker still. He'd softly whistle and at that moment a cool breeze would wash over them.

At night the community would sometimes stage joonba, the narrative performances that the Gija would at first refer to for Tony's benefit as 'corroborees'. Lit by fires and spotlight, dancers would take on the personas of Dreaming figures, transforming before the tiny audience that gathered to watch.

During a joonba about the Dreaming willy-willy it manifested before them, blowing dust around the dancing figures. Tony began to understand that the Gija lived in this space constantly, that the borders of their tangible world were constantly open to what lay beyond. 'It's a very hard Law,' the old men would say to him. They meant it was a difficult world to make your life in: it was a place of spirits, of dangerous forces, of intricate cause and effect. Often, watching night-time performances, he thought about what little he knew of the Greek tragedies, about how they balanced terrible events with levity and how the internal dramas of the human mind were named and externalised, liberated into the real world around them.

As the wet season came, the dry bed of Gum Creek, which passed nearby, filled with clear water and began to flow, everything in its wake becoming pure and fresh. Lightning split the sky as rain sent new stands of spear grass rocketing skyward. As time progressed, Hector explained the subtleties of the many seasons as they arrived. A new flower or a spray of fresh grass would signal a coming change. All of it was constant motion, and the Gija would interconnect with it as one. The Greeks created the gods, Tony realised, to map the world's complexities by name; the Gija had done the same, manifesting the social world in the constantly shifting ecology around them.

Each name spoke of a contingency. It was proof of the world's logic.

•

In the background Teapot and Little Joe were quiet presences; they observed the painting group establishing around them, but declined to take part. Instead, they would spend hours labouring over their ancient LandCruiser utility, trying to keep it roadworthy enough to make the fortnightly run to Turkey Creek to collect their pensions. Tony would watch, fascinated, as they pulled the engine apart time and time again, reaching ingenious solutions to myriad mechanical problems.

Once, camping at the gorge above the community, the two brothers lay on swags and told Tony of how they'd been born in the bush and as children had lived a traditional life with their family, even as the pastoral industry occupied the country around them. After narrowly avoiding a party sent to track them, they had walked into Doon Doon Station under the cover of darkness and sat at the homestead's periphery watching in awe as station life played out beyond the lighted kitchen window. The next morning they went in as a group: they laid down their spears and various-sized boomerangs in exchange for clothes and a life as unpaid station labour.

Now, with the station days long behind them, it was all about the LandCruiser. It was a project the brothers attacked with a singular focus. When the vehicle was running, their family would pile into the back: Little Joe's wife Susan and their daughter Madeline, and Teapot's three daughters – Milly, Brenda and Wendy. It was common to pass the LandCruiser on the road between Crocodile Hole and Warmun, stacked high with passengers, slowly grinding from gear to gear; just as common was the sight of it abandoned at the roadside, either broken down again or out of fuel. Somehow Teapot and Little Joe would fix it up enough to make the run back to Rugun, where the slow process would kick in once again.

Fat Man was a different kind of character entirely. He was born after the station era had collapsed and had known little beyond the cyclical pull of government welfare. Charismatic and personable, he was indulged by Phyllis and Big Joe, and often in trouble. Tony learnt quickly that he could talk a mile a minute and would readily spin stories for whoever was around to listen. When he drank, his stories became more and more outlandish: he once claimed to have shared a gaol cell with Mike Tyson, the American boxer. Although ridiculous, the fantasy made a strange kind of sense: Fat Man was a ready fighter, prone to drunken rages.

Tony had already witnessed bursts of violence in town and understood how casual it could be. At times it seemed as if younger men like Fat Man consciously wielded it – a means, perhaps, to earn what respect they could in lieu of the Law that granted their Elders such gravitas. But often it simply appeared a blind expression of frustration. Drinking only fuelled it and, for this reason, Crocodile Hole had clearly defined rules when it came to alcohol. If someone brought in grog they would have to seek Big Joe's permission to drink it: he'd usually send them off to Gum Creek so any disturbances could unfold at a distance

Tony would happily join groups there and drink warm cans of VB in the sandy riverbed. As with the parties at Pindan Avenue, there was a certain unrestrained joy to it, but more often than not some kind of jealousy would soon erupt into yelling and fighting. Women would rage alongside the men; everything could collapse in an instant, unravelling into chaos.

On weekends, Tony sometimes left the community behind and took runs into town with any of the old men who wanted to join him. They'd pile into a handful of vehicles and drive in ragged convoy down the highway. The last stretch, where the bitumen ran smoothly over the Ord River causeway, now felt strange. Alongside them, the landscape fell away, replaced by the clusters of low buildings that announced Kununurra's neatly plotted streets.

Initially, Tony would return to Pindan Avenue, where Simon Georgeff would welcome him and the others – they would simply pull up there, pile into the house and stay as guests for a number of days, falling into the old routine – but he would later rent rooms at the Hotel Kununurra. He'd visit the bank and post office and stock up on simple provisions at the Tuckerbox. If he had a group of paintings to send south, these would be dropped at the freight terminal, a simple shed in Kununurra's small industrial quarter. Afterwards, he and the old men would take in the relative luxury. A favoured haunt was the bakery where Tony would often sit at a table with Rusty and Hector and Paddy, all of them eating large breakfasts while they drank coffee and smoked. *This is as urbane as it gets*, he'd think wryly, recalling the long afternoons he once spent at Mario's cafe on Brunswick Street, a low-key epicentre for the mid-eighties Melbourne art scene. In the background he could feel the racist old white ladies behind the bakery's counter glowering at them.

At night they would return together to the Animal Bar and take their place among the mass of drinkers. Paddy would often claim space in a corner, where his offer of free drinks would quickly secure him a retinue of Gija women, while Rusty and Tony would hunker down in conversation.

Rusty had begun talking about painting as soon as he'd arrived at Pindan Avenue, but he'd only picked up a brush in earnest when the group relocated to Rugun. As an artist he struck Tony as insecure – whether it was because he'd worked as Rover's offsider and then as the groundsman at Waringarri Arts and was used to others holding the spotlight, Tony wasn't sure – but Rusty already painted in a distinctive, graphic style: his landscapes were places of turmoil where each shape seethed in and around another. The accompanying stories could be epic in their detail. One early work told of a malevolent figure that Rusty called 'The Little Cigarette Man'. He was long and thin like a cigarette, and about the same size. He'd sit on someone's shoulder and cause havoc with his whispered interjections.

Rusty was often guarded, but at the Animal Bar the drink would loosen him up: he and Tony would talk freely. *Waterbrain*, his multi-panel painting from 2002 that lays out in fine detail the creation of Gija knowledge over a lifespan, was first raised there as a concept, years before Rusty even put brush to canvas. Life began in water, Rusty would explain, liquid and new; later, through Law, the mind becomes fully formed. That work would eventually prove his masterpiece, a long and complex picture shown at the GrantPirrie Gallery in Sydney in 2001 and sold immediately to the Art Gallery of New South Wales. For years before he began it, he and Tony would return to the work's underlying philosophy. They'd sit together at the bar, their cans of beer before them, as Rusty slowly pulled his story into a shape he might finally set down in paint.

2.

It wasn't long after the group had relocated to Rugun that Colin and Elizabeth Laverty finally visited. They flew in from Darwin and checked into the Kununurra Country Club where Tony collected them and then drove them down the highway before finally turning onto the rutted track to Crocodile Hole.

They weren't the first visitors. The community's only working phone, located in the main house, had begun to ring regularly soon after Tony and the painters had arrived: contacts Tony had first cultivated in his initial months in Kununurra trying to either secure exhibitions or sales, or organise a visit. Simon had brought the first of them, a Perth socialite and aspiring gallerist called Jemma Stowe, who was a good friend of his mother's; she was followed by Martin Browne, a long-established art dealer from Sydney who had once consigned paintings by Colin McCahon to Tony's Melbourne gallery. Both selected work for exhibitions, but it was the Lavertys who flagged the kind of direct support Tony was after.

This was part of the overarching idea that was now beginning to take shape: gallerists would be useful in the early days – he knew that exhibitions with the right dealers would quickly build Jirrawun's profile – but ultimately he wanted to scale back this initial dependence and emphasise direct sales. Although Liz and Colin had been to Warmun, not to mention the other communities that art had drawn them to, Crocodile Hole was something else again.

Liz was struck not only by how small and hot the place was, but by how clearly Tony had been captured by it. The last time she'd seen him he had been clean-cut in a dark Italian suit; now he was dressed much like the artists he was working with: a chequered shirt (top pocket stuffed with a packet of Winfield Blue cigarettes) tucked into dirty jeans cinched at the waist with a silver-buckled belt. Boots and a stock hat completed the picture. He'd also proudly jettisoned all but the most basic notion of Western hygiene: he was washing only occasionally, usually in the waterhole, and had taken to cleaning his teeth with charcoal, a method he claimed was an old bush trick.

Tony showed the Lavertys the waterhole, where they watched a group of kids play. They then made their way to the painting shed, where they met Paddy for the first time, and Rusty too. Hector, who the Lavertys knew from Warmun, greeted them warmly.

The couple sat together in the sweltering heat of the shed, beaming as the artists gathered beside them and Tony took photos. They looked at one canvas after another, and although their visit was about more than buying, much of what they saw proved too good to turn down. They selected new paintings by Hector, more work by Paddy and a handful of new canvases by Rusty that marked his first ever sales. Over coming years they would add to this collection on a regular basis, amassing what would eventually amount to the most comprehensive array of Jirrawun work, private or otherwise.

The money that followed only added to the distinct feeling of momentum Tony had first recognised in Kununurra. Word of any sales spread fast. The large-scale card games that ballooned fortnightly in Warmun as welfare money came in began to relocate to Rugun, where painting money had the power to grow every jackpot. Battered LandCruisers would rumble in all afternoon, blue tarpaulins would be unfurled over the dusty ground, the spotlights clamped in trees would be hooked up to long extension cords and, once evening bled into night, switched on to bathe the scene in a warm glow. Games could have as many as twenty players, all of them sitting cross-legged in a circle on the tarp. Cash piles in the centre could be huge, but they were rarely held on to for long: someone would win, only to recirculate the lion's share almost immediately. It was a simple economy in motion, a redistribution of wealth in real time.

Tony would often find himself in the background, labouring away. He was happy to do it. He felt he'd been claimed by the Elders for a reason, that he needed to be as invested in the project as they were. But if there was a sense of pride shared between them, there were nonetheless immediate obstacles. For one, the venture was entirely independent. Tony found himself in the unenviable position of starting everything from scratch: there were no procedures in place; income depended solely on sales; infrastructure was almost entirely absent. It often felt an insurmountable undertaking.

Even the smallest details were blown out of all proportion. When the first rains of the wet season came Tony had to organise for demountable trailer accommodation – a 'donga' – to be delivered so he and the artists had a roof under which to sleep. It had four rooms: along the side they built a lean-to veranda from bush timber, covered it in blue tarpaulin and sat there together as if in front of a pioneer hut. To send a fax Tony would have to make the two-hour return drive to Warmun; at times he'd get back well after nightfall, only to turn around and do it again the next day. Shipping paintings meant a trip in the other direction, to Kununurra; packing them required materials that needed to be carefully ordered and maintained. Run out of something as simple as packing tape and the whole operation could grind to a halt.

To avoid the worst of the heat he quickly learnt to pack paintings at night. There was a single bulb suspended inside the painting shed and he would work away under that, dripping with sweat. Rusty at first offered to help – he had, after all, once packed paintings at Waringarri Arts – but Tony was idealistic: he readily took the opportunity to underscore the group's hierarchy. He would tell Rusty he was a painter now, not a packer. Only the next day Tony would acquiesce: as they loaded paintings into the Toyota LandCruiser utility that he had recently purchased he would stand back as Rusty and Freddie expertly tied down each load with the knots they had learnt as young men on the stations. They would then drive across the creek and back out towards the highway. It was easy for Tony to imagine they were back on the pastoral frontier, that they'd been loading cattle, not paintings, and were now off to the meatworks at Wyndham.

Tony was no stranger to hard work – at his galleries he'd done everything from painting the walls to hanging the exhibitions – but he soon found that the remoteness of Rugun added a psychological layer that could be crippling. At times the risk seemed all too clear. He often felt this most keenly at night when his anxiety levels would keep him awake, staring at the donga's ceiling, his mind swirling with the fear he might somehow step too far from his previous life to ever fully return.

Sometimes, fleeing humbug, he would drive a short distance from the community, set up his swag in the LandCruiser's trayback and lie there beneath the night sky. It was peaceful – he would watch shooting stars trace the blackness above – but it could be terrifying too. The vastness of the surrounding country would press into him. Miringi, a dingo mongrel who had adopted him not long after his arrival at Rugun, would sleep at his side, and on those nights the dog would often wake, whimpering at unseen presences in the surrounding darkness.

•

When the New Zealand–born painter Peter Adsett arrived in Rugun, not long after the Lavertys had departed, he recognised the ground Tony was negotiating. Adsett was travelling with Tony's old friend William Mora: it was late August of Jirrawun's first year and the two of them had come straight from Darwin, where they'd attended the annual National Aboriginal and Torres Strait Islander Art Award.

William had already explained to Adsett what little he knew of Tony's project in the Kimberley, and Adsett was eager to understand it more fully: he had been keenly interested in Aboriginal art since he first arrived in Australia in 1982. They spent two nights at Crocodile Hole, sleeping on swags. During the day Tony showed his visitors through a collection of recent works that were stacked in the painting shed. To Adsett it seemed Tony knew each work intimately; he could speak of how each artist had made them, even pinpoint the decisions that had guided their hands.

There was Paddy's work *Brumby Spring*, a picture of nine circular forms clustered around a waterhole's central void, and another, by Hector, that depicted stars gathered in the night sky above a horizontal sliver of moon: an obtuse, romantic image that told of the creation of the Milky Way. Adsett thought some works were not particularly successful, but given the conditions at Rugun the achievement was obvious.

It was also clear to Adsett that the relationship between Tony and Paddy already provided Jirrawun its key. Freddie obviously remained important (it was he who sat with Adsett and Mora and explained what Jirrawun as a group was trying to achieve) but, in conversation, Tony kept circling back to Paddy's work. He repeated the assertion he'd made to Simon Georgeff only months earlier, when Paddy had first arrived at Pindan Avenue to begin painting: the old man, Tony now said to Adsett, would be another Rover. Adsett saw little reason to doubt him, but although he was impressed by Tony's clear commitment, he found it hard not to wonder how long this enthusiastic visitor from Melbourne could embed himself in the community without losing his grip and the whole project collapsing around him.

For Adsett, the question wasn't simply academic. He too had felt the charismatic pull that remote places and people could enact; at first he tried to understand Tony's motivations through what he himself had experienced. As a young painter in the late 1980s, he had travelled to the Central Desert at the invitation of the famed Anangu Elder Nganyinytja, a colossal figure in the political and cultural struggles of the Anangu-Pitjantjatjara lands. Adsett's experiences there had been complex, hard to fully articulate, but Nganyinytja had guided him well: she had emphasised the importance of staying grounded in his own culture, of not moving too far beyond its borders. One had to be open, but also careful.

Adsett had since pulled away from the kind of direct experience that Tony was so clearly reaching for, but his paintings – lyrical black and white abstractions – betrayed an abiding interest. They were characterised by planar forms and graceful line-work that remained just beyond comprehension: a glimmer of a waterhole, perhaps, or a fence line tracing the curvature of a hill. It all clearly chimed with East Kimberley aesthetics, but Adsett's work was carefully analytical; Tony was clearly striving for something far more visceral: if he sensed the risk of transgression, it was something he welcomed.

During his visit, Adsett attempted to relay to Tony what he'd learnt in the desert, but if Tony caught the significance of it, he barely registered what was being said. Adsett would recall stripping down to shorts for a swim in the waterhole, and being surprised that Tony held back with the old men, watching from the shade: Adsett could later picture him with clarity, standing in his cowboy shirt and hat. The intent behind the painting project was easy enough to understand, but Tony's broader motivations struck him as far more complex, harder to grasp.

William Mora selected works for two exhibitions – a solo of Paddy's work and a group show of the others – while Adsett turned in his mind the potential of supporting them another way. He had held a position at Northern Territory University since he and his wife Susie had relocated to the northern capital in 1992, at first as a sessional lecturer and now as the co-head of painting. When he returned from the Kimberley he met with the acting Head of School, a printmaker from Tasmania called Tim Smith, and pitched an idea.

Smith was a receptive audience: he shared Adsett's interest in Aboriginal art and had already been instrumental in initiating a key shift at the art school. The challenge for him was one of focus: if the north had previously looked to Melbourne or Sydney for its measure, it now had to draw upon the surrounding region, Aboriginal Australia and Southeast Asia. The logic behind this was simple. In Australia's far north, Smith often reasoned, it was Western art that was strange, not its Aboriginal or Asian counterpart.

By the time Adsett approached him to discuss the artists he'd recently met at Crocodile Hole, this emphasis had already begun to play out: artists from a range of northern communities had recently passed through the art school studios. The renowned Yolngu artists Johnny Bulunbulun and Banduk Marika had visited from Arnhem Land; from the Kimberley they had welcomed the Jirrawun artists' immediate predecessors: Rover Thomas, Queenie McKenzie and Paddy Carlton. Initially it was printmaking that had provided the kind of exchange Smith and his artist-colleagues were striving to achieve, but the borders of engagement were wide open.

In Smith's office Adsett explained how they might offer support. He knew that any arrangement to host them onsite had to be informal enough to allow the group to come and go as they pleased, but couched in terms that recognised the Gija's cultural standing: a 'fellowship' rather than a 'residency'. The idea was initially reciprocal – Adsett soon returned to Rugun to camp with a group of art students and staff in late 1998 – but the real focus was on the following academic year, when the university would welcome the artists in Darwin. With access to the university's resources, and support from their staff, Adsett hoped the clear promise of the paintings he'd viewed in the shed at Rugun could be more fully realised. Within weeks it was confirmed: the artists would travel to Darwin where they could paint in a more supported environment.

3.

Initially it was just the men who undertook the journey: Paddy, Rusty, Hector, Freddie and Tony. They billeted at an Aboriginal Catholic church that offered cheap rooms close to the university, and caught a taxi to the campus soon after they arrived.

The university's buildings sat low to the ground, interspersed with patches of tropical greenery. Adsett met them at the art school and walked them through the facilities: here were the open-plan studios for painting; nearby, a workshop for printmaking.

Outside was an open-air concrete area that had until recently been used as the ceramics studio. It was there that the group initially drew together in the shade, tired from travelling. Paddy, who was carrying with him a handful of possessions roughly bound together in a stained cloth, was nursing a nasty hangover and wanted to unwind. He pulled a fifty-dollar note from his top pocket and handed it to one of the painting students who'd gathered in welcome: 'Go get two boxes of green cans,' he said.

Paddy then drank for a while, joined by a small group of students and staff, and then lay down on the concrete and went to sleep with his head propped on a stray brick. In a gesture towards comfort he first wrapped it in an old shirt.

Russell Lilford, a gentle and enthusiastic painter who worked as the art school's studio technician, watched with growing amazement. Adsett had earlier pulled his staff aside in preparation for the Gija's visit. 'These men are old,' Lilford would recall him saying, 'we really need to look after them.' It was hard to tally this assessment with the tough old man sleeping with a brick for a pillow on a concrete slab.

As Paddy slept fitfully, the others drank and talked, settling in to the new environment. Hector, sociable as ever, held court. Freddie and Rusty were far quieter, watching proceedings from their chairs. They let un-drunk cans line up on the concrete in front of them, waiting until they were warm enough to drink the way they liked them: 'Kimberley cold!' they explained to laughter.

The next day the painters withdrew with Tony into the air-conditioned painting studios and began work. It was a relief to be free of Rugun's stifling heat. For Tony it even felt like a holiday: it was invigorating to be surrounded with like-minded people, not just artists like Adsett, but figures like Lilford and Leon Stainer, the university's resident printmaker, who had lived and travelled in the north for years. Tony felt they understood the energy that had captured him at Rugun; he didn't constantly have to explain his motivations. Stainer had even worked closely with

Rover Thomas, and soon held a slideshow of the country Thomas had taken him to in the Kimberley. The artists sat there together in the northern capital looking at pictures of Kimberley sites and talking about Thomas, who had only just passed away the previous year, and whom they'd all known well.

•

With a provisional schedule soon established, the group began to fly back and forth between Darwin and the Kimberley. One residency might take as long as two weeks or a month, a return to country usually far longer. On the second trip Peggy, Goody Barrett and Phyllis joined them, along with another woman, Mary Thomas. At first they also billeted at the Catholic church, but they would eventually stay with their close friend, the linguist Frances Kofod, at her Darwin house, while Tony and the men found space elsewhere: sometimes Stainer or Lilford had a room or two spare; other times a student would be keen to welcome them.

All this quickly justified Adsett's initial motivations and he encouraged the interactions that were occurring. Everything was open and informal; observers came and went as the painters worked; there were discussions about the content of the paintings, even debates about the ethics of representation. The Kimberley still provided the project its engine room, but in Darwin the borders were opening: oxygen was rushing in.

The women often painted together; the men off to one side. Rusty would find space alone, where Adsett, who was drawn to the Gija artist's tendency to think deeply about each of his works, would often find time to sit with him and talk. Paddy continued as he had at Crocodile Hole. His systematic approach made him appear to observers as a stoic: once he began a work he would often determinedly see it through to the end, seated cross-legged on the studio's concrete floor. When necessary he'd turn the canvas before him, his paintbrush clasped tightly in his teeth.

As usual Tony circulated from one artist to the next, offering encouragement and guidance in equal measure. He'd now taken to wearing only black: an open-necked shirt topped by a wide-brimmed Akubra; boots and a trimmed goatee and moustache completed the picture. He looked like a figure from the Kimberley's earliest settler days. If at times it appeared a carefully scripted performance, it was nonetheless perfectly calibrated to the increasingly curious visitors who'd make time in their day to stop in at the painting studios.

Marcia Langton, the firebrand Indigenous academic who was then NTU's Professor of Aboriginal and Torres Strait Islander Studies, was among them. She met the group early and became a ready advocate for their project. To her, the artists seemed familiar: Langton had worked in the Kimberley in the early eighties, initially as a volunteer for the Kimberley Land Council tasked with encouraging Aboriginal people to vote, and knew something of Gija country. Her first visits there had quickly convinced her of the seemingly unalterable poverty and racism of the place. A clear pattern had carried over from the station days: Aboriginal life was still too often held in check by malevolent white men whose acts of cruelty and violence were random and without cause. It was a social landscape that made the relations she forged in those early days all the more memorable.

Once, during her first trip to the region in 1980, Langton had stopped her vehicle to talk to a lone figure by the highway near Kununurra. It was Peggy's brother, Timmy Timms, a Lawman held in high regard across the region. He was walking to Nineteen Mile community, carrying with him nothing at all. Although Darwin marked the first time that she'd met Paddy and the others, it was due to memories like this that Langton felt she recognised them. When she was asked to open an exhibition of their paintings at the university's small gallery, she accepted immediately, delivering an impassioned speech that stuck in the minds of those who attended.

Frances Kofod was also a regular presence. During residencies she would often arrive laden with recording equipment to sit with each artist and interview them in Gija and Kimberley Kriol. She would then painstakingly transcribe each painting's story: the beginnings of what would become a valuable archive. Kofod – a large, soft-featured woman who'd long adopted the billowing floral dresses favoured by Aboriginal matriarchs – wore glasses with tiny round lenses and wide-brimmed sunhats that she pulled low over straight brown hair. She possessed her own deep ties to Gija country and knew each of the Jirrawun artists well. After first visiting the Kimberley in 1971 to study the Miriwoong language she had gone on to work alongside Hector at Warmun's bilingual Ngalangangpum School; later, Rover had often camped on her veranda when she was living in Kununurra. Although she had left the Kimberley in 1996 following a bad road accident, Kofod had recently begun to re-establish ties there: the fact that her Gija friends were now visiting Darwin on a regular basis surely seemed part of a broader pattern that would soon draw her back to their country for good.

There were also others. George Chaloupka, the renowned rock art scholar, was among them; so too key members of the art school faculty, including Dadang Christanto, an Indonesian artist whose recent relocation to Darwin had sparked a body of work critical of his country's dark political past; and Judy Watson, the acclaimed Waanyi painter who had moved to Darwin from Queensland. Each came and watched, similarly intrigued by the artists and the strangely charismatic white man who worked with them so closely.

As finished paintings began to accrue, Adsett gave over part of his office as a space to store them. When he wasn't assisting in the studio, Tony would retreat there and call his contacts down south, doggedly securing sales or organising the next exhibition. For Adsett it was a lesson in art dealing: more than once he would overhear Tony carefully setting the market up; holding works back, building interest and demand. Each time there was a residency the phone bill would grow exponentially and, behind the scenes, Peter would have to resecure the administration's support.

He gave Tony office keys and Tony soon set up a single mattress in there. After nights with Rusty and Freddie at the bar under Darwin Casino he'd often return to Peter's office to sleep, ready to begin anew the following day. The university's open-air bar provided another outlet: together with Russell Lilford and Leon Stainer, the artists and Tony would gather there once a day's studio work was complete, drinking and talking as the long, humid afternoons stretched out towards night.

•

At the art school studios Paddy's paintings began to take on the shape that would come to define his career. His images became more reduced, more immediate. In the first works that PB created there, Tony stripped the palette to black and white alone. It was a direct response to Adsett's recent work, almost a challenge, and the limitation flagged a way forward.

Beyond the early painting from Crocodile Hole that depicted the rockhole at Winperrji, and which had stood out in its sparseness, PB's work had to date been more crowded, marked by roughly outlined landforms that jostled together. Now, a fine balance between open spaces began to dominate. A painting might be no more than a horizontal line demarcating two fields; elsewhere he'd pinch these shapes inwards, letting one push into the other. As always, each work reduced country to a kind of code, and could be deciphered as a planar representation of specific places and the Dreamings that activated them, but in Darwin such readings began to fold into others.

For one, the ghost of twentieth-century modernism now stalked the surfaces of Paddy's paintings unabated: when an image of *Untitled (White Shapes on a Black Background)*, a reduced and poised abstraction from 1917 by the French painter Jean Arp, was later reproduced alongside Bedford's early painting *Garnkoorlbany – Jack Flood*, it made unexpected sense. For those who watched PB in the studio all kinds of connections would fall into place. It was an experience of excitement, of concentrated energy: every painting appeared to riff upon the last, opening as it did endless-seeming variations.

PB's first painting from Darwin was *Red Bucket (Red Pocket)*, named for an area on his mother's and uncle's country where a deposit of red soil lies surrounded by rich, black volcanic ground: a 'pocket' of red. He had only recently painted the same site at Rugun, where he'd used black, yellow, red and white to identify that country's features, but in Darwin, with colour jettisoned entirely, he was forced to pare it back to form alone. The black shapes lay stark against unbroken white. Each still spoke of a specific geography, but their cumulative effect was now far closer to musical notation than the static cartographic rendering of a map. The ebb and flow of the country's rhythm had become an interplay between abstract form.

In *Mad Gap*, the painting that immediately followed, he made clear that the baseline of one work – perhaps a large swathe of black outlined in a ragged string of white dotting – would readily carry over to another. If the country was different, so too was the story, but PB's paintings were nonetheless beginning to fit together like a puzzle. Each piece added to an overall picture: a vast accounting of place that, to more than one observer, had begun to seem like an accounting of the old man himself.

Tony's approach, honed at Crocodile Hole and now nearing perfection, was simple: he let each artist's practice direct how he interacted with them. Although open to suggestion, Paddy approached each work as if it were preordained. Freddie similarly knew what he was doing: he had watched the first wave of East Kimberley artists at Turkey Creek and had arrived at his elegant, map-like style long before he and Tony crossed paths in Melbourne. Rusty liked to be left to his own devices and worked slowly: if he sought guidance, it was usually of the conceptual kind that he and Tony had already established during their conversations at the Animal Bar; a willing ear to help his thoughts find visual form. For their part, the women required constant banter and encouragement: for them, the studio was a social affair and their attention would sometimes lapse; as best he could Tony would draw them back to the task at hand.

In each practice he was searching for points of difference, expressions of each artist's character that might be recast as image. In Darwin, Rusty's works were becoming increasingly dense, at times unsettling in their intensity; Hector's were growing far more whimsical and often hinged upon figurative representation; in sessions with Phyllis, they'd established a soft colour palette dominated by an ochre pink intended to complement her bourgeoning practice, to find ground that was hers. The closer he became with each of them, the more clearly Tony could see their work and its potential. Sometimes he would sit alone in Peter's office and picture paintings yet to come, excited by the possibilities.

4.

The artists had always insisted to Tony that Jirrawun, once it found form, had to be about more than a painted economy. Hector had been particularly focused on this. It had to be about culture too, about history and its impact on the Gija world. Now, with the groundwork laid, the way in which painting might help realise this was taking shape.

The group were still spending long periods back in the Kimberley; it was there that Peggy's brother Timmy Timms, the Elder Marcia Langton had once picked up along the highway to Kununurra, first began to steer them in this direction. Timms's role as a Lawman usually kept him in near-constant motion throughout the greater region; now, he began to guide long night-time conversations by the campfire. The brutal story of European settlement of Gija country was broadly known – death and dispossession had soon followed the arrival of the pastoralists in the 1880s – but the details were hazy, the historical record contested.

Tony had already heard some of it. At times, the artists would make cryptic references to particular figures – vicious station owners, perhaps, or leaders of punitive killing missions – that would stick in his mind as markers for future conversation. Other times they'd been more explicit, and a broader pattern was drawing into focus: as forgiving and gentle as the Gija often seemed, to know them was to understand that, for many of them, the horrors of colonisation had solidified as barely contained anger.

He had by now cast himself as a newfound champion for the Gija cause, but he also sensed a far more complicated picture: he too was part of a lineage of interlopers set in chain by the first wave of pastoral settlers. He would wonder about painting's broader purpose. Against the Kimberley's obvious dysfunction – the drinking and fighting, the bright-eyed kids already marked by malnutrition or the ravages of fetal alcohol syndrome – the project's focus could at times seem minor. But as new stories of frontier violence began to emerge around the campfires, this began to change.

It was like they were telling ghost stories, he would later think, almost as if each teller was attempting to outdo the last. The firelight caused the faces of his friends to flicker in and out of the darkness, heightening the effect of their words.

Timmy was the first to begin.

He characterised what followed as 'hard stories'. He sketched out the detail quietly, his voice measured, carefully plotting narratives in which the frontier's brutal environment had spilled over into violent encounter. The others would listen gravely as the old man spoke, before adding their own accounts of the massacres that had been perpetrated in the region well into the twentieth century and which still held fast in their collective memory. Initially, Tony didn't know what to think, sitting there as the only white, listening. If anything, his presence seemed purposeful, as if much of his time in the Kimberley had been leading him unknowingly to this point.

At first he was horrified by what he heard – a feeling that would always stay with him – but as the stories continued from one night to the next, he began to see the borders of a project: an ambitious exhibition that would turn each artist's distinctive voice towards a shared purpose. Rover Thomas had painted a widely celebrated series in the early 1990s that had touched on similar events – Tony had seen them in Thomas's survey at the National Gallery of Australia in 1994 – but since then the subject had gone cold. Now, Tony began to imagine that, if it was done correctly, the artists could achieve far more: they would provide an historical reckoning, a riposte to a nation that had too often turned away from the darker facts of its colonial past. To know something of that history was to understand that the reality of Aboriginal dispossession bore intergenerational effects.

The first massacre paintings came not long afterwards. Timmy and Paddy were staying in Darwin with Tony at the house of Jason Davidson, a young Aboriginal man who had once been a strapper in the horse racing industry in Adelaide and was now a photography student at the art school. It was Timmy's first visit and, following the way in which the stories themselves had come to light, he was the first to put brush to canvas.

Tony watched intently. At first the old man marked out stark black lines across the open expanse of white. Even at that stage Timms clearly knew what he was doing. Tracing the shape of a story he'd long known, his hand barely hesitated.

The composition soon extended as a long unbroken line. It looped upwards and down, its borders delineating landforms, and beneath them marking out two sites. Here, once again, was Garnannayien, the same place that PB painted where the ancestral emu had become stuck in a cleft of rock. But Timms left that site unmarked. Instead he painted the gorge itself, the peak of Mount King and the place just below where a group of Gija had been poisoned and burnt in reprisal for spearing a breeding cow at Bedford Downs Station.

Only a week before, Timmy and Paddy had sat for an interview with Frances Kofod and revealed the existence of a joonba for this same story: a song cycle and accompanying performance which encoded the story's terrible details as movement and sound. Both men knew the history: Timmy had been a toddler when the massacre had occurred; Paddy was born a short two years later. Now, seeing the story revealed in visual form felt to Tony like further revelation. Here was an image that could be presented as fact, evidence of colonial atrocity writ large.

Timmy had recounted the events to Kofod in unsparing detail. The Gija were directed by their murderers to collect wood for a bonfire; lunch, once they were done, was strychnine-laced bread. Two old men escaped death, but the others were not so lucky.

Kofod would soon carefully transcribe Timmy's Kriol account. He told of how his poisoned ancestors lay twitching on the ground, of how they were then bludgeoned with sticks until they were 'finished', and carried to the woodheap where they were doused with kerosene and set on fire.

PB painted the same site soon afterwards. It was his story too: his former Bedford Downs boss, Paddy Quilty, had been the one to order the atrocity. It was Quilty's name that Paddy carried. According to the story that Tony had now heard often, Quilty had appeared in the Gija station camp soon after Paddy took his first breaths and enquired whether the new arrival were a boy or a girl. When told, he'd given a simple instruction: 'You can call him Paddy after me.'

Bedford knew the country that Timms had painted, but the story he mapped carried different details: high on Mount King, well above the killing ground, PB showed the cave in which the spirits of the victims had gathered together as shadows and danced. It was here, sheltered from view by a small rock fig, that they had for the first time sung the joonba's verses.

Afterwards, the shadow-spirits travelled west towards the setting sun; an encounter with a white settler forced them east again, where they met a 'clever man', Wirrinyjangu, who heard their song and was alerted to their presence.

He told them they didn't belong there, that they needed to go back to Bedford Downs.

Once again they returned to Mount King; they came to rest there in the cave and looked down upon the massacre site. Since then, Timmy and Paddy explained, the joonba had been kept alive in secret. As it passed from one generation to the next, whites had never seen it.

•

Peter Adsett was at this time travelling often. He'd been awarded a studio residency in Indonesia in late 1999; soon after an opportunity arose to exhibit his paintings at the Australian Consulate in New York. Amid it all, his mind had also turned towards the potential Jirrawun might carry for collaboration and exchange. His approach was markedly different to Tony's – with a job and family in Darwin, Adsett was far from the centre of Kimberley life – but he had nonetheless begun to picture a future iteration for the collective that might include artists like himself: figures whose knowledge of Western art might merge with the East Kimberley's existing aesthetic and conceptual traditions to forge something new.

William Mora had suggested that Adsett develop a project with Rusty when they had first visited Crocodile Hole, but it was only once the two of them had got to know each other that the idea had developed: a series of works in which each of them might explore the legitimacy of painting as a means to stage cross-cultural conversations. Rusty was at first reticent, but while Adsett was in New York, he heard word that the Gija artist was ready. On his return to Darwin they met and Rusty agreed that he would stay with Adsett and his wife Susie at their property in semi-rural Humpty Doo, forty kilometres outside Darwin. Adsett worked there on the wide veranda overlooking a small billabong, and had hosted Aboriginal artists before.

He and Rusty talked it over with Tony and the three of them together set the rules of engagement: although not strictly a Jirrawun project, any work that might result had to make sense within the collective's overarching vision. Tony argued that all the paintings should be the same dimensions and the palette be restricted to white, black and red.

At one level this was a pragmatic directive: by limiting the possibilities for each work, Tony was aiming to sharpen their overall effect, to draw them into focus. But the limitations would also act to bind the works together into a cohesive whole. They would emphasise the project's serial nature, the cumulative effect of each painting placed one beside another. Remove one from the sequence and the network of connections would collapse.

All up, Rusty spent three weeks with Peter and his family at Humpty Doo. The first week he spent in quiet contemplation. There was no grog; Peter and Susie, who worked as a midwife at Darwin Hospital, made sure he ate well. Rusty was a gentle presence, but once drawn out he could discuss the nuances of painting for hours. In Adsett he found a willing ear: for him painting was a medium of poetic and intellectual potential; to talk about it was almost as good as making it.

Slowly they mapped an approach. Rusty would make one painting and the next day Peter would respond, each of them working with the canvas laid flat before them: Peter on the veranda; Rusty under the shade of a tree nearby. Each evening they lined finished works up against the wall to view as they sat around a large table with Peter's family for dinner. After an initial tentativeness, it became hard to break the flow; the nature of the work, marked by a heightened concentration, took over.

Rusty began with a painting of his birthplace: a comb-like red form crowning a white field; below it he sketched a red circle striated by white lines. Soon he was talking about dreams, about accessing the threshold spaces of the Ngarranggarni, about what painting should and shouldn't do. Colours seemed especially charged. 'Black can't do that,' he'd say cryptically, looking at Adsett's work. This continued for two weeks, until fourteen canvases had been completed and the project's possibilities exhausted.

From the beginning Adsett had decided to respond to the space in Rusty's paintings, to the way the Gija artist split his compositions into a complex of puzzle-like shapes. At face value his own works were starkly geometric: shards of bright white that cut across black grounds; architectural against Rusty's roiling bodily forms. Each of Rusty's paintings was eventually titled with a name that spoke of its broader philosophical and cultural significance – *Different languages for Aboriginal and non-Aboriginal people*, or *Father and Grandfather Teaching Place for Me* – but for Adsett this content wasn't the point. It was the sense that somewhere between these two painted languages a ground could be sketched that spoke to the potential of cultural entanglement.

The questions sparked by the resulting work would soon be clear: how might a painting relay the fine balance between two separate minds? How might a visual composition speak to the vagaries of exchange, to both the pitfalls and opportunities, to the bright moments and the dark?

Rusty carried his own answers. For him the Law was not an abstract concept enacted by a third-party institution, but a tangible condition as central to life as breath itself. It concerned the kind of unassailable truth revealed in dreams; the doctrine cradled in the site of his birth; the language passed to him by his grandfather. That old man, Rusty would later recall, had put it to him in the simplest of terms: if you don't follow your Law, you're lost.

Rusty named the series *Two Laws... One Big Spirit*. It referred to his belief that the laws of each culture bleed into each other and can either be collaborative, or antagonistic. For his part, Adsett was careful to characterise *Two Laws* as a visual conversation. He'd point out that the project wasn't a collaboration, that it was instead a 'dialogue' that left each man's cultural identity distinct. Adsett had once again gone to the point of rapprochement but held back.

The kind of questions that guided Adsett were of little appeal to Tony: he was seeking something more immediate. The title he chose for the massacre project, *Blood on the Spinifex*, referred to Bruce Elder's 1988 history *Blood on the Wattle*, a book that broke new ground in the broad recognition of the systemic violence that had driven Australia's colonial settlement. Work on it was slowly gathering energy – Rusty and Phyllis Thomas had recently added their own accounts of historical events to stand alongside the Bedford Downs paintings by Paddy and Timmy – and over the coming eighteen months the project would find its final expressions back in the Kimberley.

Two Laws undoubtedly conveyed a shared intensity, a sense that pure form might stand for something far greater, but it remained easy to see where one artist's vision ended and the other's began. *Blood on the Spinifex* would be premised on no such distinction. One culture would appropriate the other in its entirety: through Tony the project would bend the aesthetics of Western modernism to Gija ends; it would be subsumed, devoured whole.

There would be a grand sense of scale and fields of open colour: one work would even deploy the repeated forms of pop art. But if *Two Laws* had laid bare the process of exchange, Tony knew instinctively that for *Blood on the Spinifex* the opposite had to be true. His voice needed to be hidden in all but the most implicit of ways: the driving force of Gija storytelling had to take centre stage.

Juwulinypany / Bow River

1.

The accident happened early one morning, when the sun was still bright in the east and shining sharply across the highway.

Tony and Hector were following Rusty, who was driving Freddie's truck. He was alternating erratically between fast and slow: just as they seemed about to catch him, he would speed up again and disappear beyond the next rise.

Their day had begun suddenly. Just before dawn there'd been gunshots at Crocodile Hole and then Peggy banging on the side of the painters' donga, yelling. After a night of raucous drinking in one of the houses, conflict had ensued and escalated. Someone had grabbed a rifle.

Peggy told Tony to call the police stationed at the Argyle mine and stood there talking at him as he tried to get through. The phone rang out three times before he gave up and tried the station at Kununurra.

'What kind of rifle is it?' the sergeant who answered wanted to know.

When pressed for more details Tony tried to hand the phone to Peggy but she refused to take it. A call like that was a contentious move: when police arrived, blame for their presence would readily be placed.

The painters, who had by now all risen, reached a consensus quickly: Tony understood they'd all seen conflict escalate before and sensed the danger. Rather than wait and see, it was best to go. They piled into two vehicles – Rusty, Freddie and Paddy in Freddie's Hilux; Hector and Tony in his trayback – and left the community in convoy. By now, daylight was just breaking over the hills.

•

On the highway Tony could still feel the adrenalin coursing through him. His mind was racing; he'd had no coffee. Rusty had again accelerated out of sight and, as they approached the one-lane bridge that carried the Great Northern Highway across a tiny Ord River tributary called Arthur Creek, Tony saw the bright glint of sun reflecting off an oncoming road train.

In a second he made the decision to keep going, to try and beat it across, but as soon as they hit the bridge he realised with a sudden weight in his gut that he'd been wrong.

Hector tensed in the seat beside him as the road train, unable to stop, entered at the opposite end. Tony slammed on the brakes and flung his truck in reverse, but achieved little: the gears ground and they kept moving forwards. Hector held his arm out in front of him, ramrod straight, as if he could stop the impact that was certain to come; Tony looked up and, through the road train's windscreen, he could see clearly the driver's face, distorted in panic.

The next moments would only ever return to him as images strung tenuously as a sequence. Everything was uncertain, impressionistic in tone: it was hard not to question what he'd seen and heard. Did everything go quiet? Did he feel the vehicle lift up and turn in the air? Did his vision cloud over and darken, or was everything suddenly cast with a terrible clarity?

He would even wonder if he had registered the image that the next day would make the front page of *The Kimberley Echo*: the road train concertinaed on the verge of the highway, its cabin upside down, its contents – explosive ammonium nitrate destined for the Argyle mine – piled under the upturned trailers like tiny mountains of snow.

Afterwards, Tony pulled himself from the wreckage and lay dazed by the roadside; he could see Hector nearby, under the shade of a tree, seemingly unharmed. The LandCruiser had come to rest right side up, its roof and windscreen caved in. Tony was covered in blood and was sure, at the very least, that his ribs were broken. He struggled to light a cigarette.

Hector was shouting to him: 'Ngaji! Ngaji!', Brother, Brother, 'Are your brains all right? Are your brains all right?'

As he lay there, Tony realised he shouldn't move another inch.

In the background, the truck's driver kicked free from his upturned cabin in a stream of expletives.

•

The first passersby were the managers of Doon Doon Station, who knew Tony from visits he would occasionally make during back and forth trips between Crocodile Hole and Kununurra. They radioed for an ambulance and then rigged up a tarpaulin to protect him from the morning heat, which had by now begun to beat down.

Later, in the ambulance, Tony simply lay and watched the clouds. They hung there perfectly white, massed in the sky. The windows on the doors framed them just so.

He was badly injured – he'd spend the coming days in hospital – and was teetering at the edge of consciousness, but he recognised the clouds almost immediately. As a child in southern Gippsland he had seen them often.

The house in Gippsland was surrounded by the rolling hills of dairy country and the sky was vast: clouds like that moved as a mass across the landscape, sometimes swiftly, sometimes slow enough to appear almost motionless. They would grow in volume as they went.

As a child Tony used to walk alone through those hills, his beloved cattle dog Scamp running scent patterns around him. As he went, he collected impressions that would solidify over the years into vivid memories: these, he found, could be placed together into all sorts of narratives.

In the Kimberley, one memory would return to him with particular insistence. No older than six, he takes leave from the comforting warmth of his mother's kitchen and wanders out across the family farm.

It's winter and the hills around him unfold under grey skies.

His walk takes him to the low corrugated-iron water tank where a midden of tiny white crow skulls lie bleached and fragile. His grandfather had shot the birds the season before, during a visit from the city. Tony picks them up, one by one, his imagination drawn by the flawless intensity of each. As he turns them in his hands he wonders where each bird's life has gone. He touches his face and traces the shape of his own skull beneath the surface of his winter flesh.

Once he knows a place like the Kimberley, he claims a memory like that as pivotal. It's vivid, he says, because the landscape reached out to his child self and touched his thoughts so clearly.

It was the marked absence that did it: the feeling, which he then couldn't name, that landscapes like that cradled the darkness of colonisation.

In their emptiness lay pronounced loss.

•

Hector was beside him in the ambulance.

'Ngaji!' he kept calling, 'Ngaji!'

That's what Tony heard as the driver sped down the Great Northern Highway towards Kununurra. He watched the clouds hanging there, slowly tracing the vehicle's passage, and he listened to Hector.

'Ngaji!'

That night, with Tony laid up in a hospital bed, Hector stayed with Simon Georgeff at Pindan Avenue. Sitting at the kitchen table, too upset to sleep, Hector reached into his shirt pocket and came out unexpectedly with a handful of glass pebbles: remnants of shattered windscreen.

2.

Tony spent ten days in Kununurra, where he moved between the hospital and Georgeff's house. It was clear that, with the accident and the events leading up to it, the respite Crocodile Hole had initially offered was now gone. When he eventually returned, the tenor of the place had shifted: everyone had heard how bad the accident had been and as he walked around, still in a neck-brace, they stared at him in silence from their verandas; he felt like a ghost.

In the days and weeks that followed, he would at times drift off to sleep, only for the terrible rush of adrenalin he'd felt just before the road train hit to return to him, shocking him awake. Other times, it would be the feeling of being thrown about in his vehicle's cabin, little more than a fleshy rag doll. But as much as the memory would haunt him, he knew that the darkness of the Kimberley was often leavened by humour. He would think of how Rusty, Freddie and Paddy had visited him in the hospital, not long after he'd been admitted: how it had seemed as if he'd awoken with the three of them already there, standing over him in their stock hats and dusty clothes like apparitions against the bleached clean surrounds.

It would be touching to later recall how each of the men's faces had been traced by concern; how it seemed that Freddie had been on the verge of tears and Paddy had openly cried. But once it became clear he was okay, it was business as usual, at least for Paddy. He had leaned forward towards Tony conspiratorially, softly rumbling something about money. It took Tony a moment to catch on, but when he did he couldn't help but laugh, even with the pain of his ribs: Old Man was asking him to sign a cheque, so he could pass some money on to family for a vehicle.

Humbug. Even there, trussed up in hospital.

•

Although Tony would come to see the accident as the reason for the group's eventual departure from Rugun, actual events were more complex. When Balangarri, the Aboriginal corporation in Warmun responsible for managing the far-flung network of Gija outstations, suddenly collapsed, the effect in the tiny community was profound: it's this that eventually pushed them away.

By then, Tony knew Balangarri well. His regular trips between Crocodile Hole and Warmun had often hinged on visits to its rundown offices for administrative assistance. Sometimes this was as simple as accessing the fax machine; other times it would be more complex. At the end of Tony's first year, Kevin Curnow, Balangarri's larger-than-life manager, had helped him put together Jirrawun's successful application to the Registrar of Aboriginal Corporations.

At face value, Curnow, an ex-lawyer, was responsible for a simple yet essential service: via the Aboriginal and Torres Strait Islander Commission, the federal government funnelled $3.6 million in annual funding through the tiny corporation, which dispersed it to local ends. It administered

Community Development and Employment Program wages for a range of local workers, and purchased and maintained the machinery and infrastructure essential in meeting the demands of remote life. Like the region's other outstations, Rugun's viability was largely contingent upon this support.

Later, the full story would emerge by way of a report by ABC television's flagship investigative news program, *Four Corners*. It was true Curnow had practised as a lawyer, but two recent convictions for fraud and theft had seen him incarcerated at Darwin's Berrimah Prison, after which he'd been bankrupted and disbarred in quick succession. At Balangarri he had spun the Warmun community into a wild dream. It included the government-funded buyback of surrounding cattle leases, a Gija takeover of the Argyle diamond mine and the floating of the company on the stock exchange. In step, he cut a byzantine deal with a tiny East Timorese province to trade cattle for concrete, which, as he later argued, he intended to market for a steep profit back in Australia.

Balangarri's Gija advisers – among their ranks Phyllis's husband Big Joe – had jumped on board, galvanised by the promise of once again owning their traditional countries and, from this base, determining their futures. But beneath it all lay a far more mundane intent: Balangarri's funds began to disappear. When an ATSIC-appointed auditor finally disentangled the administrative records it became clear that Balangarri had been claiming wages for at least 100 more CDEP positions than officially existed. The shortfall was unaccounted for.

Curnow soon fled, leaving behind him $1.5 million in debt. Liquidators moved in and began to repossess Balangarri-owned assets from the outstations. Generators, vehicles and machinery all went; the fuel tanks Balangarri had once kept filled were emptied. With no generator at Crocodile Hole the power and running water went out; without fuel on hand, residents could easily find themselves marooned, unable to travel to get food and other supplies. After nightfall the only light came from campfires. The painting collective had only been based at Crocodile Hole for not much longer than a year, part of which had been spent travelling to Darwin and back, but continuing to paint in those conditions seemed impossible: they soon left.

At first, Tony stayed for a short period in Warmun with one of his few white friends, a woman called Julie who had worked for Balangarri and from whom he would first hear much of the scandal's detail. She was different to the regular white worker in Aboriginal communities, neither exploitative nor blindly selfless, but although he enjoyed her company he felt aimless. He involved himself in the Balangarri saga as it unfolded – when the story was picked up by *Four Corners*, he was mistakenly interviewed as a 'community advisor' – but beyond that he spent his days wandering about, casting his mind to the daunting question of how the painting project might endure. Remika Nocketta, a young girl who had often been at Crocodile Hole and, along with her sisters, called Tony 'uncle', would visit with friends and play with newborn kittens that a mother cat had lodged under the house.

Initially the artists gave Tony space. They came and went between Warmun, Rugun and Kununurra, but their project was hanging in limbo: no one was painting. It was Timmy Timms who first seemed to recognise the impasse and put forward a solution. He was the chairman at Bow River, a community as tiny and remote as Rugun, and he suggested the group simply cut their losses and relocate there.

Known in Gija as Juwurlinji, or Juwulinypany, Bow River was in many ways like Crocodile Hole. It lay far from the highway: a rutted dirt track led into the wilderness before petering out among a handful of the simple tin-clad community houses that Tony now knew well. But whereas Crocodile Hole had first been established as an outstation, Bow River's history extended to the pastoral era. Originally part of Greenvale Station, the surrounding country had been annexed in the land grabs that drove the region's colonisation, run by whites, and handed back to Aboriginal control in 1984. The collection of houses had been built where the old homestead had once stood. That had been the home of Maggie and Sam Lilly, early settlers who purchased the excised station in 1945. Nearby, a large marble headstone marked the burial site of the two white brothers, Richard and Walter Macale, who'd first overseen Greenvale. The river, a wide sandy bed that lay dry for most of the year, wound its way below. At night wild horses would gather there under the paperbarks, seeking out small pools of permanent water.

Rammey Ramsey, a renowned dancer in his early seventies who would now join Jirrawun as a painter, was prominent among the handful of residents. Tony had first met him not long after his arrival in the Kimberley, when Freddie had taken him to Bow River, and still carried an indelible image of the old man sitting like a statue at the front of his house, his face inscrutable behind wraparound sunglasses as he watched the vehicle lurch its way across the creek bed and up towards the community. It would have been a grave and slightly foreboding greeting but for one detail: someone had daubed the phrase 'LOVE SHACK' in large letters across the wall behind him.

Rammey had recently moved to another house, where he lived with his young wife Beverley and their young daughters. His first wife Mona Ramsey, Timmy's daughter, lived close by, as did her and Rammey's adult children. Tony would soon learn Rammey's story in some detail – how he'd been born at Old Greenvale; how as an infant he'd lost both his parents in quick succession: his mother to snakebite, his father to tribal retribution of unknown cause that saw him clubbed to death. Timmy, who had served as the Lillys' head stockman, had first brought Rammey to Bow River to work on the station. When it was finally ceded to Aboriginal control, Rammey had been among the first to return; now, he rarely left. The uncertainties of Warmun had been relatively brief, but Bow River seemed to Tony like a return to something vital: the sense of family was strong.

•

The painters moved their project into the love shack, which was now vacant and lay close to the riverbank, a short walk from the nearest house. They knew this was a good place: Paddy explained that the cameleers who once plied their wares between Kimberley stations had in the old days camped there in the shade of a large gum. It still stood just beyond the veranda.

Tony already had in mind a project by which the group might mark their relocation – a suite of new works by the old men – and although it would take time to set in motion, he would in later years most readily recall the resulting paintings when he thought of their early days in the community. Hector had recently returned to Warmun, where he'd been focusing his energies on Warmun's fledgling community art centre. This had replaced Narrangunny Art Traders and was being run out of the old post office by a young Melbourne couple. For Hector, the shift was preordained. Warmun lay on his traditional country, which included Texas Downs Station, where he'd worked for much of his life. Although he readily pledged Tony his ongoing counsel, he had to align himself with the new art centre.

Tony wanted Hector to be involved in a final run of work that he hoped would reach back to the beautifully provisional dance boards that were painted for Rover Thomas's *Guirr-Guirr* by the initial wave of East Kimberley artists. He sourced sheets of plywood in Kununurra and had them cut into a range of body-scaled dimensions. The largest were sixty centimetres by almost two metres: long, horizontal fields that echoed the Kimberley's panoramic landscapes. At first, he sought the original materials that might once have been used: the white ochre, the charcoal, the kangaroo blood. Hector took him to collect natural gum binder in the surrounding bush, but when it proved too difficult Tony simply kept the palette tight, this time in deference to the limits within which the early paintings had been made. The only colours he mixed were red, black and white.

Rammey, who proved to be a quiet and profoundly good-natured man, realised his first paintings on the love shack's low veranda, working alongside Hector, Timmy and Paddy. There was no ceremony involved in him joining the group: he simply walked down from his house on the low rise above and told Tony that he wanted to paint too. His voice immediately proved as distinctive as the others: it was clear that he knew how to plot out a composition, that he too was guided by the dictates of Gija Law. As with the others, for Rammey the question of what to paint seemed non-existent: he immediately turned his attention to his ancestral territories, a remote area near the Elgee Cliffs known as Warlawoon, a word that Tony soon learnt doubled as Rammey's own bush name. But whereas the works of the other painters most often comprised loose, organic-seeming forms, Rammey favoured angular shapes: he was just as likely to map out the rectangles of a stockyard as he was to depict the arc of a hill.

Rammey's works were good, and it was exciting to watch him find his footing in the studio, but it was Timmy who proved the revelation.

Tony had only recently been on hand when Timmy had made his very first paintings in Darwin; he now sensed a visual confidence in him to rival Paddy's. Here, he thought, was another master.

Timms worked with a kind of dogged commitment to each image. Like PB, he filled his compositions casually, but nonetheless often arrived at what seemed a perfect balance between figure and ground. He also let shapes push outwards from the edges of the picture plane, opening them into the space beyond. In one work – nothing more than stark black forms on a red background – he mapped the contours of country that ran north from Rugun to the Dunham River. This had been his uncle's country, a place he'd walked as a young man, eating fish and crocodile as he went. He knew it as Jimbirlan: the name for the spearheads his people had once crafted from the deposits of white stone the ancestors had scattered there.

In another painting Timmy reversed his palette, this time plotting out the forms in red against a black ground. This work touched on one of the stories of frontier violence that had by now begun circulating around Bow River's campfires and were just beginning to underscore the slow-building *Blood on the Spinifex* project. At the painting's centre he showed the distinctive rock formation known to Gija as Neminuwarlin, and to settlers as Pompey's Pillar: the place where the Aboriginal bushranger called Major once hid during the height of the region's frontier wars.

Freddie, who was Timmy's nephew, had already made a series of works that cast Major as an Aboriginal version of Ned Kelly, and would soon return to the story again, but Timmy folded it softly into a broader picture. He included a long range called Gernimboowoorrin and in the left-hand corner a dark aperture in a hill that marked the Dreaming site for bush honey. For Timmy, everything flowed easily: the only hiccup came when a young family member took it upon themselves to 'touch up' one of his paintings, neatening the dotting and flattening the beautifully rough brushwork. Although Tony was incensed, he couldn't help but note that, for Timmy, it was a non-issue. He could only imagine the reason: if the work still showed the same site, its power must be as strong as ever.

•

The paintings on plywood would soon be gathered together in an exhibition at William Mora's gallery in Melbourne, a tough group of works that signalled, once again, the seriousness of Jirrawun's vision. The artists titled it *Gaagembi*, a Gija word that translates as 'poor things', or 'poor fella' – a lament for those whose lands were lost as the first wave of settlers fanned out across their ancestral countries.

Working into this space seemed to somehow draw the pre-settler world closer: Tony sensed that in the process something was revived. He would recall one night in particular, when he and Paddy were settling into their swags on the love shack's veranda, paintings in progress stacked to one side.

Silence had long stretched between them when Old Man suddenly broke the reverie with an unprompted string of language directed at the darkness beyond. He wasn't yelling, but he was speaking with a resonance that carried into the night: it appeared that Paddy was addressing the stars that lay a glittering blanket above them.

As he fell silent the frogs and crickets resumed the night's raucous business: a scattering of single sounds that soon built to a wall. At first, the dense, almost symphonic energy seemed a kind of answer to Paddy's call, as if the surrounding country was calling back. But in the distance another string of Gija soon rang out, faint but clear. It was Rammey, lying on his own veranda on the rise above.

The old men called out like this once or twice more, before the sounds of the night rose up again and the noise became indistinguishable from the silence itself. Only later would Tony learn that this is how the old people had once communicated between bush camps, calling out to the ancestors in the night, one after the other.

3.

At Rugun, Hector had spent hours with Tony discussing the challenges of Gija life, much as he'd once done at Pindan Avenue, or before that at Warmun. As always he'd taken digressive, elliptical routes through whatever subject was at hand, but if Hector had previously framed his thinking for

Tony in broadly philosophical terms, his conversation had recently turned towards more pragmatic ends: how, the old man would wonder, might his people disengage from the vagaries of government funding? How might they build something to truly last? In the wake of the Balangarri collapse, such questions had only become more pressing.

As Hector disengaged in favour of Warmun, Tony suspected a greater design behind Timmy's increased presence, almost as if Hector had ensured someone would continue shaping the Jirrawun vision beyond the limits of the painting project. Timmy played the part well and brought with him a different tenor of authority. He readily picked up Hector's concerns and began to explain to Tony that the answer to the question of what his people might do lay all around them. He saw a future for Bow River in which it would achieve its independence from Warmun. He wanted the pastoral business to be re-established in a meaningful way; for the infrastructure to be repaired and the community's young men schooled in the hard work he himself had spent much of his life performing: this, he knew, could deliver them a stable economy. From there all kinds of ideas might be achievable.

Timmy was no stranger to the kind of innovation forced by necessity. When he and his people had originally been driven from Bow River in the mid-1970s, they'd found themselves exiled to Guda-Guda, a camp at Nine Mile, near Wyndham, that now lay abandoned. Even then, he had led by example: he built much of that community's humble infrastructure with his own hands, all while helping to establish the Kimberley Land Council and lobbying for his people's return to their ancestral country. He also took odd jobs to support his family: he once found himself suspended beneath the Wyndham wharf, painting its girders white while saltwater crocodiles moved about in the waters below.

Timmy's ideas about Bow River were widely shared. Peggy, who was now visiting regularly, clearly understood her brother's vision: she soon expressed a desire to establish an independent school like that which had once run at Rugun, the remains of which had formed the painter's shed there. It was hoped that kids could learn both Gija and gardiya knowledge, side by side, and go on to help establish a new, bi-cultural world.

Tony purchased a notebook in Kununurra and began to record the ideas that would come up in nightly conversation. He had started to formulate his own plan, and he saw the rhyme in what was now emerging. If Bow River's infrastructure developed in the way that Timmy, Peggy and the others dreamt, why couldn't it also house an ambitious painting studio? Sales could be fed directly back into the community, providing another facet for an independent economy. Frances Kofod could translate the culture in real time, returning to what she'd once done at Warmun's Ngalangangpum School. Alongside, there was an obvious role for Peggy that suited her energy to a tee: she would be the charismatic lead of a Gija dance company that would be based at Bow River and could one day perform around the country. There were other possibilities too, cultural tourism key among them. Surely wealthy art collectors would pay handsomely for the privilege of visiting the country in which artists like Paddy worked.

On their next trip to Darwin Tony began to type up his notes. He was assisted in this by Leon Morris, a sharply intelligent young law graduate Marcia Langton had introduced to him during the initial residencies. Morris was a good fit for the task: he had volunteered for the Kimberley Land Council in the late 1970s, when it was still a tiny organisation run from a back office in the Derby YMCA, and had known both Timmy and Peggy since those early, charged days. A subsequent role with the Kimberley Aboriginal Law and Culture Centre – another not-for-profit advocacy and support body – had seen Morris become a champion of the Gija cause. By the time he met Tony, the painters and their families already knew Morris well. Even though he was now based in Darwin, he understood the challenges that were going unmet in communities like Bow River and Rugun far better than most.

The notes eventually became a document: a proposal for a strategic partnership between the Gija and the multinational mining company Rio Tinto, which would be accessed through the Argyle diamond mine. Marcia Langton had left Darwin for a position in Melbourne, but she had recently been engaged by the mine's new management to help address the long-simmering tensions that had attended its approach to community relations over the past two decades – as the proposal took shape, her presence there proved key. So too did that of the mine's recently appointed general manager of operations, Brendan Hammond, a white South African who had previously worked in management at the vast open-pit Rössing uranium mine in Namibia. His belief in the value of good community engagement marked a distinct shift in the mine's culture.

Hammond, who'd been in his role for just three years, understood what was at stake at both ends of the equation: community engagement was about business sense as much as social justice. To date, the mine had been restricted to the surface, where it had slowly carved away at the resting place of Daiwul, the Dreaming barramundi, until the ridge line of the surrounding range had taken on its distinctive stepped silhouette. The diamonds at this level were now near exhausted, but although Hammond had initially been tasked with slowly winding the whole project down, he had readily seen another opportunity: if operations moved underground, the project might be extended by another two decades.

Tony began to send Langton detailed updates via fax about their discussions with the mine's management. At first it was disheartening – the incumbent community relations team were, in Tony's words, 'dinosaurs' – but a newly appointed liaison officer called Fred Murray soon made it known he was different. He carried a skin name from a previous role in the Tanami and proved a deeply pragmatic figure who understood that relationships were built at the granular level of human interaction. To make headway you had to be on the ground, you had to have a feeling for the minutiae of the social world. During one visit that Langton undertook to the Kimberley as part of her consulting role, she toured local communities with Murray and recognised his genius at knitting together connections, at making even the most unexpected things fall into place. There were stories of him driving all day just to visit with a far-flung Gija stakeholder, or assist in a community activity. In the immediate aftermath of the Balangarri collapse, Murray had quietly drawn on Argyle's resources to help address the fallout: he'd organised for local people to refuel their vehicles at the mine and undertaken food drops to places like Rugun and Bow River.

Tony's first encounter with Murray came during a community meeting about new housing, and was low key. Later, he wondered if Murray had been holding back, sizing him up – stray white men in Aboriginal communities rarely had the best intentions – but it was soon clear he'd passed whatever test Murray had in mind: the two became close. Murray would offer charmingly blunt advice that always seemed to arrive at the correct moment.

'Mate,' he'd say once Tony had been living in the community for weeks or months on end, 'go and have a wash: you stink.'

He would then drive Tony to one of the air-conditioned miner's dongas at Argyle for the night. After Bow River it seemed luxurious: not only could Tony shower, but he could also eat whatever he wanted from the mess hall's smorgasbord. He could even have a cold beer at the small bar.

The final proposal drew on these connections to sketch an ambitious structure against which the Gija's vision could be carefully arranged. Everything would be funnelled through a new state-of-the-art resource centre. It would service both Bow River and Crocodile Hole, severing the dependence the two outlying communities had upon Warmun's government-funded administrative infrastructure. It was hoped that this would also help draw people back from the social vacuum of places like Kununurra and Halls Creek.

A number of corporations would exist underneath the resource centre's umbrella, each of which would address one facet of the Elders' overarching vision: each community would be overseen by separate entities; arrayed between them would be the Jirrawun Aboriginal Art Corporation, the Juwulinypany Cattle Station, the Walumbarn Independent Aboriginal School and the Jirrawun Aboriginal Performance Corporation. Finally, the resource centre would house the Warlpawun Tourist and Cross Culture Corporation.

A site for the centre had already been identified: a beautiful, flat area of ground just south of where the Great Northern Highway ran across the sandy bed of Bow River. It had been considered carefully. Access would come straight from the highway, and would lead to a neutral space between the two communities. The site was strategic – it could be glimpsed by passing traffic and would draw visitors in – but ancestral logic had also guided the choice. Timmy explained this to Frances Kofod and she dutifully transcribed it for inclusion in the final document.

As Leon Morris worked on the document with Tony in Darwin, he drew on his long experience writing funding proposals. The key would be sustainable partnership: a collaborative space forged between corporate and Gija interests.

Peggy's widely shared hope for a Gija school became 'culturally appropriate education' that would be integrated within a 'mixed-use' economy that drew on pastoralism, tourism and cultural practice. The final proposal read for the most part like an annual report: clear and concise, measured in its insistence that the status quo for Gija people needed to shift. It was perfectly in keeping with the impersonal language of the corporate world – the Gija vision couched in the language of the Aboriginal industry, carefully calibrated to appeal to private and public sector patrons alike – but nonetheless communicated the urgency that had carried it into being.

It was soon printed five times and bound at the university. It came out looking like a thesis, its black fabric cover embossed with gold lettering: WARLPAWUN, it read, *The Place of the River Wallaby.*

4.

One of the stated aims of the Warlpawun proposal was the performance group. In that light, the fact that Timmy and Paddy had only recently revealed the existence of the Bedford Downs massacre joonba for the first time made sense: it was this that would surely provide the spark from which a fully fledged dance company might grow.

At Bow River, Peggy – already identified as the likely lead player – had quickly turned her energies towards drawing the joonba back into focus. She had been a little girl at Greenvale Station when the performance had found its way back to that country, and had first heard the associated songs when a group of senior men had returned her brother, a young Timmy, to the station, fresh from a cycle of ceremony. Now, a dance ground was marked out in the dirt between Bow River's dilapidated houses, roles were delegated and supplies were brought in to support a growing number of participants.

Hector began to visit from Warmun to provide advice on the performance's conceptual architecture, conferring with Timmy, Paddy,

Big Joe and others. Dottie Watbi, a senior woman whose father had once been the owner of the joonba's songs, was brought in as an adviser. Mona Ramsey – Timmy's daughter and Rammey's first wife – began work on the phrasing; so too did Phyllis and Timmy, who added the insistent tone of clapsticks to the circular, repetitive verses that were fast emerging. Button Jones, a Miriwoong Elder whom Tony knew only in passing, arrived to play the didgeridoo, which in Gija country was known as the maluk.

Painting sessions relied heavily on Tony's presence, but, with the performance, he stepped back as activity swirled around him. He observed proceedings with a feeling of contentment: relegated to observer status, he was for once stress free. He simply sat there under the stars from one night to the next and watched. Sometimes Frances would be there too, laden with recording equipment, but beyond that Tony was usually the only white in attendance. If nothing happened, it was fine: he'd long learnt that things nonetheless fell into place.

Some nights he would listen as the Gija argued among themselves in language, trying to agree on the best way to shape the joonba's emerging form. To them it clearly had a life of its own. When they spoke in Kriol or English they chose striking, poetically toned phrases to describe what it was they were attempting to do: the joonba needed to be 'brought back'; it had to be 'woken up' as if it were a sentient being called from deep slumber. To do this required 'straightening' its 'legs' – the separate verses upon which the whole performance would stand. Timmy would happily explain that the whole thing needed to be 'sweetened': 'You have to sugar it properly,' he'd say. Recordings were made on cassette, passed around and then rerecorded as key cadences and phrases shifted towards finished form. Slowly they began to dance it out in front of those gathered to watch: piece by piece it began to take shape.

Initially the narrative was unformed. To the uninitiated viewer its content remained largely hidden: the only obvious reference to the actual massacre arrived when its victims succumbed to the poison and the dancers dropped writhing to the ground. For the children whom the Elders had begun to tutor in the joonba's intricacies, this was always a cause for hilarity. They'd fall to the dust, giggling as they enacted the drama of their ancestors' final moments.

All of it rested beautifully against the surrounding country, as if finely calibrated to the nuances constantly at play across the land's surface: a shift in light could in an instant make the landscape expansive; just as quickly clouds might come over and everything would seem to draw in around them. Hector and Peggy explained to Tony that the best time to begin a joonba was just as the sun was sinking below the surrounding ranges and golden light was cutting low across the performance ground. Traditionally, they said, it would continue all night, ebbing and flowing in waves that would only recede once daybreak signalled the ceremony's true end. Although he never witnessed such a marathon, the joonba at Bow River seemed always to begin at the right moment: the light of the lowering sun could carry through all that followed. These early moments provided the performance its poetic key. It was here when the meanings underlying symbols and gestures began to double, where they pulled away from any absolute interpretation and instead lodged somewhere far more fluid.

The icon of this was a dance object called the woorrangoo, a standard-like emblem constructed from a scaffold of three sticks – two crossing perpendicular over the other – wound with many strings of brightly coloured wool. For the initial rehearsals these were crafted by Rammey and Rusty. There were small ones which the dancers held horizontally in the fire's light; larger ones they grasped either side of the bottom cross bar, swaying back and forth as the coloured prism of the woorrangoo rose vertically over their shoulders like a totem.

The dancers would begin by emerging from behind a screen of freshly cut gum branches. They would be holding small woorrangoo, slowly turning them this way and that. The objects called forth the spirits of the dead but, as Tony learnt more, he sensed a greater complexity. The dancers would turn the woorrangoo ever more swiftly in the light of the setting sun, creating a mesmerising blur of colour. In this moment, the woorrangoo manifested the bodies of the victims burning on the pyre of freshly cut wood. But they also revealed more: the shadow-spirits of the dead simultaneously looking back from the safety of the cave on Mount King, watching as the fire burnt brightly on the plain below.

The accompanying song was deceptively oblique: a series of Gija phrases, tightly related, repeated with minor variation. Tony would first experience it as a hypnotic run of language, each part hanging sharply in the air before cascading into the next. Only later would he read a transcription prepared by Frances and understand how those passages spoke of the sparks rising from the flames, of how they merged together with the sunset itself, of how they then once again folded back into the blaze of the fire. Each phenomenon strung together with the next, creating a circular effect that mirrored the coloured blur of the woorrangoo moving backwards and forwards amid the dust raised by the dancers.

Here was something timeless, he'd think. With the darkness drawing ever tighter around them, everything was compounded in the moment unfolding before him: not only the song, the movement of the dancers and the blur of the woorrangoo, but history too.

•

Marcia Langton had continued to fly back and forth between the Kimberley and Melbourne. Along with another anthropologist, Kim Doohan, she was by now developing a model of engagement at the Argyle mine – one based on the ideal of 'informed consent' – that attempted to reflect the finer details of community politics. But even as a new agreement was taking shape, the tenuous quality of relations became shockingly clear: grog runners in Warmun viciously assaulted two Argyle-stationed police officers, a husband and wife, and left them hospitalised.

In response, a number of the Jirrawun artists were invited to paint a series of large boulders that were arranged around the mine's police station. The joonba's first public performance soon took place against this backdrop, not only as a gesture of reconciliation, but to enact a tangible Gija presence within the mine's grounds, to underscore that Gija Law ran there too. Afterwards, Langton would recall watching in real time as relations strengthened: suddenly there were more meaningful interactions between people like Brendan Hammond and the Elders; now each knew the other's names and there was an emergent respect for the relative chains of authority. The mine, which would soon negotiate an agreement to take operations underground, would in coming years implement a groundbreaking process of cultural induction for its employees: on arrival every new worker would have to go through the manthe, the smoking ceremony that confers safe passage to strangers in Gija country. Soon, groups of brawny mine workers clad in fluorescent safety wear would be stooping through thick clouds of eucalyptus smoke, pushed this way and that by the group of women and girls tasked with the ceremony's execution. From the waist up the women would usually be clad only in bras, their bodies painted with the white u-shapes of Daiwul's scales. Most often Peggy would lead proceedings, while in the background other senior women, key among them Phyllis, Goody Barrett and Mona Ramsey, sang the associated song cycles.

But before any of that, the joonba continued its steady progression from one place to the next. Following the performance at the mine, an invitation was received to present it at the opening of the 2000 National Aboriginal and Torres Strait Islander Art Award in Darwin, the annual showcase exhibition held at the Museum and Art Gallery of the Northern Territory. In the world of Aboriginal art, the exhibition was a big deal: it drew together artists from around the country, along with art collectors and museum curators searching for the next big thing. For this, Rio Tinto honoured their nascent partnership with the Gija. Fred Murray rented the group a coach and driver to ferry the performers – more than thirty people, including a group of children and Elders like Timmy, Peggy and Hector – to the northern capital and back. They stayed en masse at Frances Kofod's house in suburban Rapid Creek, rolling out swags, foam mattresses and bedding under her large double carport and using her garden as a space to finesse their performance. Tony and Paddy, who had driven together from Kununurra, joined them there and settled in.

By now, Tony and Kofod had kindled a strange, slightly unwieldy friendship. Tony had found her hard to get to know during the initial residencies at the art school, but their shared investment in Jirrawun had slowly softened any barriers. He recognised that the vast reserves of cultural knowledge Kofod had gathered over her three decades of Kimberley work were a priceless asset to the project. Her clear fondness for the artists and their families was also deeply felt, and reciprocated: except for the white nuns in Warmun, few gardiya had been involved in the Gija world as long as Kofod. To the Gija she was Nampitjin, a skin name that placed her firmly in their world.

As the rehearsals took over her garden, her generosity was on full display: she organised to feed the Gija and worked tirelessly to record and translate. Timmy laid down the rules for those among the Gija who might find the lure of town too strong and end up drunk in the long grass. Faced with the old man's unquestionable authority, they toed the line. The performance night grew nearer.

Tony felt the stress of it rising. To him the performance still seemed raw; he struggled to sense its overall shape; feared that on stage it would make little sense. Fred Murray arrived and lent a hand, shuttling props to the performance site, an open-air amphitheatre on the museum's lawn that rolled softly down towards the pandanus-fringed beach of Darwin Harbour. He held things in check with an admirable sense of calm, but on the night panic nonetheless set in. Everything merged together in the tropical heat – a blur of activity – until suddenly, as the sun sank at just the right moment, Tony found himself in the audience with Murray, watching as the joonba's first performance outside the Kimberley took place, and the sky, at first sketched with colour, faded to black above.

Around them were gathered the art award's usual attendees: Aboriginal artists from across the desert centre and top end accompanied by harried-looking art coordinators; fashionably dressed curators and collectors from down south sweating in the humidity; a broad cross-section of Darwin locals. Peggy, almost preternaturally at ease before an audience of strangers, gave opening remarks before Timmy's clapsticks rang out clearly and the singers' sharp, keening voices began to trace each of the joonba's 'legs'.

As the dancers performed – stamping their feet as they moved together in rough sequence – Tony let himself relax. In the moment, it all suddenly seemed perfectly pitched.

•

Only a day later Rusty and Peter Adsett's collaborative series, *Two Laws… One Big Spirit*, celebrated the end of a fortnight-long run at 24hr Art, a publicly funded contemporary art space in the well-heeled Darwin suburb of Parap. The works had been finished almost five months before, but the exhibition had marked their first public unveiling.

The paintings were hung in the sequence they'd been made: it was possible to follow Peter and Rusty's painted 'dialogue' from left to right and back again. Here was one of the Gija painter's dense compositions, each shape carefully stitched with white dots; next to it, one of Peter's strangely fluid untitled pictures: the starkly sectioned black and white drawn somehow onto the same plane, neither of them sitting above or below the other.

Word of the series had spread slowly, but in recent weeks interest had become more pronounced. Peggy, painted up for ceremony, performed an abbreviated rendition of the previous night's joonba for the small crowd that gathered. Many had seen the full performance on the museum's lawn, but the space in the gallery was more intimate, the acoustics of the concrete floor far more intense. It was early afternoon: light flooded in through the large windows; in the heat of the build-up the press of bodies was sweltering.

Afterwards Peggy and Rusty both spoke and, as if the gates had now been opened, both told of frontier massacres that had directly affected their families. Peggy spoke with a striking theatricality. Her emotion was raw: she implored those gathered to believe the story of the massacre and to respect the notion of two laws that played out in Peter and Rusty's work. As she did, tears scored black lines down her ochre-painted cheeks. By comparison Rusty was more subdued, but his deep rumbling voice worked a certain magic: as he spoke the predominantly white crowd before him was transfixed.

5.

The rest of the year came quickly: the artists returned to the Kimberley where they dispersed between Kununurra, Rugun and Turkey Creek. Tony, once again, lodged at Bow River.

In September, a recent series by Paddy opened at Martin Browne's gallery in Sydney, timed to coincide with the 2000 Olympic Games: a sharp, graphically direct group of works that doubled down on the old man's emerging reputation as a master. Browne managed to get one reproduced on the cover of the United Airlines in-flight magazine. A month later the

Gaagembi exhibition opened in Melbourne. Afterwards, as Christmas approached, Tony flew south for a break.

Later, he could recall the day of his departure with striking clarity. Before he left he travelled to Turkey Creek to say his farewells to Timmy and Paddy, who were both staying there. He found them sitting together in the shade of a large tree among a group of countrymen and women, all of them in the midst of a high-stakes card game. It seemed to Tony that his departure was no big deal, that the old men knew he'd be back soon, but Timmy nonetheless had clear instructions: on his return, he wanted Tony to drive to Fitzroy Crossing, a town 450 kilometres to the south-west. He and Paddy would be there for men's Law, he explained, and he wanted Tony to see it.

Tony's time back in Victoria was brief. He spent New Year's Eve at Somers, a coastal town on the Mornington Peninsula, where a group of old friends often drew together at the home of Jose Alfano, an architect, and his artist partner, Christabel Wigley. It was there Tony received the news: on 31 December Timmy had died. It had happened suddenly: he had been in Warmun with Peggy; she'd made him a large cup of tea and he'd gone inside to lie down, feeling ill. He never got up.

Tony flew back to Kununurra and as he drove into Bow River he passed Chocolate Thomas's LandCruiser coming out. Each slowed to a halt: the dust settled around them. Rammey was sitting quietly in the passenger seat beside Chocolate; the back seat was overtaken by a group of Bow River kids. For much of his return trip Tony had held the news of Timmy's death at bay: now, seeing his friends, it broke over him like a wave; he rested his head on the steering wheel and cried. 'Poor fella,' he heard the kids in the back seat of Chocolate's vehicle murmur.

For the Gija community, Timmy's death carried profound consequences. He had been the key Lawman: the carrier of the songs that mapped complex networks of responsibility across many Kimberley language groups and beyond. As one of the region's most important political leaders he had also long been the go-to figure for any whites wanting to negotiate with the Gija: a regular presence at land council meetings and mining negotiations; a spokesman brilliantly versed in articulating community aspirations. Now, the questions were clear: who among the community could step into this space with similar ability? Who would welcome the pressures that followed?

At Bow River there was a general feeling of numbness: even here, where funerals were regular, the loss of someone as significant as Timmy left people reeling. When Tony arrived, preparations were just beginning. In recent decades the dead had most often been buried at Turkey Creek, but the Bow River mob were insisting that Timmy be laid to rest at the place he loved.

The existing cemetery occupied a small reserve a short drive above the community: a long-abandoned handful of graves only faintly marked out in the spear grass by arrangements of pebbles and stones. Beyond that there was nothing to denote the area's significance. Tony joined preparations for the funeral, working with a number of Timmy's family members to clear the ground. They fenced the area and made a sign to hang over the simple gate: 'Juwulinypany Cemetery'. Later, he and Jeffrey Clifton, Freddie's son-in-law, dug the grave together. Clifton, who had worked on CDEP road crews, operated a front-end loader loaned by the Argyle mine before both of them cleared the red earth with shovels. Anticipating a large turnout, he then bulldozed a car park nearby.

On the day, Fred Murray drove Timmy's coffin the three hours from the Kununurra morgue in the back of a troopy, its air-conditioning blasting full force. They laid the old man out in Bow River's large open-sided machinery shed; on the wall behind hung a red and black painting that Tony had made with the Bow River kids on a large tarpaulin: a version of one of the old man's recent works.

By now, vehicles had been arriving for a day or more. Mourners came from across the country and both sides of the political and cultural divide. It would later be claimed there had been as many as a thousand in attendance, a figure made up of not just Gija, but of Aboriginal leaders from the Kimberley and beyond, of political figures past and present.

If the whole scene appeared unwieldy, it was nonetheless marked by a certain elegance. Paddy dipped into his recent painting income to provide new clothes for the core group of Gija mourners: black and white stockman outfits for the men, new dresses for the women, little bow ties for the young boys. Marcia Langton made the journey to pay her respects; so too did the high-profile political brothers Patrick and Mick Dodson. Pat, a magisterial figure whose long white beard spilled over his black-clad chest, rose during proceedings and read a letter from the federal Labor leader Kim Beazley, who was well aware of Timmy's wide-reaching influence in the Aboriginal sphere. Senior management from Argyle rubbed shoulders with Warmun's Catholic nuns; a small ABC television crew filmed footage for a documentary that would air a year later. NAISDA, the Sydney dance college that provided the Bangarra Dance Company many of its most talented members, and which had hosted both Timmy and Peggy as guest instructors, sent a dancer to perform a short sequence that had been specially choreographed for the occasion.

Tony watched as the initial ceremony drew to a close and people lined up to splash a blessing of water on the coffin's lid. When Hector's turn came he was inconsolable: 'Now we got no song man!' Tony would recall him shouting as he lay his head on the polished wood. 'We got no culture man!' Later, as her brother was lowered into the earth, Peggy fell to her knees.

As the crowd dispersed, and the afternoon shadows began to stretch out towards evening, it became clear that, in the direction of Timmy's father's country, a large storm was gathering.

Within moments the sky was dark; a swift, cold wind signalled the ferocity of the rain to come. Performances had been planned for the coming hours, but it was now clear that to stay was to risk being flooded in: people began to pile hastily into their vehicles and make a run for it, skidding across the riverbed just as the heavens broke.

Leon Morris, who had recently helped form the Warlpawun proposal in Darwin, and had known Timmy since the early days of the Kimberley Land Council, watched from a passenger seat in amazement as the first moments of rain opened into a torrent and thunder cracked around them. Morris, who'd lived in Darwin and the Kimberley for years, was the veteran of many a wet-season tempest, but this was beyond anything he'd experienced.

In the coming days he would publish an obituary for Timmy in *The Sydney Morning Herald* that would fill out Timmy's character with a series of finely observed details. It was true the old man had been a formidable political presence in the region, but Morris was careful to underscore that his stature as a performer was similarly profound. He wrote of how Timmy's passion for culture, which had bound together the key events of his life, had carried through to his final days. Not long after Timmy had shepherded the joonba through its public premiere in Darwin, he had undertaken his final public performance at a meeting at Kupartiya, an Aboriginal-owned station near Fitzroy Crossing. That day, as Timmy had left in a minibus, he was clearly eager to stay immersed in the moment. He put a cassette on for the long drive home: a recording of Gija music and song on which his own voice rose unmistakably above the other performers. The old man, Morris would recount, was smiling broadly: this was to be their soundtrack as they drove back towards Turkey Creek and the country unfurled around them.

Now, with the storm reaching full force, it was hard not to see Timmy's passing in elemental terms. By the time Morris's vehicle reached the highway the water was flooding down the hills and through the gullies. Lightning was coming in a barrage of swift, horizontal flashes. Everything was lit up, every rock and tree picked out in exquisite detail.

•

Tony had stayed at Bow River and watched as the convoy of vehicles beat their hasty retreat. As night fell, he and Paddy sat together, listening as the storm dissipated around them in the darkness and the thick, fecund smell of the freshly sodden country washed over them.

Paddy was clearly in a reflective mood, quietly smoking and turning Timmy's loss and its implications over in his mind.

'I hope the country weeps for me when I die like it did for my wardoo,' he said of his brother-in-law.

Bedford Downs

1.

Along the highway, the signs for pastoral leases rose up against the landscape at regular intervals: Texas Downs, Violet Valley, Mabel Downs. Each stood taller than a man and spelt the settler names for that country in curved letters bent and welded from tubular steel and painted bright white.

Jason Davidson, the young Aboriginal photographer from Darwin who had sometimes hosted Tony and the old men during their university residency, was driving: it was his vehicle, a single-cab LandCruiser utility. Paddy was sitting in the middle seat, Tony was next to him. As each pastoral sign flashed by, it brought them closer to their destination: the entry to Springvale Station, which led on to Bedford Downs.

When they finally turned onto the unsealed entry road the gates began. There must have been twenty in all, but it was hard to keep count. The gates brought a maddening staccato rhythm: the car stopping and starting in the heat, one gate after another closing behind them and pushing them deeper into country. It wasn't the first time Paddy and Tony had made the trip – they had already undertaken it as part of a larger group including Frances Kofod, Chocolate Thomas and Peggy – but there was something about the intensity of it being just the three of them that heightened the experience. This was true for Davidson too: at one stage he watched as Paddy got out of the cabin, and returned with tears in his eyes: being back clearly brought with it strong emotion.

Springvale homestead soon drew into view in the distance, but they kept going. The homestead at Bedford Downs, when it appeared, was roofed in red, the walls of its outbuildings rendered white against the dark foliage of a partially irrigated garden: palms, large shade trees, frangipani, patches of lawn struggling under the Kimberley sun.

A cattle grate at the front split a fence line of white tubular steel on which the now familiar welded letters spelt the station's name. From a steel arm hung a cut-tin silhouette of a humped Brahmin bull. It was painted black: a perfect bull-shaped void softly swinging against the endless blue sky.

•

In its first years Bedford Downs had been a wild place. When the Western Australian government had first begun issuing leases over the 'unoccupied' land of the East Kimberley in the early 1880s, it was the more fertile country around the Ord River basin that had initially been taken. By the time the lease to Bedford Downs was officially granted to a small group of investors in 1906, the Kimberley's far-flung network of white towns had already been established: Fitzroy Crossing and Halls Creek to the south; Wyndham to the north. Linking them was the patchwork of stations – among them Texas Downs, Greenvale, Lissadell and Violet Valley – which by then had already begun pushing a steady stream of Kimberley cattle across country to Wyndham.

Together with Tablelands Station, which abutted Bedford Downs to the north-west, and the smaller leases of Karungie Downs and Galway Downs, their borders extended outside the patrol area covered by the Halls Creek and Fitzroy Crossing police. They were on the periphery and, for this reason, settlers feared the area. Cattle killing was rife: in the year Bedford Downs was established Aboriginal people camping near the newly built homestead were arrested on the charge. Measures taken elsewhere, including regular police patrols and the establishment of ration depots like the one at Turkey Creek, were impossible. Largely unpoliced, Bedford Downs lay for its first years at the centre of what was then colloquially known as 'the back-blocks', or more ominously, 'the underworld'.

Perhaps for this reason the station passed hands quickly. 'Texas Jack' Kelly, the mercantile and brutal overseer of Texas Downs, which in 1897 had been among the first stations established in the East Kimberley, purchased it with a partner, Bob Sexton, in 1908. They constructed a new homestead a day's ride to the north of the provisional structure the first owners had erected, before selling to another conglomerate of interests for £16,000. Paddy Quilty's family bought Bedford Downs two years later. He was one of six children of Irish settlers who'd previously worked their way from Sydney to Croydon on the Queensland gulf, a vast area that in the mid-1800s marked the edge of the most lawless and violent stretch of the country's frontier. The pastoralists pushed westward year by year: mounted parties comprised of police and black trackers announced their arrival; murder and massacre often followed. The Quilty family secured two large-scale leases, Oakland Park and Euroka Springs: the money they made allowed the family to invest in Sydney property and, in turn, for Paddy Quilty and eventually his brother Thomas to once again meet the frontier in the East Kimberley half a generation later and expand their family's holdings.

By the time Quilty arrived at Bedford Downs, the station, although still incomparably remote, was well established. In addition to the homestead there were 17,000 head of cattle roaming its low hills and shallow gullies. Alongside Quilty, there were at first only two Europeans employed there: the rest of the labour was undertaken by the local Aboriginal people now indentured to the country's new 'owner'. By 1920 a carpenter and a cook had been added to the whites employed; beyond that, it remained Aboriginal labour that provided the station its fuel. Quilty was only forty-seven years old when he died in the late 1930s, but Bedford Downs didn't pass from his family for another four decades. By that time the Quiltys held 4.5 million acres of land between Western Australia and the Northern Territory.

As a child Paddy had lived with his countrymen and women in the Gija camp near the homestead. He'd been born at Bedford Downs only three years after Paddy Quilty had first arrived, and as he grew he joined his people in the work by which their lives were now largely defined: making Bedford Downs profitable for the whites who had taken it from them.

The women worked at the homestead. They cooked for Quilty and his white workers and washed their clothes; they tended the kitchen garden and scrubbed clean the homestead's whitewashed walls. The men, meanwhile, performed the many tasks of cattlework: mustering stock, building and mending fences, constructing cattle yards of cut timber. They also learnt the art of working with horses: how to break in young colts and fillies, how to shoe and saddle them. All of it spoke of the kind of simple yet deeply lopsided exchange economy that had built colonial empires the world over. In return for their labour, Paddy and his people were simply given food, clothing and tobacco; their children and Elders were fed and clothed too. Beyond that, the wealth they laboured to create went to others.

In the wet season came the reprieve that in coming decades – once the industry, for Aboriginal people at least, had collapsed – allowed the Gija of Paddy's generation to view the station era with something approaching fondness. Those from Bedford Downs joined the majority of the region's Aboriginal station workers in collecting the last of the year's rations and walking together in family groups, as many as twenty strong, back to the country's remotest corners.

Most years they'd be gone for months, during which time they'd cover vast distances on foot. As they went, the stories that made the Gija world unfurled in step with all that they passed. It was these kinds of places that Paddy would one day paint. To the south-west, for instance, lay Barlooban, an area marked by a flat stone and known in the settler world as Motorcar Yard. This was where the frill-necked lizard ancestor once lived with the brown falcon. The lizard lit a fire to ward off the dry-season cold and set a meal of yams cooking among the coals. The falcon swooped down and stole both the food and the fire, and the two of them fought there until the falcon was defeated and walked away down the river, throwing the fire around him and setting the country to burn as he went.

Stories like that were everywhere. To look up at night was to recall Kunjin, the new moon, who'd once meant to marry a star but had been drawn instead to his cousin, the black-headed python. He could still be seen, frozen in death as a rounded hill, in an area now annexed by the south-west spread of Springvale Station.

In country, Paddy's people shed the clothing they wore on the station: the loose workpants, cinched tight at the waist, the sweat-stained rough cotton shirts and the wide-brimmed hats. In their place the men wore nothing but nagas: squares of cut cloth tied over the hips. The women stripped to skirts and went bare breasted above. Rations were interspersed with a cornucopia of bush food. There was flour ground from seeds the women would harvest in handfuls from clumps of native grass. This would be made into a simple dough and either cooked flat on top of the coals, or dug in under them to bake. There would be kangaroo and bush turkey and the wild potato called ngawanye. In the waterholes lived fish, which could be speared, and freshwater crocodile, which could be grabbed from the clear water and clubbed. There was also freshwater turtle, goanna and flying fox. Billen trees had honeysuckle-like flowers that could be pulled apart to reveal the sweet nectar inside. Native bees could be tracked to their honey-rich hives which hung clumped in trees, or were secreted in the split of a rock or burrowed into an abandoned termite mound where only the tiniest of entry holes betrayed their existence.

In country, they met others from the surrounding stations. Together they performed ceremony and initiation: this was the season's real business. In between the long and complex performances undertaken by the adults, children would be painted up and given space to practise the songs and dances that they themselves would one day lead. Initiated deeper into Gija Law each year, their lives opened before them in hard-won increments: piece by piece the world fell into place. Knowledge was power; for this reason it was granted in only the most careful of fashions. Only at a certain age, for instance, would boys learn from fathers how to make spears. First, the art of collecting spinifex gum, and grinding it again and again until it became supple and wax-like before setting harder than rock. If it needed to be reworked it had to be heated in the fire. They would then learn to strip long sinews from kangaroo tails: these would be chewed flat and dried into thin leather-like strapping which, along with the wax, was used to attach sharp flint to long lengths of springy wood. The straightest spears were the most coveted: they could fly through the air with deadly accuracy. A handful like that near guaranteed a successful hunt.

The many lessons of the wet season were intended to achieve far more than teaching a new generation the skills of bush survival. They provided the Gija a means to keep alive the place that sustained them, to keep the heart of the country beating. It's for this reason Paddy and his people danced and sang the country's stories. All of it was directed towards the life of the country they loved: its seasonal patterns and the food bounties that followed, the generations of people yet to come.

•

The visit with Jason Davidson occurred early on, but over the years that Tony and Paddy worked together, the two of them would return together to Bedford Downs again and again. Each time was different: as his renown as a painter grew, Paddy brought with him a deeper confidence. He was soon accompanied by a spiralling cast, among them honoured guests, confidants and advocates for the Gija cause, all of them evidence of his growing influence.

Stories from such later visits would come to seem like parables for Paddy's late-life success. There was the trip in 2003, for instance, when Tony and Paddy had been accompanied by the lawyer Peter Seidel and his wife Karen Czech. Seidel, a partner at the high-end Melbourne firm Arnold Bloch Leibler, had then recently become Jirrawun's key pro-bono legal advocate: he would soon draft wills for the senior artists. That day, as their vehicle pulled up to the homestead, one of the owners emerged to meet the unexpected visitors.

Paddy lowered his window. He didn't even wait for the woman to speak. 'I'm Paddy Bedford,' he rumbled. '*I* own this country.'

He waited for what struck Tony as a carefully timed comic beat, before gesturing into the back seat at Seidel.

'And this is my lawyer.'

But on the day Paddy drove in with Tony and Jason Davidson the dominant archetypes of the frontier – the white bosses and the black workers, the fear and subjugation – were clearly still fresh in his mind. He appeared circumspect and nervous, as if unsure what to expect. They drove past the homestead without stopping; Paddy directed them instead to the old eucalypt under which his mother had given birth to him.

The white trunk of it was folded and creased. Although Tony knew that Paddy had also worked on Greenvale and Bow River as a young man, and knew those stations too, to look at the tree was to realise how much the old man's identity ran back to Bedford Downs.

As they drove on, Mount King, the site of the Emu Dreaming that had already given many of Paddy's paintings their subject, hung close on the horizon; on its flank somewhere was the cave to which the spirits of the massacre victims had fled. It was a slow drive now; the LandCruiser rocked backwards and forwards across shallow gullies and up over small rises.

Soon, Paddy began to direct quiet strings of Gija from the window. He was telling the ancestors of their approach, explaining why they'd come. When they finally arrived the three men got out into the immense silence of the surrounding country. This was the massacre site. It was marked by a steel star-picket that had clearly been driven into the ground long ago: it was rusted and bent, overgrown by spindly acacia. Tony would always think of how innocuous the whole scene appeared – clusters of white-trunked gums, spear grass rising from rocky ground – until Paddy pointed out its identifying features and the terrible history of the place drew into focus.

Here, deep grey with age, were the ironwood stumps from which the victims had cut the firewood; close by was the rough circle of ground where the fire had burnt. Rendered fat had left it barren among the surrounding spinifex.

As the old man stood there Davidson shot a sequence of photographs. Paddy appears oddly boyish: a small figure in an oversized hat, his pants hanging on his thin frame, his shirt's top pocket overstuffed as always with Winfield Blues.

He and Tony put their arms around each other and stood there looking down at the ground before them.

2.

Only a few months after Timmy Timms's funeral, full-scale rehearsals for a new, more theatrical version of the joonba began. The speed of this was at one level unusual, but although songs associated with someone recently deceased would usually be 'covered over' by the Gija for at least two years, the sense of urgency that had led to the performance in Darwin clearly remained: Peggy would later recall that, in continuing this momentum, they were only fulfilling Timmy's wishes, that her brother had been insistent they keep going no matter what.

A site was chosen a short distance from Bow River, and a flat area of ground carved out by the community grader. Those eager to participate soon arrived, their vehicles negotiating the winding track that led up past the newly opened cemetery where the plastic flowers on Timmy's grave were still bright under the Kimberley sun. Once at the site, they disgorged their vehicles' contents across the freshly graded earth: piles of mattresses and old blankets; bright silver and blue tarpaulins; here and there a battered dome tent or pitched rain-fly. Most of the prospective players were Gija, but there were a handful of Miriwoong mixed among them: it seemed word of what was planned had spread far.

On the first morning, Tony met Fred Murray there, and the two of them watched as the mob set up. Faced with the apparent chaos, Murray, who had built on the Argyle mine's initial support and secured funding for the enterprise unfolding before them, now expressed some doubt. But Tony would recall being confident: 'It'll work,' he told Fred.

Sure, what was happening now was more ambitious, but the Gija had already woken the joonba up at Bow River the year before; they'd pieced it together and performed it in Darwin, where it had been received well. Plus there was the fact they now had a professional director on hand: Andrish Saint-Clare, a Darwin-based self-styled maestro of intercultural theatre who had developed his most recent project, a gloriously unwieldy hybrid piece called *Trepang*, over five years with Yolngu collaborators in Arnhem Land. Billed as a 'Yolngu opera', that production had told of the complex network of ties that once existed between the coastal Yolngu people and the Macassan traders who for centuries had sailed their distinctive praus in on the advance monsoonal winds to collect sea cucumber. Tony had been in the audience when it had opened at the Darwin festival two years earlier and was enthused by what he'd seen.

Saint-Clare was a striking figure who most often wore his long hair in a ponytail, and his features in a brooding scowl. A child of Hungarian immigrants, he'd grown up in Sydney and was a relatively fresh northern recruit. By the time the Jirrawun group had settled into their residency in Darwin, he was working at the university in an office only a short walk from the painting studios; he'd been among those who'd often dropped past. When the joonba had premiered in Darwin the previous August, Tony had been sure to encourage Saint-Clare to attend, and although Saint-Clare left unimpressed (it was, he'd later claim, far too 'processional' to carry much weight on a traditional theatre stage), he had sensed its possibility.

He'd met Timmy soon afterwards, and Peggy too, and had been struck by both of them.

By the time proper rehearsals began in May 2001, Saint-Clare had visited the Kimberley twice; on one trip Tony and Paddy accompanied him on a two-night reconnaissance mission to the massacre site. Frances Kofod was there too: she had recently returned to Kununurra to live and would play a central role in the joonba's further development. Saint-Clare would recall it as the simplest and most direct way to be on country: the four of them travelling in two LandCruisers along with a broader group including Peggy, Phyllis and Mona Ramsey. They took with them a .22 and shot kangaroo for dinner; they drank from creeks and slept in swags. The first night they camped at the gorge that marked the upper reaches of the Ord River, where the creek trickled through a sheer rock face and the setting sun was captured against the high walls. They set up on the sandy bank and lit the evening's cooking fires.

As the blue above faded to pinks and oranges, and stars came out one by one, Paddy gave Saint-Clare the narrative bones of what would eventually be realised on stage. He spoke about the different country of his mother and father, of how the travels of the victims' spirits had driven them as shadows towards the setting sun, of how their return to the cave on Mount King had linked together a sequence of interrelated stories. Later, Peggy and Phyllis sang passages of a song called the Warnalirri, and their voices bounced off the rock walls around them, doubling as they did into strange cadences that carried into the darkness of the landscape beyond. By then, the moon had risen and had sent its staggered patterns across the surface of the water in front of them.

The next day, at the massacre site, the Gija women performed the manthe smoking ceremony to clear the malevolent ancestral power of the place. Peggy and Mona sang the first verse of the joonba and explained to the spirits why they were there and what it was they planned to do with their story. They pointed out the weathered stumps, the roughly circular area of ground.

Watching, Tony couldn't help but think of how the story was spreading, of how Frances had first recorded it the year before in Darwin, of how he'd soon after seen it take shape in Timmy's and Paddy's paintings:

with Saint-Clare on board it now promised to go further still. But, like many whites who became close to Paddy, he would always be surprised by what the old man thought of the perpetrators of the massacre. This only became clearer as Paddy's interactions with visitors like Saint-Clare became more common. Only occasionally would his anger be apparent: more often he was strikingly balanced in his assessment, almost as if he felt it was wrong to spear the cow, that even if the punishment outweighed the crime, within the Kimberley's established landscape of colonial horror such retribution could only be expected.

At times, Paddy would reserve his most generous assessment for his namesake, Paddy Quilty. Since he'd only ordered one massacre, Quilty was 'only a little bit bad'.

•

There was soon a fully functional camp at the Bow River rehearsal ground. A handful of canvas pup tents were brought in and a long bough shelter was constructed from freshly cut gums to shade people from the heat of the day. Nearby, an elaborate bush kitchen was pieced together from materials drawn from Bow River's two rubbish dumps.

Food was to be cooked on open fires; there was a small generator to power a refrigerator and a handful of dim lights. Toilets were kerosene drums topped with white plastic seats and surrounded by curved corrugated-iron privacy walls that spiralled inwards. The Gija showed Saint-Clare, still a Kimberley novice, how to check for the tracks of snakes in the earth at the toilet's entrance, just in case one had found its way in and was lying there ready to be startled.

As with the painting camp at Crocodile Hole, the first to rise each morning were usually a group of old men: the habits of the station days were widely shared. They would sit and smoke under the still-dark sky as water for tea rose to a boil on a small fire beside them. Tony would often join them: over the coming months much of his energy would be directed towards the production and, although the artists were all participating, painting took a back seat. He and Saint-Clare soon found a creative rhythm that they would both remember fondly. During downtime, they found novel distractions. Saint-Clare would recall the two of them driving off-road at speed through the flat country near Bow River, crashing through dry timber saplings as they went.

As rehearsals developed, Saint-Clare began to picture the performance in two distinct parts. The first would be more conventionally theatrical. It would tell the linear sequence of events that led to the massacre: the spearing of the cow, the fateful return to Bedford Downs, the poisoning and the flames. A short interval would be followed by a ninety-second run of impressionistic video footage before a back-to-back sequence of unadorned joonba described in abstract terms the cross-country flight undertaken by the spirits of the victims. In this way, the communal, collective quality of the joonba's form would be pushed hard against what had preceded it. Saint-Clare knew this was an opportunity to build upon the core achievement of *Trepang*: he wanted to exploit the differences between Western and Aboriginal modes of storytelling to arrive at something entirely new.

Tony was eager to participate immediately, but *Trepang* had taught Saint-Clare to tread lightly in a production's early stages. He believed that theatre's initial challenge lay in how to open a space of mute interaction, that if this was employed as a basic principle it would establish the intimacy required to move forward. In this way his role as director could take on a far more nuanced and organic character. On a return trip to Darwin he had a friend cut and assemble a series of simple props, including two long rifles with black-painted pipe for muzzles. He visited a hardware store and purchased lengths of chain, anything that might provide the narrative with something tangible: points of contact from which they might as a group work outwards.

Back at Bow River he gathered the mob and dumped the mismatched collection of props before them in a pile. Everyone began to play around, turning certain objects in their hands and connecting them to story. In this way key figures emerged; improvisation carried with it flashes of narrative: the largely unknown terrain between what the joonba initially was and what it might become slowly became more familiar.

Tony jumped in too, as enthused as anyone. From the pile of props, he picked up a white plastic mask. It was near featureless, the kind of thing that might be purchased at a novelty store to scare children. He passed it to Peggy's son, Ray, who pulled it over his face and donned Tony's battered black Akubra. There was also a peaked civil war cap, replete with gold buttons and leather strapping; Tony put it on, and then he and Ray each picked up a rifle. They stood side by side as Saint-Clare took a photograph: Tony with his gun resting over his shoulder, casually threatening; Ray's gun held low, as if ready to cut someone down at the waist with a blast from both barrels. It was all in jest, but each of them embodied their characters with enthusiasm: they appeared as history's demons set loose against the wilderness beyond.

A key sequence of the joonba's narrative soon emerged. It came in the first half of the performance and told of how, after spearing the cow, the group of Gija had first been arrested and gaoled in Wyndham. On release they were given death-warrant notices to wear around their necks and directed back towards Bedford Downs on foot, a journey of some 250 kilometres. They encountered an Afghan and a Chinese man; both read the notices and attempted to warn the Gija of the waiting danger, but the majority continued onwards nonetheless; unable to read, they were convinced the notices were harmless, that they simply granted them safe passage.

As moments like this became clearer, Rusty, who was not a performer, worked together with Tony on more elaborate props. Tony took on the first of the macabre death notices, which the Gija referred to as 'tickets'. According to the joonba the originals had been written – it was this that had veiled their meaning to the massacre's eventual victims – but Tony eschewed text altogether and instead roughly brushed on cut squares of cardboard that universal symbol of looming death, a skull and crossbones. He finished each with a white outline of Kimberley dots. Rusty turned his attention to an ingenious two-dimensional cart that he constructed from warped lengths of dead ironwood and an old wheel. This contraption signalled the appearance of the station supervisor, who would corral the victims around it and take them off to chop the firewood that would in turn be used to burn their corpses. The cart was designed to be packed down and reassembled. It was a beautiful, instantly iconic object that would soon sit in the middle of the stage during the fully realised performances as a kind of character in and of itself.

Paddy was there every day as well, watching from a carefully placed chair in the shade. He was quiet, but it was clear that from behind his dark wraparounds he was watching like a hawk. The Gija may have granted Saint-Clare theatrical licence to make something new from the joonba's raw form, but Paddy was already thinking ahead. Not long before rehearsals drew to a close he told Tony about a sequence of dreams he'd had that extended the narrative that had been playing out before him. One thing fed the other: the joonba had informed the dreams, just as the paintings had led to the joonba's re-emergence the year before.

The process was circular, generative. Here, at Bow River, with the late afternoon sun heavy on the horizon, and the now-familiar light cutting its golden swathe across the rehearsal ground, it made perfect sense. More than once since the two had drawn together, Tony had woken beside Paddy to find him deep in conversation with ancestors who'd come to him in his sleep, or softly singing a new passage of song they'd given him. Tony now took such developments in his stride: if another joonba was presenting itself through Paddy even as the current one struggled to find new shape, it was simply further evidence of how the Gija world worked.

•

After five weeks, an early version of the final production was performed at the rehearsal ground; by then the cast had in large part been identified. David Turner, another of the region's senior Lawmen, took the role of Trevor Smith, Paddy Quilty's boundary-riding head stockman who had poisoned the victims. As with many of the others, Turner had worked as a stockman across the region, including with Timmy and Rammey on Bow River Station, and knew the culture of that time well. He created much of his character's dialogue himself: hard, abusive phrases that had marked his interactions with the white bosses he'd once laboured under: 'black cunt', 'useless bastard'. In an echo of the featureless white mask that Ray Patrick had donned during the early rehearsals, Turner eventually played the man in whiteface, his eyes reduced to skull-like black sockets under the shadow of his felt hat. He looked like something from a horror film.

Tiger Moore, a renowned song man who lived at Doon Doon, danced in the sequences of unadorned joonba. Dougie Macale, an enthusiastic, personable figure who had grown up on Texas Downs, played the bullock, the animal's horns sweeping back from his forehead in a double arabesque. Timmy's grandson, John Gallagher, a talented young stockman from Bow River, would be the Chinese man who tried in vain to warn the victims of the massacre to come. Gallagher's brother Kevin had also been drawn into the production. As children the two had been well schooled by their grandfather: Timmy had taken them often to Law meetings and set them dancing among their countrymen. For years, they'd been by far the youngest performers.

Peggy kept everything ticking over with the sheer force of her personality. She led the songs with Goody Barrett and Button Jones, and would bookend each future performance with an opening or closing address, sometimes both. Not only had she and Timmy brought forth the joonba the previous year but her son Clancy was widely understood to be the reincarnation of one of the massacre's victims, Mamanda. In the version of events told in the joonba, Mamanda had been the last of the Gija to be murdered. In one verse it was he who sang out: 'I can see myself burning there in the smoke.' In a finely judged inversion of history, Clancy would play the station owner – Paddy Quilty in spirit, if not name – and on stage would order the death of his ancestor.

In keeping with the joonba's collective production there were no stars, but each player brought their own talents. Rammey, for example, who danced the long-bearded Jowarri devils with his grandson Vincent in the final production, was an almost unbelievably delicate performer. He danced with an evocative economy entirely his own. Saint-Clare would later recall in Rammey's performance the poised minimalism of Japanese design: the bare essentials deployed with absolute precision. Tiger Moore, by contrast, quickly proved himself a natural comedic talent: it was almost as if he could stand on a stage and do nothing and he'd have the audience in stitches.

The first version, consisting of different parts of the joonba and the beginning of the 'play', was performed at the rehearsal ground for an audience drawn from the surrounding communities. Family came from

Frog Hollow, Warmun, Doon Doon and Kununurra. ABC television Darwin sent two videographers; Roger Foley-Fogg, a lighting designer from Sydney who had joined rehearsals early on, lit the performance under the Kimberley stars.

Foley-Fogg added his own touch: in his youth he had worked on psychedelic 'happenings' at the famed Yellow House in Sydney, and had later lit a stage production Saint-Clare had worked on in the 1980s. Saint-Clare had encouraged him to freight a phalanx of equipment to the Kimberley – smoke machines, strobes and lasers – but he ultimately settled on something far simpler. He bathed the open stage in carefully controlled light and placed a smoke machine at each end. There was a fire lit at the centre and when the smoke from the machines hit its updraft it formed a neat column. David Turner saw this and recognised it immediately: 'That's the spirit rising', Foley-Fogg would recall him saying, as if it were the clearest thing in the world.

For his part, Saint-Clare was careful to begin with something that could shock the audience to attention: the kind of cold open that would, in a sense, 'bite them' unexpectedly. He and Tony crafted a figure of a man from chicken wire and dressed it in old clothing before stuffing the head with straw and spraying it black. They attached two long wires to the 'shoulders' and laid the grim contraption atop a pile of cut spinifex before soaking it in fuel and running a wick off stage.

The opening moments of what was now called *Marnem Marnem Dililib Benuwarrenji* – or in translation, *Fire, Fire Burning Bright* – consisted of the figure being engulfed in flames. As the strings were pulled, it sat up with a jerk in the fire. It sent ribbons of sparks spiralling into the sky above.

3.

On her return to Kununurra, Frances had secured a rental on Ironwood Drive, a street that marked the edge of a reserve that surrounded a stacked tower of jutting red rock known by whites as Kelly's Knob, and by the Miriwoong people as Thegoowiyeng.

This was a Dreaming site for the head-lice ancestor and, according to Rover Thomas's *Guirr-Guirr*, the very vantage point from which the travelling spirit of his mother-in-law had looked far off to the north-east and watched Cyclone Tracy laying waste to Darwin. It was possible to drive halfway up and walk the rest of the distance to the peak where, if one looked to the north, the irrigated patchwork of the Ord Valley disappeared into the haze that marked the far wilderness.

Kofod's new house was almost identical to the one Tony had lived in with Simon Georgeff on Pindan Avenue: an unassuming fibro that stood back from the road, raised slightly off the ground on blocks. A large raintree stood near the gate, beside which a concrete drive ran down the side of the property to a tin shed. By chance it was next door to the very house Kofod had sold when she first left the Kimberley four years earlier. That house would soon come up for sale and she would purchase it and move back in, but for now she was sharing the rental with a colleague; Tony began to stay there too, at first setting up a mattress in the shed.

During rehearsals, the exhibition of massacre stories, *Blood on the Spinifex*, never strayed far from Tony's mind. It was the perfect accompaniment to the joonba's theatrical development: another way in which to articulate the shadow histories of the region that had first emerged around the campfires at Bow River. He understood the two projects as intertwined: the energies of one couldn't help but feed the other. The openly collaborative process of developing the stage production only emphasised the potential connections.

Work on the associated paintings had been sporadic since Timmy and Paddy had painted the first of them at the university in Darwin. First off, there had been a minor disruption that had ultimately brought to a close the open-ended arrangement that the artists and Tony had enjoyed there. Tony, who hated the idea that there might be barriers to creativity in the studio, had physically assisted Timmy with his work. A visitor had seen and had complained to university staff.

Tony's assistance had occurred organically; to him it felt like a natural extension of the working relationships he'd already established. Timmy was painting the first two works he realised in Darwin. Both were large, one and a half metres by almost two, and from his cross-legged position he was struggling to reach the centre of the canvas. When it came to filling in the background with blood-red ochre, he instead directed Tony, who could move around the work with relative ease. Tony took the task seriously: he loaded the brush heavily and pushed the pigment across the white expanse in staggered increments.

The ensuing complaint boiled down to nothing – Peter Adsett had met with other staff members to discuss the issue, and together they'd ultimately been unconcerned with Tony's approach – but it left Tony unsettled. He felt he'd simply followed Timmy's wishes, that his assistance was nothing beyond what a white artist of similar stature would accept without thinking; Timmy struck him as perplexed by the complaint as well, even upset that his authority as a Lawman had been drawn into question.

It was for this reason that the group had sought out more private surrounds on their next trip to Darwin. Leon Stainer, the printmaker who had quickly become close to Tony and the artists, found them a large shed in Coconut Grove, a suburb in the city's north. Inside, however, it was sweltering, almost impossible to work: memories of the brief time spent painting there would be dark and troubled. The next paintings that would form part of *Blood on the Spinifex* were made in the more conducive surrounds provided by Frances Kofod's driveway in nearby Rapid Creek.

This time it was Rusty and Phyllis. Both had their own stories to tell. Rusty painted a work that detailed a massacre at a site known as Chinaman's Garden, an area to the north-east of Halls Creek where his family had once lived and where, in the years following the discovery of gold in the region, a Chinese settler had established a plot of vegetables to trade among the influx of fortune hunters. Rusty had taken Frances to the site in 1988, during her initial time in the Kimberley. He'd shown her the ground where a group of Gija had been shot and burnt and, in a low range across a sandy creek bed, a cave where his uncle had fled to evade death. The perpetrators had lit a fire there in an attempt to kill him too. Kofod would later recount how she had climbed up and found the entrance still blackened by flame.

Phyllis painted a work that was eventually titled *The Escape*. It showed a story about her own uncle, about how he fled by foot from an armed white man who pursued him on horseback across the open red plains of country known to the Gija as Riya. It was a long way, she explained to Frances once the painting had been completed: her uncle ran and ran and ran. When he got to water he jumped in and hid himself among the roots of large trees growing at the edge. He stayed there for much of the day, and in the late afternoon emerged to safety.

In the top half of her canvas Phyllis mapped out against a pink background a simple planar view of her uncle's escape: his fleeing figure, boomerang and spear in hand, pursued by a rifle-bearing man on a horse caught mid-gallop. The area her uncle had run through had later become the site of a small bush airstrip. There, another family member, treacherously ill, had been evacuated by the flying doctor's service, destined for Wyndham Hospital, only to die en route. These details were deployed simply by reference to the place itself: to paint a specific site was to capture all of its stories at once, explicitly or not.

In his work, Rusty used a reduced palette of red, black and white. He depicted the hills and landforms around Chinaman's Garden in characteristically intense fashion: distinctive, anamorphic shapes that seemed to grapple one another for control. He too included figurative elements: a small colonial homestead on one side; on the other, a pair of tortured-looking trees standing witness at the massacre site.

•

It now made sense for painting to continue at Kofod's house in Kununurra: as in Darwin, she could be on hand to record the stories that accompanied each work. The next paintings for *Blood on the Spinifex* occurred in a flurry of carefully orchestrated activity that spilled over the driveway at the front. Goody Barrett visited with her younger sister, Lena Nyadbi, and together they worked on their own canvases. Tony had first met Nyadbi during the second of his initial visits to the Kimberley, and she was now affiliated with the art centre in Warmun. Like her sister she was a gentle woman, easy natured, quick to smile. Tony knew that Nyadbi and Goody shared a story, and he wanted them to revisit it together.

As with Phyllis's painting, Goody's also depicted two narratives. One told of the ancestral man who stood high on a hill calling out to his lost dogs: they had chased a kangaroo to water and once there had turned to stone. The man called out across the country until he too met the same fate.

But it was the depiction of a limestone cave known as Geminybany, on Lissadell Station, that tied Goody's painting to the exhibition's broader theme. This was where, as a child, her family had hidden her each time white men rode through that country: she was taken there, swaddled in paperbark, and told to keep quiet until the interlopers had departed. Nyadbi knew the same story: she painted the same cave among a cluster of stark black-and-white forms gathered beneath a field of patterning. This showed the spearheads that came from country near Crocodile Hole, arrayed as vertical dashes beside arched representations of barramundi scales: Daiwul, once again, whose final resting place marked the site of the Argyle mine.

Peggy took part too. She painted a story that Timmy had first covered in one of the works he'd made in Darwin: the 1915 massacre at Mistake Creek in which the colonial policeman Mick Rhatigan had been implicated. In his painting, Timmy had shown the huge boab tree that still grew there: a gnarled figure massed beneath a sequence of curved hills, its branches echoing the shapes of the landscape beyond. Peggy instead focused in on the tree alone: in her painting the branches were rendered stark and graphic against a soft pink ochre ground.

Without the accompanying story the painting was innocuous, even seemingly decorative, but as a prompt for oral history it carried with it another sobering version of the region's settlement. All the paintings that would soon be gathered together as *Blood on the Spinifex* acted in this way: initially they may have seemed harmless – a play of sinuous form and dusty colour familiar to anyone with even a passing interest in East Kimberley art – but once decoded they spoke an inventory of horror.

Over the coming months, Frances would assemble interviews she'd recorded as the project progressed around her, and painstakingly transcribe them, one by one, for publication in the exhibition catalogue. But first, as Tony watched each painting take shape, the stories came out as fragments that soon merged into a monstrous whole: babies killed with a stick;

white men trapping Gija in a gorge and finishing them by gunshot; an old woman crawling wounded down a creek bed.

If the impressionistic images of the joonba were still fresh in Tony's mind, they now found further expression. He thought of Goody as a child, sheltering in the cave as whites rode below; he thought of Paddy too, of how the old man had carried Paddy Quilty's name his whole life, proof that the massacre lay at the very centre of his identity. This time Paddy had painted the story of Bedford Downs to include two old ladies who had hidden in the spinifex and watched terrified as the massacre took place.

It always seemed there was something new. Tony would retreat to his bed at night, much as he'd done when such stories had first begun to emerge, unsettled by the chatter of testimonials swirling in his head.

4.

'What are you going to do to those black cunts?

'What are you going to do to them?

'Paddy Quilty is really angry. What are you going to do?'

This is how the performances of *Fire, Fire Burning Bright* in Melbourne began each night. David Turner had painted his face white and taken on his character of Trevor Smith, Quilty's head stockman. He was sitting backstage at Melbourne's State Theatre. Through the stage door, the audience was waiting in anticipation.

Turner was seated in front of a make-up mirror ringed in lightbulbs. Each night Tony would stand behind him, just to the left. He was revving Turner up for the performance to come.

'What are you going to do to those black cunts?' Tony would ask. 'Quilty is *really* pissed off!'

'I'm going to fucking kill them,' Turner would eventually growl in response.

All of it was timed for maximum effect. In the theatre outside, the house lights were going down as music swelled over the speakers: Górecki's *Symphony of Sorrowful Songs*. The music was Saint-Clare's choosing: he had wanted it at the start because it built slowly and beautifully. It was important for the audience to wait there in darkness, for their eyes to adjust to it, for them to begin to feel uncomfortable.

He would judge how long this would take night by night: it might be two minutes, or five.

Tony would receive Saint-Clare's signal over a set of headphones and he'd guide Turner to the edge of the stage. He'd hand Turner a hat and a wooden pipe: props that by now had taken on an almost talismanic aura. The pipe, especially, seemed as if it cradled the power of Law for Turner; it was his, and his alone: touch it at your own peril. Before one performance an unassuming stagehand made the mistake of picking it up from Turner's make-up table, and Tony had watched in surprise as Turner-as-Trevor-Smith had almost bitten his head off.

But now, with the music reaching its crescendo, Turner would be completely focused, laser-sharp. Last of all, Tony would push a box of matches into his hand; he'd leave two sticking out from the top so Turner could find them easily in the darkness.

'It's time,' Tony would whisper. 'Go!'

Then Turner would be stepping out into the theatre's void. He'd walk silently across the stage, until, at the right spot, he'd stop.

In the darkness he'd take out the pipe.

The music would draw to a close; silence would press in. Over the speakers came a boom of thunder, followed by a flash of lightning. If it all worked perfectly, Turner, in the moments that followed, would light his pipe from a struck match and his white-painted face would flicker at the middle of the stage, disembodied in the dark.

He'd toss the match and a fire, this time carefully stage-managed gas, would quickly engulf the black figure laid out atop the heap of wood. As the flames built, the figure would rise up among them, before the stage once again faded to darkness.

In this way, it began at the end. The next scene would reset the story, and the inexorable sequence of events would be set in motion.

•

Reviews, when they came, were mixed. They were playing the 2002 Melbourne Festival – one of the biggest arts events in the country – and the production was by now judged against a high bar, but experience among the cast remained limited.

The project's first theatrical run had occurred only recently in Perth, as part of that city's annual festival. But although Robyn Archer, the acclaimed festival director, had seen the production there and immediately programmed it for the same year in Melbourne – a dream outcome – the experience had been difficult for many involved, almost impossibly so. Funding had to be found from a range of sources, and permission sought from relevant Elders so the joonba could travel in the requisite direction. Once that was done, there had to be a new spate of rehearsals to soften the production's sharp edges. Finally, the full cast of twenty-two needed to travel 3200 kilometres to Perth and back; many among them had never left the Kimberley and were drastically unfamiliar with the city: homesickness was rife.

Added to that was the now absent line of authority that had previously run back to Timmy. If cast members wanted to drink in Perth, they did: there were stories of drunken violence, of people disappearing into the city for days at a time, of performance wages being spent on junk cars that then had to be transported back to the Kimberley. As a result, the run of performances in Perth varied in quality from one night to the next and, although many among the production team were often impressed by how some of the performers could find poise and beauty at exactly the right moment, it was ultimately an uneven affair.

By Melbourne, the lesson had been learnt. The drinkers among the cast first spent two weeks at a dry-out camp near Kununurra, where they passed through the worst period of withdrawal. With the assistance of Bernard Galbally, an old friend of Tony's who was the son of one of Melbourne's most famous criminal lawyers, they secured the use of Xavier College's bush retreat at Buxton, a small town near Healesville to Melbourne's north-east. Russell Lilford, the painter from Darwin who had first met the group at the university, had served as project cook in Perth; he now flew to Melbourne ahead of the main group and drove out to Buxton to prepare. He stocked the large camp kitchen with food and made sure the sleeping arrangements would be suitable for the thirty-six cast and extended family who were on their way.

The idea behind setting up out of town was simple. Not only would the temptations of drink be held at bay, but the Gija would surely appreciate being away from the city. But any hope they would be calmed by nature was soon dashed. Lilford welcomed the performers when they arrived and it was immediately clear that the Victorian bush – thickly treed and choked by undergrowth – was to them a threatening, uncertain place. Stand anywhere in the Kimberley and you were almost guaranteed to see all the way to the horizon. Here the country hid its secrets; it was shadowy and cold. Who could tell what spirits lurked among the trees?

A woman from the local Aboriginal community was brought in to perform a welcome to country, but for the Gija it didn't go far enough. Peggy and the others directed her through the more elaborate ritual of the manthe – the green branches and the smoke – and afterwards they seemed more settled, but it was only partial. During the month they stayed there preparing for the production's Melbourne run, the Gija rarely ventured outside.

Along with well-appointed timber cabins, the Buxton camp had a huge canvas marquee in which they could rehearse: Saint-Clare was pleased to find it roughly matched the size and scale of the State Theatre's stage. As rehearsals kicked in once again, the support staff worked hard to make the cast comfortable. For food, Lilford leaned heavily on the Kimberley staples of damper and soup. He already knew how badly many of the Gija ate back in country – the ubiquitous boxes of fried chicken and chips from the Turkey Creek roadhouse – and even though there was a deep fryer onsite he refused to use it. Instead, he worked with the camp's caretaker to replicate Kimberley bush tucker. One weekend, they went as a group to a local trout farm, where rods could be hired and well-stocked ponds made fishing an easy sport. The mob brought back to camp over a hundred fish, which Lilford roasted in the kitchen's large industrial ovens. One night they even organised for local hunters to bring in a freshly shot kangaroo. The Gija men directed Lilford to singe the fur from the carcass and together they dug a fire pit: when it was ready they filled the kangaroo's body cavity with hot rocks, buried it under the coals and covered it with sheets of corrugated iron and shovels of soil. It cooked there for hours and, when uncovered, was perfect. The only complaint Lilford heard that night came from Paddy: by the time he was served, his favourite Kimberley delicacy – the animal's brain – was missing.

Evenings were most often quiet affairs. Some nights there was organised entertainment. At times this was as simple as a classic Western on video, but other times it would be something far more elaborate. One night the Melbourne Italian Women's Choir sang: a large group of good-humoured ladies who drew even the shyest among the Aboriginal cast out of themselves. Another night it was Paul Kelly, the singer-songwriter who with Kev Carmody had written 'From Little Things, Big Things Grow', the song that had been like an anthem as the painters first drew together in Kununurra.

The Gija all knew Kelly's music well. The night he played, the requests came readily, not only for 'From Little Things, Big Things Grow', but also 'To Her Door', Kelly's mournful 1992 hit about a broken relationship. That too had played often in the Kimberley. Paddy and Hector both loved it. Driving together with Tony, they would listen to it as the landscape scrolled past. Now Paul Kelly himself was playing it for them, just him on guitar, as the unfamiliar bush pressed in around the campground outside.

In coming years, it was memories like these that would most often return to the minds of those who participated: the friendships that could spark in an instant; the social dramas that at times seemed to colour everything; the constant mistranslations between Gija and settler worlds.

These moments could be poignant. Tony, for instance, would recall Phyllis Thomas on the opening night, almost cowering at the stage's edge. She was one of the singers, and was painted up, ready to go on. 'Jungurra,' she asked, 'which way do we look?'

For her part, Robyn Archer, the festival's director, would barely think twice about the mixed reviews that *Fire, Fire Burning Bright* would eventually attract: to her it was a great piece of theatrical storytelling that exceeded her hopes. In recent years she had often programmed with the reconciliation movement in mind, seeking events or productions that emphasised a coming together between Aboriginal and non-Aboriginal Australia.

At the performance's end the audience would seem shocked. They would applaud vigorously, but it was as if people were unsure of how to acknowledge the gravity of what they'd just seen, nor of how they themselves might be implicated in that history.

Then Peggy would walk out on stage and deliver her charmingly off-the-cuff address to the audience in her thick Gija accent. She'd always begin with something like: 'Well, what did you think?'

Her whole approach would be so disarming and charismatic that it seemed to Archer as if the tension in the theatre would be immediately defused, that a flood of relief would wash over everyone. For Archer this was part of the proof the production had hit its mark.

Yet, as sweet as it was, the success of *Fire, Fire Burning Bright* was short-lived. Although many of the difficulties faced in Perth had been overcome in Melbourne, the pressures of holding everything together had remained immense; as performances drew to a close the white production team began to fray: the regular disagreements and bickering that were a mark of theatre's social intensity solidified into outright arguments; in a number of instances the resulting animosities would never be resolved.

The fact they were left with a large debt only added to the discord. Theatre was expensive at the best of times, but in this case there were many additional costs: wages for extra support staff, flights back and forth from the Kimberley, clothing for the colder climate. The stage design had also been more elaborate than it had been in Perth. It all added up. Recouping their initial investment had hinged upon a run of sold-out performances, but the first night had been full of comps and the second marred by a patchwork of empty seats. It was only the final night that they'd played to a truly full house.

To bail them out, Robyn Archer eventually cut into the festival's broader budget but, although resolved, for Saint-Clare the debt remained a professional embarrassment. Recriminations flew. Saint-Clare soon recognised that the strain on his non-Gija collaborators was terminal: in the weeks following the production Tony dropped from contact entirely; by then Saint-Clare and Frances, who had been there on a daily basis, had long ceased talking. Any sense that the performance group might endure as a permanent part of Jirrawun's overarching project grew fainter and fainter.

Initially, Saint-Clare remained eager to continue what had been set in motion, but what future projects he pictured with the Gija would never be realised. His clearest idea was a solo production about Rover Thomas, which he intended to hinge upon his working relationship with Tiger Moore. That one was cut down in the bluntest of ways: Moore was a drinker, and, although like most of his co-performers he had abstained while in Melbourne, his return to the Kimberley was once again marked by excess. One night in Kununurra he pushed particularly hard: the following morning he was found dead on a median strip.

5.

Blood on the Spinifex opened in Melbourne in December 2002, two months after *Fire, Fire Burning Bright* completed its theatrical run. Marcia Langton had made a connection to the Ian Potter Museum of Art at The University of Melbourne and the exhibition had been programmed across the two ground-floor galleries.

It was an ideal venue. Redesigned in 1998 by the architect Nonda Katsalidis, the Potter was a stark, crisply contemporary space: the epitome of the white cube. The black concrete floors were deeply polished; sheer white walls rose to high ceilings. Outside, the city strained upwards from its neat grid, while behind the museum the gothic pomp of the university's oldest buildings provided an ungainly historical counterpoint. It was hard to imagine a context further removed from the Kimberley's open landscapes, nor from the sprawling human tangle in which *Blood on the Spinifex* had taken shape.

In the exhibition's final stages all this had been at the fore of Tony's mind. Like Andrish Saint-Clare had done for *Fire, Fire Burning Bright*, he too knew he could work with the starkness of this contrast. For one, he wanted to exploit the austerity of the high modernism he still loved – the way in which the best paintings of the period had found their most powerful expression isolated on white walls like those of the Museum of Modern Art in New York. He pictured the paintings of *Blood on the Spinifex* hanging in the Potter surrounded by immaculate white space. He wanted to play on scale as much as anything: he knew that big paintings could hit the viewer in the guts. For an exhibition about colonial atrocity surely this would be perfect.

One of the two largest paintings in the exhibition was a composite work formed of eighteen separate canvases, each of them a half metre square. Hung in two long rows, they covered more than five metres of pristine gallery wall. These were the 'tickets' that Tony had first painted as props for *Fire, Fire Burning Bright*, but here they'd been painted by Desma Sampi, Remika Nocketta, Freddie and Phyllis.

Remika and Desma were only thirteen, but their Elders and Tony had guided them well. Each image, a rough skull and crossbones, was painted with graphic immediacy in black and red and white. The variations between them added a distinctive looseness, but the debt to the repetition of pop art was clear: they appeared as if Warhol's serial portraits had been stripped clean of flesh and passed through the Kimberley's dark historical filter.

Stage-managed or not, it was an impressive work, but it was far from the exhibition's best. Timmy's two paintings – the works that had kicked off the entire project in Darwin – looked as strong as ever. So too did Paddy's masterfully oblique pictures of Bedford Downs: their overlaid, angular shapes appeared as paper cut-outs, crisp and flat under the gallery's cool lighting. Rusty was represented by the painting he'd completed almost two years earlier, *Chinaman's Garden Massacre*, but he'd recently added another that was more characteristically cerebral: an idea rather than a story. He had set up a table and chair away from the main buzz of activity at Ironwood Drive and sat there hunched over a blank canvas until he got the work straight in his head. When he finally committed it to paint, it appeared simpler than much of what he had already done, but it too was underpinned by a dark vision. He chose for it the most direct of names: *Blackfella Murdered in Australia*. It consisted of an oddly misshapen outline of the continent, black on a red field. Its centre was a dotted circle. It marked the whole country as a massacre site.

All the works were large and given ample space, but the exhibition was dominated by a vast painting of Freddie's called *Blackfella Creek*. Freddie had only been peripherally involved in the production of *Fire, Fire Burning*

Bright: he'd stayed at the Buxton camp, and attended the final performances, but like Paddy he identified far more as a painter than a performer. He had by now built a strong reputation, and had in recent years shown widely, but *Blackfella Creek* struck many as a high watermark. It recounted a story that Freddie had carried for much of his life, and which here he treated as a Gija epic over six panels. In all, it was nine metres long: a mournful flow of lines and ellipses in matt velvet black and grey.

Freddie had also completed his work at Ironwood Drive. Watching, Tony had been once again impressed by his friend's ability to hold an entire composition in his mind and then draw it out in a series of gestures so fluid it was as if he'd practised each a thousand times. The work in progress was arranged on trestles beneath the large raintree that shaded the driveway, but there were only ever enough trestles to set out three of the six panels at any one time: as Freddie ran through the painting panel by panel he never saw the whole image at once.

On the museum's wall the accomplishment of it was striking. Amniotic forms drifted through the composition like oil moving slowly across the surface of water. It could well have been something tiny blown up to massive proportions – a bacterial slide seen through a microscope's lens – but it was, of course, an aerial map. As with many of Freddie's best paintings, it was cropped in a way that suggested it pushed far beyond the edges of the canvas and into the world beyond. Creek beds extended as tendrils beneath the black forms of hills; the grey ground showed the plains that ran between them. On the extreme right-hand edge, a series of small circles, three in total, fell away from the picture until the last was only glimpsed. The two top circles were red and gave the work its only flash of colour.

The work took as its subject the same story Timmy had once painted for the *Gaagembi* exhibition in 2000, but Freddie expanded the detail in full. The first of the three circles showed the hideout of Major, the Aboriginal outlaw who in his final days had counted among his entourage Freddie's grandmother and her older sister. Major's story, a kind of Kimberley legend, was widely known. It was present in both oral and historical record, passed widely across the region by Aboriginal people and Europeans alike. Freddie had often listened to his grandmother tell it when he was a child;

later, working on Lissadell Station, the older Gija stockmen had added to her accounts.

The details shifted and changed from one version to the next, but there was a sequence of shared features. Major was widely believed to be from the Wardaman people of the Daly River region; he was brought as a child to Texas Downs Station, where he proved himself fearless. For this he was given his name by the station whites. They jokingly saluted the boy; the station's overseer, 'Texas Jack' Kelly, brutalised him: as Major grew, he retaliated.

Kelly, seeking to pull Major back into line, eventually had a policeman called Jock Miller blindfold and tie him to a tree, before the two of them took turns beating him with a length of sapling. Miller then took Major in chains to a camp at Wyndham Six Mile. When Miller departed several weeks later, enough trust had grown between the two that he gave Major a rifle and ammunition and directed him back towards Texas Downs alone. Instead of returning to ingratiate himself to Kelly, Major chose the life of an outlaw.

When Tony and Freddie first met in Melbourne, and were staying together in Ivanhoe, they had gone together to the Heide Museum of Modern Art in suburban Bulleen. There they'd viewed Sidney Nolan's Ned Kelly series, those instantly recognisable pictures that depicted the colonial Irish bushranger as a black cut-out against yellow landscapes. Freddie had immediately made the connection; he recognised in Ned Kelly what he valued in Major's story: the underdog who kicked out against his oppressors. He completed his first painting about Major not long afterwards; within two years, he had made a series. It was a point of great pride to Freddie when two of these works were included alongside Kelly's famous armour in an exhibition at the State Library of Victoria in 2003.

For Freddie, Kelly and Major were cut from the same cloth: in his paintings, Major wore Kelly's iconic slitted helmet and, as with Nolan's famous rendition, was shown as an abbreviated black figure, often with the stylised form of a rifle at hand. In *Major at Growler Gully*, from 1999, Freddie painted Major standing between the rolling forms of two hills. It was here the outlaw claimed his first victim: a settler called Scotty MacDonald who lived at an outstation on Texas Downs. After retreating to the hills Major would soon reappear to raid another outstation, this time on Lissadell, where he was held responsible for the deaths of the caretaker and the cook. According to some, he dispatched the latter with a hammer and the former with a sharpened wheel-spoke.

Afterwards, Major and his companions travelled on foot together through Lissadell. They passed Mount Evelyn, Rain Bottle Tree and Boxer Spring, where the water was known to be hot enough to brew tea. A skirmish followed at Dunham River Station; Major's party once again disappeared into the remote hill country of the Gija and their immediate linguistic neighbours, the Jaru. They stayed there in a cave high on a limestone cliff and constructed a wooden access ladder that could be pulled up behind them. They stole bullocks from the surrounding station, and from the top of his hideaway Major could see the country all around. Travellers and stockmen who passed below were fired upon; they were robbed of their weapons and food.

As fear set in, wild rumours spread through the tiny settler enclaves scattered between Texas Downs and Wyndham to the north. It was said that Major intended to kill them all, that he wanted to cleanse the place of whites; once he did, he would step up and become a king to his people. The reality was more prosaic. Hungry and tired, Major made a desperate bid to return to his own ancestral country. It meant passing through territory now heavily policed: he was seen and a punitive party of constables, Aboriginal trackers and station workers quickly assembled.

When Major's end came it was suitably cinematic: a pitched gun battle on a remote corner of Texas Downs. He and his fellow travellers had been surrounded at dawn and, as they moved from camp, the punitive party set upon them. Although outgunned, they didn't go quietly. The official police account, written by PC Fanning on 28 September 1908, recounted that 'Major & party had 40-odd rounds of ammunition left and about 150 shots were fired altogether'.

In some versions of the story, Major was shot multiple times: once in the arm, twice in the body and then a final round to the head as he lay helpless on the ground. Some claimed that his arm (or in other accounts, his hand) was severed and taken by police as proof of his demise. In a painting from 1999 Freddie went one step further: he showed Major lying in a pool of blood, his helmeted head cut from his body. True or not in Major's case, this had been the well-publicised fate of another famed Aboriginal outlaw, Jandamarra, a Bunuba man also known as 'Pigeon', who came from the south of Gija country and had been killed a decade earlier. Jandamarra's skull was sent to England where it entered the collection of the gun manufacturer William Greener: a grim testament to the effectiveness of his weapons.

Blackfella Creek only alluded to the grisly details. Freddie instead focused on the majesty of the landscape that bore witness to Major's struggle. Across the top of the left-hand panels he showed the hill country known as Gawurrngarntin, which was the Dreaming place for the female hill kangaroo; underneath ran a range called Wuluny that led on to a spiritually dangerous site associated with the blowfly. He also showed how his own life traced that country, how he too had been written into its shapes and forms. Here, in the painting's lower left was a mustering camp he had stayed in when working cattle as a young man on Lissadell.

Like many of the paintings in *Blood on the Spinifex*, *Blackfella Creek* found a home almost immediately. It ended up in the collection of Arnold Bloch Leibler, where it would soon be installed in their main Melbourne boardroom: an ongoing witness to the pro-bono Native Title work the law firm was known for. Rusty's *Chinaman's Garden Massacre* was purchased by the Art Gallery of New South Wales; *Blackfella Murdered in Australia* went to a private collection in Sydney. The large-scale *Tickets* was bought by the painter David Larwill, an old friend of Tony's whose neo-expressionist work had formed the backbone of the 1980s Melbourne artist collective ROAR studios.

Sir William Deane, a white-haired man of generous spirit who'd stepped down as Australia's governor-general the previous year, delivered the exhibition's opening remarks. Deane had been a persuasive and dogged advocate for Aboriginal rights throughout his long career, and before leaving his role had made sure to use the symbolic power of his last official engagement wisely. He had travelled to the Kimberley and visited the Mistake Creek boab in the company of the ABC television reporter Kerry O'Brien, a small camera crew and Peggy. He had stood there and offered his apologies for the massacre.

That visit had drawn the ire of Keith Windschuttle, the conservative ideologue historian, and sparked one of the most vicious chapters in Australia's history wars, but Deane had stood firm. Now, in retirement, he was focused on the reconciliation movement; to this end, he'd recently accepted the invitation to become the Neminuwarlin Performance Group's patron and would soon take on the same role for Jirrawun. As the opening night's crowd stood quiet among the massacre paintings, Deane gestured towards the promise he saw in the Jirrawun project with a characteristic mix of hope and gravity. To him, it was ready evidence of reconciliation at the absolute grassroots level.

After *Fire, Fire Burning Bright*, the majority of the artists had returned to the Kimberley and stayed: Freddie alone attended the museum opening. As Deane spoke, Tony watched his Gija friend from across the crowded room. Freddie looked beautiful. He was dressed in a new suit and a dark felt fedora, and standing near motionless amid the surrounding crowd: a black man in a mass of white.

To Tony, he looked like a king among men.

Ironwood Drive

1.

Paddy was now famous.

Looking back, it had happened almost unbelievably fast: the meeting with Tony at Warmun, the dedicated painting sessions, the exhibitions and the acclaim that quickly followed.

Tony liked to recount a story that he dated to Paddy's earliest windfall: the sale of his very first boards to Colin and Elizabeth Laverty. The cheque had cleared, Paddy had taken his cash from the bank and, in the midst of a party at Pindan Avenue, had disappeared. When he was found he was drinking in the small park behind the Coles supermarket. He was sitting on the dry grass like a newly minted king, a group of much younger Gija women surrounding him, each of them holding evidence of his largesse: their very own cask of moselle.

'I'm a millionaire!' Paddy was yelling.

He was on his back, addressing the expanse of afternoon blue sky that spread out above him. 'You can all go get fucked: I'm a millionaire!'

There were variations on the story but, even if the details shifted, the point was always clear: Paddy's dramatic turn of fortune was like a bolt from the blue. He'd only recently been destitute: he had depended either on family, or on the fortnightly trickle of welfare that disappeared almost before it arrived. A good feed, a beer, a new hat: all of it had been conditional. Paddy had been dependent, powerless; now, in what must have seemed a moment, he was independently wealthy. He'd used paint to transcribe his Dreamings and received in exchange a thick wad of fifty-dollar notes.

The feeling of vindication that one might imagine buoying the old man's words upwards to no one in particular is immense: 'I'm a millionaire, you cunts!'

He wasn't, of course, at least not yet. But back then even a thousand dollars was enough to break the cycle: to Paddy even that level of wealth had been previously unimaginable.

In the two years following their successes in Melbourne, Jirrawun would grow swiftly. By 2004, their annual painting sales would reach $800,000; a year later, they would push over $2 million. In light of their humble beginnings it seemed to many observers a stunning achievement, and it was, but in the early years of the new millennium this was the pattern across the industry. Aboriginal art had long been celebrated, but the market, strong in the 1990s, had now only grown. Dealers across Australia were clamouring for work, collectors were lining up, their wallets as good as open. But although Paddy clearly relished his newfound wealth, he lived almost as simply as ever. His clothes were still threadbare, ill-fitting and speckled with paint. He rarely wore shoes: if he did they were invariably battered and worn. Occasionally he replaced his old hat with a new one. One of his few indulgences was a gleaming white Toyota LandCruiser, in which he was driven around like royalty.

The detail set out in the Warlpawun proposal had proven elusive at Bow River – the core vision of it was almost immediately constrained by the difficulties of remote life – and Jirrawun had once again moved its operations. Paddy now lived on Frances Kofod's veranda in Kununurra, at the house she'd previously owned and had now repurchased, next door to her initial rental property. Tony had moved in too. From the vantage of his bed on the veranda Paddy could survey the passing traffic on the street outside, but, with the gate closed at the front, and Frances or Tony as informal gatekeepers, he was protected from the family humbug that his good fortune had attracted.

It was a small place, but Frances had set it up well: she had given one room over to her office, the cluttered living area was dominated by a piano, a wide veranda extended around much of the house; at one point it had been built around a thick-trunked gum. There would soon be an ornamental fishpond at the front, surrounded by a wash of tropical greenery. Tony and Frances's friendship was as good then as it ever would be, and in Paddy they had a mutual passion. It was, Tony would later recall fondly, almost a family unit in the simple rhythms they established together.

During the day Frances would most often work while Paddy and Tony painted on the veranda; at night they would usually come together for meals. Paddy would eat early. He was a man of set habits and liked one dish served with little variation: fried kidneys, with or without onion. Tony and Frances would take turns preparing them; Tony would sometimes slip in a teaspoon or two of dijon mustard at the end so it would thicken the offal's natural cooking juices into a simple sauce. Old Man liked that.

Later, once Paddy had wrapped himself in his blankets and fallen asleep at the far end of the veranda, Tony and Frances would often sit up, talking and drinking white wine. Sometimes Tony would hear Frances playing the piano. She had trained seriously as a young woman and remained talented, but the car accident that had initially compelled her to leave the Kimberley had left one hand damaged, unable to move freely over the keys. As a result she rarely played, but when she did, it felt special: the notes tumbled across Ironwood Drive and drifted up towards the monolithic face of Kelly's Knob. At night it was little more than a black silhouette picked out against the star-scattered sky.

•

The decision to leave Bow River had been far from easy: Freddie was especially incensed. He had briefly taken on the community chairmanship not long after Timmy had died and had thrown himself with some enthusiasm into realising his uncle's vision. Tony had watched, helping where he could. He had known for years that Freddie held dreams of setting up an independent enterprise by which he could support his family, and the plan to reinvigorate the station at Bow River had seemed to briefly fulfil this aspiration.

After the completion of the Warlpawun proposal, establishing Jirrawun's next stage in the community initially seemed possible. Although the collapse of Balangarri had only highlighted the failings of the Aboriginal and Torres Strait Islander Commission, which was then in its final, troubled stages, in the aftermath the commission had sent a consultant to the East Kimberley to survey the damage Kevin Curnow's reign had caused.

With the freshly bound proposal at hand, Bow River had been able to secure significant funds for community infrastructure.

With money, things had moved quickly: two new houses were built and a new bore sunk for drinking water. The old homestead, a near ruin, was renovated as a community office. Through the Kimberley Aboriginal Pastoral Association the station received a cache of fencing materials and new water tanks. Tony had been shocked by how fast the ATSIC funds had been soaked up by white subcontractors, but there was nonetheless a feeling that things could change: not long afterwards, the Aboriginal Independent Community Schools Association came to Bow River to discuss a local alternative to the Catholic-run school at Warmun.

But it was soon clear that establishing the Warlpawun vision in an Aboriginal community faced an insurmountable challenge. Under Native Title legislation, freehold title was not possible, a fact that made private enterprise all the more difficult. If the resource centre and gallery were built on Aboriginal land, who would own the infrastructure? How would they secure the kind of bank loans that any aspiring business needed, or assure corporate benefactors that any investment was sound? If it was backed by government funding, how would this shape the vision of it, and to what ends?

Gija politics only seemed to compound the challenge. Community councils across the Kimberley were often marred by infighting and nepotism. Single families could easily stack the ranks and unequally reap the benefits of community resources. Power in the Gija community had long been centralised through Warmun, a place in which Tony had come to learn two families held near-total control: even under Timmy's leadership, Bow River had struggled to untether itself from that influence in any meaningful way. The Bow River mob might have held it together if they too weren't afflicted by the same tendencies, but conflict could also take hold there.

When Freddie travelled with Tony to Darwin for an engagement and returned to Bow River to find he had been unceremoniously voted out of the chairmanship, it had been the final straw. He was furious: to Tony it seemed almost as if something in Freddie had snapped.

'Let's go gardiya way,' he would recall Freddie saying.

Not that there was anything inherently Gija about the way the community ran: Tony had now seen enough to know that it was gardiya administration – itself trucked in on the back of the region's colonisation – that had resulted in such a dysfunctional system. Plus the kind of whites who took jobs in places like Warmun often set the worst of examples. Gija had learnt from watching them as much as anyone. It didn't take much to make the link back to the mess of Balangarri. Before that it was the starkness of the station days, the slave-like labour for white 'owners' who took as they deemed fit.

At times, sitting out at Bow River at dusk, with the generator-powered lights flickering and the smoke of cooking fires moving slowly between the dilapidated houses, everything could become clear: the Aboriginal industry supported the livelihoods of countless whites, but from this perspective it could seem confounding at best. At worst it was simply another layer to smother the kind of truly self-determined life that Elders like Timmy had imagined.

As much as Tony loved the place, by then he understood it as a patchwork of unresolved histories, a mess of competing visions calcified. Who knew, really, how it ran, or what strange energies fed its lurching momentum at any given time?

It was true that money could at times be funnelled into Bow River – the ATSIC funding had been secured with seeming ease, and by most measures was a windfall – but it could equally be washed away at the stroke of a pen. What remained in the aftermath appeared like flotsam after a storm, broken infrastructure to mark a high tide's brief reach.

A new house to counterpoint those sinking into decay beside it.

A bright children's playground erected on the dry earth, the metal of it treacherously hot in the sun.

Broken vehicles.

A pile of unused fencing materials rusting away under the wet season's rains.

In this light, Freddie's message seemed clear:

Fuck the constraints government placed upon the Aboriginal world.

Fuck the petty politics that only served to keep communities like Bow River stuck in their cycles of poverty.

Fuck Warmun.

Fuck the government funding that treated Aboriginal art as little more than a cottage craft industry.

Fuck the Aboriginal industry and those it served; for that matter, fuck government in its entirety.

Tony heard all this in Freddie's statement for the simple reason that it was exactly the sentiment that he himself had come to feel. The message he took from it was simpler still.

Let's buy property.

Let's do it ourselves.

It was with this at the forefront of his mind that he soon turned Jirrawun's energies towards purchasing the house on Ironwood Drive in Kununurra. It was the very same place that Frances had until recently been renting, where Tony had stayed on and off, and where the final paintings for *Blood on the Spinifex* had been made. Securing the property wouldn't be easy – obtaining a loan for an independent Aboriginal art collective took far longer than he or others ever imagined – but once they had signed the paperwork, and he and Freddie had each taken a room, he would realise they had secured the closest thing to a permanent home they'd yet found.

2.

All the painters were by now benefitting from the booming market, but the majority of the money came from Paddy's work.

It seemed that in every group exhibition it was his paintings that stood out; even in the early days collectors had moved swiftly. Soon there was a waiting list for his work and an exhibition was near guaranteed to sell out, oftentimes before it opened.

The temptation was clear. It was the same issue that community art centres also faced when one artist from those they worked with somehow found that hard-to-define combination of critical acclaim and commercial demand: flood the market, reap the financial benefits that followed. Instead, Tony acted with restraint. It was the long game that interested him. By the time combined sales were poised to push past a million dollars a year, only six solo exhibitions had been held in Paddy's name, all of them carefully selected, all of them put together with the eye for detail that Tony had first exercised at Reconnaissance.

Tony had always been the key for any outsider hoping to connect with the artists, but as the tiny collective's early achievements solidified into broad-scale acclaim he became, in the eyes of many, increasingly auteur-like. He was known to be both visionary and mercurial: tendencies he had always carried, but which Jirrawun's growing profile had clearly served to draw out and intensify. The carefully selected galleries they worked with were expected to toe the line. It was a simple equation: the fewer the dealers who held Paddy's paintings in their stockrooms the better. Although it was soon clear that Paddy would be able to sell everything he put to market, Tony believed that collectors *should* have to wait: ideally they would contact him directly and he could vet them, draw the best of them close, just as he'd already done with collectors like the Lavertys. That way he could build a relationship that would pay dividends over a number of years.

It was an approach that seemed supremely easy to justify. If Tony's life at Crocodile Hole and Bow River had doubled as a mark of his commitment to the Gija world, he now expected some small measure of the same from gallerists. A show of Paddy or Rammey or Freddie's work (or, for that matter, the work of any of the others) was never business as usual: it had to be treated like an event to eclipse all others. Full-page ads in the best art magazines needed to be approved by Tony. He chose the work, sometimes even dictated how each exhibition was hung. Push back and a gallerist would quickly find themselves excised, sometimes for years at a time.

Some already knew the pattern well. Dallas Gold, for instance, a dealer who had opened his Darwin gallery, Raft Artspace, in direct response to the wave of interest that attended Jirrawun's residency at Northern Territory University, experienced the best and worst of Tony's personality early on. Gold had moved to Darwin to study painting after an initial career in hospitality, and was close to Peter Adsett: he had often taken his young family to visit Adsett's home studio at Humpty Doo during Adsett's work with Rusty on *Two Laws... One Big Spirit* and had shared in the excitement that for many marked that work's development.

Although he soon gave his own practice away, Gold – a thoughtful, somewhat reticent man – loved painting. Like Tony, he believed in its poetic intensity: his gallery's name even referred to the infamous near-fatal journey on a homemade raft that one of the most acclaimed Antipodean modernists, Ian Fairweather, had once made between Darwin and Rote Island in the Indonesian archipelago. Raft's inaugural show in 2001 was *Four Men, Four Paintings*, a blunt and effective hang of new works by Freddie, Rammey, Paddy and Rusty. It sold well, but for Tony this wasn't enough: when Gold expressed interest in staging a solo exhibition of Rammey's paintings soon afterwards, Tony had laid down the gauntlet. 'If you want the show,' he told Dallas, 'you have to sell Rammey your car.'

Gold couldn't – he was then operating on a tiny budget – but he took the second option that Tony offered: 'You want the show, you do the work.'

So it was that Rammey travelled to Darwin with his wife Beverley and their young daughter Raelene and stayed with Gold's family to make the paintings: eight in total, angular and roughly symmetrical compositions in ochre brown and black. As Rammey worked, Gold and his wife Lorna had cooked for their visitors, taken them shopping and made sure the painting materials were right.

Tony's intent was as clear as it was blunt: if you wanted to make money off the paintings, you had to understand something of what it took to make the project happen on the ground. Dallas would fall in and out of Tony's favour in the years that followed, but his gallery, backed in part by the Lavertys, became an institution in the Aboriginal art world. He built relationships with every major community art centre and sold work by their most acclaimed artists. But he would later claim that he'd felt he was involved in something bigger than simple commerce with Jirrawun: the way Tony shaped the whole project made it feel as if history was being made, that every exhibition was one of significance and import. Dallas would later admit that, by prompting him to open a gallery, Jirrawun had changed his life.

Dallas became familiar with each of the artists – Paddy, for instance, would often pull him aside when the two crossed paths and say to him, 'Rammey's looking for you', as if to help make sure Rammey and Dallas remained close – but it didn't render him any less vulnerable to Tony's whims: things could easily turn; charismatic one moment, Tony would be cold the next. After a handful of exhibitions in the years that followed, the two eventually fell out. When Dallas reconnected with Tony in Kununurra, begging for another show, it was as if they had moved back to square one.

'You have to buy the girls a washing machine,' he told Dallas in no uncertain terms. He was referring to the close group of Gija sisters aged between fifteen and twenty who had by then drawn together under Jirrawun's broader canopy. Soon to briefly enter the art world, where they would take on the self-chosen moniker the Jirrawun Chicks, the girls were the granddaughters of Phyllis's sister Nora Nocketta. Tony had first met them at Crocodile Hole; in recent months the eldest, Vondean, a supremely elegant young woman who had an infant daughter called Leshante, had secured an unadorned government house in town. Tony was now encouraging them to paint, and if Dallas first thought he was joking, it was soon clear he wasn't: no washing machine for the girls, no show.

Dallas did as he was told, and Tony delivered on his word, but their relationship was soon once again on the rocks: frozen out for reasons he would never quite grasp, Dallas would watch Jirrawun's most successful years unfold from a distance.

•

There was a simpler measure of a gallery's commitment, less personal, more direct in its terms. Tony asked them to accept a lesser commission than they did with community art centres. If they refused, they too would be shut out. It was another demand he found easy to justify. Those who protested only made clear the inequities of the system. Push most gallerists into a corner and they would all too easily make clear their true colours. They were mercenaries, most of them: they profited from Aboriginal labour and did little in return.

'It's just like the station days,' Tony was now known to argue in one particularly biting take on the Aboriginal art industry. And at one level he was right: the apparent imbalances of the system were hard to reconcile. The fact remained that with the commission to the gallery and the proportion the art centre retained, an Aboriginal artist usually received only thirty to forty cents of every dollar that was made from their work. The art centres were for the most part heavily subsided by government arts grants, but still needed everything they could get: they were famously unwieldy organisations that worked with spiralling casts of artists among whom only a handful were ever profitable. Commercial gallerists readily made a similar argument – that they needed what they took to run – but the optics of it were hard to defend: although they lived a world away from the artists they purported to represent, the galleries could nonetheless receive the largest cut.

But regardless of the ideology that drove Tony's approach, it also made undeniable business sense. With the work so sure to sell, he was in a strong position to negotiate: the Jirrawun artists would never receive less than fifty per cent of the wall price, no deviation. Of what remained, thirty per cent would go to the gallery and twenty to Jirrawun itself. In the instance of sales negotiated directly by Tony, the artists would receive sixty per cent and Jirrawun forty. If the whole project was about building a new kind of art economy, it was already clear where its focus lay. Everything should be directed back to country: the goal was that the artists controlled not only the means of production, but the money that was generated from their work.

But there was more to it than that. With sales rising, all sorts of ideas came to the surface. Even if the specific details of the Warlpawun proposal would not be realised, the core intention of it continued to guide their progress.

With the addition of corporate benefactors, Jirrawun could co-fund a health worker who could sidestep the flawed community health system by visiting the artists at home and responding to their needs through a network of specialists. Jirrawun could take each of the artists off welfare and more than replace that meagre income with painting money. Jirrawun could build a purpose-designed studio and encourage a roster of wealthy collectors to visit them in country and buy their paintings direct. Now that Paddy's work was selling at ever increasing prices, Jirrawun could establish a painting trust for him. They would put away a selection of his best work, so when Old Man needed to stop painting for good he could live off a trickle of judiciously made sales, every imaginable need provided for.

All of it seemed possible, and in some form or another much of it was. Controlling the money was about teasing forth such outcomes, making them real. Tony and the artists could surely do some of it alone, but he knew it would be near impossible to achieve it all. He had already raised much of this with Jirrawun's loose network of supporters and a consensus had soon emerged: the organisation needed a board of directors to help usher its most ambitious visions into being.

It was surely a measure of their existing success that this happened as easily as it did. Helene Teichmann, a left-leaning Melbourne lobbyist who had come to Jirrawun through Jirrawun's connection to the Argyle mine, provided the first piece of the puzzle. She wielded considerable influence: not only did she have Melbourne establishment connections, she'd long enjoyed a direct line of communication to the prime minister's office, along with any number of federal members of parliament.

Teichmann was known to be as charming or ruthless as circumstance demanded. She was a striking woman with stacked blonde hair, red-painted lips and nails, a scattering of gold and pearls. Jirrawun first came to her attention when she was passed the Warlpawun proposal by Bruce Harvey, the Chief Advisor of Community Relations for Rio Tinto Australia. She had read it in one sitting, struck by the clarity contained within. Tony was in her Melbourne office not long afterwards and, although it was already then clear that Bow River was no longer an option, she offered her assistance: she assured him that if he could guarantee the operation on the ground, she could provide him the contacts he needed.

The first connection Teichmann made was to the Melbourne law firm Arnold Bloch Leibler, which had been established by its principal partner, Mark Leibler, as a leader in pro-bono Native Title work. ABL soon appointed Peter Seidel, a lawyer with an impressive array of casework behind him, to the Jirrawun cause, and he quickly set to work designing a company constitution with his ABL associate Rosie Pane. This would be an essential step in making the board a reality, but it also intended to be more than that. Seidel and Pane consulted with the Jirrawun artists, and inflected the resulting document with the notion of Two Way that had underpinned the development of the painting collective since its earliest days. Once that was done, Helene took the board chairmanship (unwillingly, she would often argue). Then there was Brendan Hammond, who was still working towards an agreement to open the Argyle mine's underground resources, Marcia Langton, and Fred Murray, who came on as an unofficial adviser. Along with Frances, who took the roles of company secretary and public officer, and Tony, they brought a much-needed understanding of the local context.

From there, membership extended by way of the expected conduits. There was Ian Smith, an archly conservative lobbyist from Adelaide: it was hoped that his presence would allow the company to more readily access the other side of the political world to Helene's. Seidel and Pane continued to provide pro-bono legal counsel; a financial adviser from Melbourne called Michael Naphtali, who for years had played right-hand man to the billionaire packaging magnate Richard Pratt, came on as treasurer. A wealthy property developer turned art world socialite called Linda Gregoriou reached out through the GrantPirrie Gallery in Sydney and took another seat, promising to wrangle art world influence.

To Tony, the group immediately felt like a kind of buffer, a means to not only realise the project's potential, but to protect both the organisation and himself from criticism (the rumour mill of the Aboriginal art world had not met Jirrawun's model with enthusiasm). And although they would ultimately struggle to fully implement the collective's vision, the newly drafted constitution nonetheless enshrined Gija participation in all decisions. It was stipulated that two board positions be held by those for whom Gija was a traditional language. Freddie came on as president, Rusty as vice-president. A third position was created on uniquely Gija terms: a manambarrany, or a Lawman. This role was Paddy's.

The first meeting took place at the tiny business centre in the heart of Kununurra, a low building with rattling air-conditioning and wood veneer meeting tables. It was by then May 2004; Jirrawun had finally secured the house on Ironwood Drive only three months earlier. Langton linked in from Melbourne, but the others made the trip especially. Later, they would meet in country again, but meetings would just as readily occur in Sydney, Melbourne and Adelaide.

With few exceptions, Paddy would be there in person for all of them, sitting and watching, near silent. The beauty of it was not lost on those who knew his history in any detail: a bunch of powerful whites working away under his watchful gaze. He had once been little more than a slave in the pastoral industry, and now this.

3.

Although staying at Frances's house had limited what was possible in the studio, Paddy's work had nonetheless developed by the time the new Jirrawun house was a reality. Most exciting were his gouaches. Old Man's large paintings demanded absolute focus; Frances's veranda, not even a step removed from Paddy's bed, required something both more direct and more informal. For this reason, Paddy had returned in earnest to a body of work he'd begun almost five years earlier, but not made with any regularity until now: works on large sheets of paper composition board executed in brightly coloured water-based gouache.

The first of them had simply provided a distraction from the weather as much as anything. It was early on, 1999, during a trip Tony took to Melbourne with Paddy, Hector and Rusty. It was autumn, and Melbourne's winter was busy announcing itself in the heavy grey skies. They stayed with Tony's old friend Robert Hirschmann, a painter who had a studio in a Brunswick back alley: a raw industrial space kitted out simply with the barest of comforts – a couple of couches, a kitchenette, walls hung with drawings and paintings in varying stages of completion.

Hirschmann worked part-time for Colin and Elizabeth Laverty, assisting them with their collection at their Sydney home – rehanging their perfectly crowded walls on a regular basis, unpacking and cataloguing new purchases. When Tony brought the artists to stay with him in Melbourne, it was less than a year since Robert had been in Sydney with Colin when the very first of Paddy's boards had arrived, the small group the Lavertys had purchased from Tony sight unseen. They'd unpacked them together with a sense of growing awe. Hirschmann's own work was abstract: he favoured rough brush-marks and heavy impasto-laden surfaces. It was hard to get work like that right, to find a balance between intention and immediacy. In Sydney, as Hirschmann had taken the layers of cardboard from one of PB's boards after another, he couldn't help but think that this old Gija artist had already achieved what he himself was reaching for.

With those works still fresh in his mind, he was thrilled to have the artists to stay. He proved a gracious, enthusiastic host: immediately he busied himself making cups of sweet tea and preparing the simple food his guests would most readily appreciate. Tony took them all to see a friend, the art collector Zoltan Friedman, who owned a clothing factory in Richmond, and all of them, including Hirschmann, returned with gifts of new coats: spun wool in bright tartan, high collared; warm enough to keep the threat of winter at bay.

Hirschmann's partner Kim Westcott, a well-regarded printmaker and painter, soon arrived with a range of art supplies: thick composition paper in black and white, along with tubes of gouache in a focused range of colours and a handful of pastel artist crayons. To date, the artists had painted on either board or canvas; works on paper were faster, more provisional, one could work through ideas in a more direct fashion. The hope was that in the process things previously unthought might arise.

Westcott had a studio nearby. It was more comfortable than Hirschmann's: not only was it heated, but with the support of a collector she had furnished the space with a large printing press and wide working tables that one could stand at to labour over etching plates and review proofs. That's where Paddy, Hector and Rusty began work: they each sat on a high stool at the tables and made their first tentative steps through a new medium. The resulting works were without exception interesting, but when Tony and Hirschmann began to pin groups on the studio wall it was immediately clear that Paddy had taken to gouache with the most ease. Rusty and Hector's works were characteristic of both their styles, but they remained somehow unresolved. PB's, by contrast, already seemed effortless. Their energy was immediately reminiscent of his paintings on canvas, but the old man clearly had a feel for the different scale offered by the paper: they were not simply small versions of larger works, but something else again.

On one of his first works PB pushed his familiar roving line in red onto black paper. He ran it close to one edge and carried it in slow descent towards a corner. There he unwound it into three open circles, one after the other.

He had chosen a thick brush and loaded it well with the watery gouache: the paper was uncoated and soaked in the paint's moisture almost as soon as the brush alighted, leaving the matt pigment almost dusty on the surface. Where the paint was thicker it pooled; it held its moisture longer. He took another brush – this one thinner – and loaded it this time with white. He used it to roughly trace the edges of each red line, granting the composition a shaky white aura that made it sing out against the black ground. He painted another two circles floating free and then took a stick of yellow pastel and sketched in each of them internal echoes, thin and wavering.

As he worked, PB constructed each composition slowly and methodically, but compared to his canvases the sheets of paper were small; the labour of them diminished accordingly. As his first work neared completion there was some discussion about whether the composition should be ringed in dots, but they decided against it: the lines alone seemed to capture each image's intensity.

All up, each of the works PB made that day took less than twenty minutes: he finished, and fixed each composition with a mute stare before looking up at Tony and Hirschmann.

Old Man's sandpaper voice: 'Done.'

•

The gouaches offered further proof that PB thought in symbols that seemed only to fully come into being as his brush moved across the open expanse of a new ground.

This was the talent that would carry through his short career – this roughness, this directness, this immediate relationship between thought and action. He'd sit in front of a new work and look at its emptiness before simply cutting right through it; a pristine space intersected by his wandering line, archetypal in its immediacy. The gouaches PB made in Melbourne had only emphasised this quality; by the time he returned to them on Frances's veranda, little had changed. Tony had materials sent from Melbourne: boxes of the composition board (once again, both black and white), along with gouache in a carefully selected range of primary tones. PB would watch as Tony mixed the paint in either used food tins or the ubiquitous enamelled mugs, squeezing a colour straight from the tube and adding the right amount of water for transparency and flow: black for the line-work; a cool red, a turquoise blue, a lemon yellow, a chalky white. In each he rested a new brush; to the side he set out a container of water.

Once that was done, making the actual works was easy: Tony would simply stand and watch as PB sat at the long painting table and plotted out one work after another. It was clear that Paddy loved the immediacy and colour of them. Each was resolved quickly: no mucking around, no overthinking. He followed the method he'd set in Melbourne: marking in the lines, and then the circles and half-ellipses that nearly always counterpointed them. As always, his compositions appeared endlessly variable, but whereas his canvases were for the most part marked by a certain sombre gravity, the gouaches were often endearingly clumsy, even comic. A cluster of loosely drawn circles might gather at the end of a wavering line, or a large circle loom almost threateningly over a diminutive counterpart cowering in a corner. Although finely balanced, the effect was not so much poised as tenuous, almost as if each composition might collapse at any moment.

Once the lines were down, the works would be set aside, often as many as six or eight at a time. The infilled colour would come later, and if parts of the line-work were still wet where the gouache had pooled thicker, Paddy's brush would sometimes catch it, blurring the black into the expanse of colour beside it: a beautiful accident of the kind Tony always encouraged him to leave. In some he blocked in full areas with a roughly brushed quadrant of yellow, or red, or turquoise blue. Others he left open, the bare white or black of the composition board only occasionally disrupted by a stray drop of colour. On black, PB would most often mark out his compositions in red or blue. One series consisted simply of red lines to which he added thin outlines of white pastel crayon, graphic and concise.

As works were finished, Tony would place them all around to dry: he'd spread them over Old Man's bed, lean them against the side of the house, against the veranda posts, against the trunk of the tree that grew through the veranda.

By the end of a session the effect of all these small paintings strewn about radiating their off-kilter energies was stunning, almost as if the abstraction of PB's thoughts had been set loose in bright colour to colonise the world around him. To Tony the best of them reclaimed the directness of PB's first boards from Warmun: like those masterworks of offhanded restraint the gouaches were breathtakingly simple.

Frances would often be there too, offering words of admiration, but if it was just Paddy and Tony, the two of them would sit there in near silence, looking at the new works en masse. They would smile. If there was cold beer in the fridge they would each open a can and settle in.

Conversation was kept to a minimum. 'Good colour,' PB might offer with a wheezing laugh. 'Good colour,' Tony would readily agree. It was a pleasure to simply look.

Seen against the ochre palette of East Kimberley painting, the brightness of the gouaches was a shock. But photographs taken of these informal sessions showed that colour was all around Paddy and Tony as they painted, even sequestered away on the veranda in the cool of the shadows, one step removed from the landscape that unfurled directly across Ironwood Drive.

In the late afternoon, sunlight would cut horizontally through the dusty air. It would set aglow the red woollen blanket on Paddy's bed, pick out the edges of the green blanket beneath it, his eggshell-blue shirt, the blue plastic milk-crate on which rested his overloaded ashtray. As he and Tony sat there, each with a lit cigarette, the colours rang out clearly: even the tendrils of smoke that wove their way around them were picked out by the sun as slow-moving snakes of bright blue.

If Paddy's best canvases were passages played by a full symphony, Tony soon came to understand the works on paper as tonal variations teased out by simpler, far more direct means: an oboe's short burst followed by the thump of a drum, or a descending note bowed roughly over a cello's strings. They were sketches that might later find further form on canvas, but the gouaches were never simply scaled up into larger works. They were free of the constraints that attended representation; they were country reduced to form and reconfigured, stacked and shuffled.

An early group of gouaches were titled for areas of Paddy's country, but this soon seemed unnecessary. It seemed to break their playful magic, so Tony simply stopped asking Old Man for titles, and Old Man simply stopped telling him.

From that point they went unnamed; they were located not as pictures of country, but as asides, flourishes, runs of activity that provided PB's larger paintings a kind of spiritual addendum.

•

Working on the gouaches was easy compared to full-scale canvases. A proper painting session was harder, more involved.

In the lead-up, no matter which artist he was setting out to assist in the studio, Tony would first have to negotiate his own thick atmosphere of anxiety: excitement curdled by doubt. His expectations would always be high, but it was impossible at the outset to know what would unfold. It was the same feeling that once clutched at him as a teenager before running out on the field to play in the under-nineteen's of the Victorian Football League. It was about entering a space in which he would have to be alive to various possibilities. He would have to react, to make decisions in real time, and then adapt to the consequences.

The ritual of preparation helped. He had learnt early that each artist demanded something different: since the residencies in Darwin, he had for this reason never worked with the whole group at once. There was no way he could grant everyone the attention they needed; the few times he tried, something would invariably go awry.

At their new home on Ironwood Drive there was room enough inside to paint, but work just as often took place along the driveway at the front, and down the side of the house to the shed, which now doubled as a haphazard storage space for materials and finished works. But as humble as each session might have appeared to untrained eyes, each was nonetheless methodically planned. Tony ensured that whatever space they were using was set out in a way that suited each artist. Then it was the same process he had first begun at Pindan Avenue: the pigment carefully mixed with the painting medium, various amounts of water added to get each colour to the exact consistency. He had long thought of it as a kind of alchemy, one that repetition refined: by now he felt he'd almost perfected it.

The artists would often visit, but painting wasn't always the driving reason. Peggy rarely had any time to spare. Her life was the same as it had been when she and Tony had first met: a flurry of activity spread haphazardly among her large extended family. She barely rested. Her visits often coincided with language or culture work next door with Frances, or were simply motivated by a pressing need to use the telephone or find some money.

'Jungurra!' Tony would hear her call from the street outside, and he'd brace himself for the whirlwind of her company.

Freddie was also overtaken by family, but for him there was also the drinking and partying and the pressures that followed: like most of the others he could go for extended periods without even picking up a brush. Rammey was usually sequestered with his family at Bow River and had only realised a handful of his distinctively angular paintings since he'd produced the solo exhibition for Dallas Gold in Darwin.

Paddy was different. For one, he was older than his fellow Jirrawun members, which meant he had fewer responsibilities and his time was often his to spend as he liked. He had continued living on Frances's veranda, where he remained a step removed from the most urgent community concerns that so captured the attentions of his countrymen and women. He could paint every day if he wanted, and for the most part that's exactly what he did: rise before dawn, eat a meal of fried kidneys for breakfast and make his way next door to the studio. He'd sit smoking as Tony readied the first canvases of the day.

It was this closeness that set people talking. Paddy and Tony had been together near constantly since they had first met in Warmun, but with Paddy's ever-rising profile had come a newfound visibility. Not everyone liked what they saw. At Ironwood Drive, Tony found himself fielding the same kinds of questions that had ultimately attended the residency in Darwin, where the casual assistance he'd offered Timmy Timms had caused a minor stir. But this time the questions were more pointed. How had Paddy become so wealthy so quickly? Why was his work always so well gauged? Other artists had risen to acclaim at Warmun, where the community art centre was now under the management of another couple from the southern states – the second since opening – but their careers were far more haphazard. What was Tony's secret? Why did he control everything so closely? What was in it for him?

Any question of financial benefit was easy enough to answer. Now there was something approaching a conventional administrative structure around Jirrawun, Tony was being paid a modest wage in keeping with manager positions at community art centres. Frances did the bookkeeping, the board signed off on major expenses. Beforehand, his wage had been ad hoc and minimal: enough to get by, but rarely more than that.

But the Aboriginal art world was as prone to gossip and innuendo as any social scene, a tendency only fanned in recent years by a run of high-profile authorship-centred scandals. And this was what the questions all gestured towards, obliquely or not: that Tony somehow enacted an undue influence on Paddy's work, and that this was somehow responsible for the success of the paintings. Like many, Tony was aware of the recent history that shadowed such suggestions. The 1996 National Aboriginal and Torres Strait Islander Art Award in Darwin had, for instance, been marred by controversy when the winning painting – Kathleen Petyarre's *Storm in Atnangkere Country II* – was drawn into question by the artist's de facto husband, a man of Welsh heritage called Ray Beamish, who claimed he'd made much of the work himself. When the doyen of desert painting, Emily Kame Kngwarreye, died in the same year her funeral had been mobbed by competing art dealers: the flood of paintings that soon appeared on the market were often of questionable provenance; rumours of forgeries were rife.

There were more recent reports of paintings made to order in backyard sheds in places like Alice Springs, of payment being tendered in dodgy second-hand cars and alcohol, of famous artists being coerced to put their name to canvases painted by others. It all suggested the existence of an entire shadow industry, but this was perhaps too simple a picture.

There was ready evidence that artists at times moved from one end of the scene to the other with little discernment: many painted as readily for so-called carpetbaggers as they did for more reputable intermediaries.

Much of what Tony was attempting to do with Jirrawun, particularly through championing more equitable payments to the artists, was intended to underscore its difference to exactly this. But he'd also positioned the organisation in distinction to the network of government-funded art centres: that part of the scene was as scored by professional and personal jealousies as the rest of it. Controlling the narrative with any precision was an impossible undertaking. In this light, he was rarely surprised that his close working relationship with an artist like Paddy would at times be viewed with suspicion – it played, after all, into his increasingly jaundiced view of the whole market – but it didn't make it any easier to stomach.

He would come to see it in terms of authenticity, that his presence somehow ruptured the myth of Aboriginal art, the idea that it arrived in the world unbidden from the minds of Elders like Paddy. For the well-oiled market the presence of a white hand, real or imagined, was from this perspective irreconcilable, but for Tony, such a position was reductive in the worst of ways. It entirely missed the nuance of what he and Paddy had established together in the studio. He tried to ignore the whole thing; if he responded, he would do so by questioning the very notion of authenticity. *By what authority does the market define it? Whose vision does it serve?*

He would point out that questions of authorship were an insult not just to him, but to Paddy too. This was something far removed from the narratives that had played out elsewhere across the industry. All that seemed to Tony to be about ethics, about dubious practice and exploitation; the questions that would reach him about his work with Paddy were far more about keeping Aboriginal art confined within carefully policed borders. It seemed the height of hypocrisy to encourage Elders like Paddy to engage with the Western art market, and then cry scandal when their work somehow challenged misplaced convention.

Even so, Tony recognised the rumours could damage both his and Paddy's reputations and did what he could. More than one self-appointed commentator would receive a strongly worded legal letter following remarks about the veracity of Paddy's practice that had somehow trickled back to Tony. With the weight of the board behind them, the missives' intended effect was usually swift: apology and silence would follow. It wasn't simply the inference that he and Paddy would be party to some kind of deception that unsettled Tony. Old Man knew his country: it was his mother's and his father's and now it was his. He owned it, knew the contours of it intimately, could draw those contours forth as shapes and lines in his mind as clear as day. No one else carried that authority: this much had been clear from the beginning of his and Tony's work together. From the perspective of the Ngarranggarni every painting was in this way Paddy's, and his alone.

But there was more to it than that, a fact that most of Tony's detractors missed entirely. He had always understood the intimacy of the studio and loved it: that alone set him apart from most whites who performed similar roles across the Aboriginal art industry. They usually hung back, fearful that any intervention, no matter how finely judged, might somehow be misconstrued. But for Tony such concerns were counterproductive, and always had been. As a dealer in Melbourne he'd drawn unusually close to a number of artists he'd represented, had at times spent hours with them in the studio, entering into the kind of creative dialogue that for at least one of them walked a wavering line between liberation and control. There was an intensity to it, and, although it was always different from one artist to the next, Tony's feeling for it was clear: for him the magic lay in that moment when an artist hung poised before their work, sensing the way in which to move forward. True creativity always cut its own path. If he wasn't on board for that, why was he even there?

For some who had known him in Melbourne it was easy to imagine that something similar was now occurring in the Kimberley, but the openness Tony had discovered with the Gija was different to anything he'd experienced. Freddie, for one, had always recognised the possibilities that followed their discussions. Since the two first met at the house in Ivanhoe, Tony had become for him a rare kind of studio confidant: on hand to advise or assist if asked, or simply to offer encouragement at the right moment in a work's development. Once they were working at Ironwood Drive, and large-scale works were commonplace, Freddie would at times ask Tony to underpaint areas of infill. Freddie would map out each picture almost casually, a thin brush dipped in black held loosely in his hand. He would decide which section was painted what colour, and then sit back as Tony performed the task.

These areas were flat – it was simple work that Freddie was asking Tony to do. But as much as Tony loved painting, if he came up with any suggestions during his sessions with Freddie – perhaps a particular colour to counterpoint a sombre palette – Freddie would always have the final say. It was as simple as that.

In this way, Freddie would eventually arrive at two beautifully subtle touches. On certain works Tony would paint a dark grey undercoat, and Freddie would follow with a lighter grey. The second layer was thinner, almost a wash, and it allowed the darkness to ever so slightly leach through, an effect that granted an otherwise flat ground a faintly turbulent undercurrent.

On other paintings a similarly dark grey would appear black until a true black was painted next to it and the relative weight of each hue intensified the whole composition. Again, it added a touch of depth that could ever so slightly shift the tenor of a finished work. Things like that made the resulting paintings sing out clearly on the pristine white walls they would eventually adorn, but they were only ever a refinement of what was already there: Tony had learnt more from Freddie than Freddie had ever learnt from him.

He would explain this years later, long after he'd left the Kimberley for good, pointing out what for him was obvious: none of it was his, not really. 'Only Freddie had those fucking genius pictures in his mind,' he would tell people, incredulous after seeing an exhibition of his old friend's sinuous paintings looking so fresh after all those years.

Freddie had died by then – taken early by alcohol – and those beautiful compositions that tangled together in one corner, and then leapt so gracefully across the canvas as single arcing lines, were so distinctly Freddie's that Tony almost cried when he saw them.

•

In the studio none of the gossip mattered. For Tony, it was simple: *Fuck them*, he'd think. *This is private.*

When things really took off he and Paddy would be intensely focused. By that stage they would be poised together over a work in progress. It's easy to picture that same wordless exchange that guided the gouaches: Tony looking and smiling, softly nodding his head, Paddy looking back, at times smiling too. Then the lines that reach out across the white field, the brushed infill that follows, the staggered dots that flag a work's final stage.

It was now as if Paddy was showing Tony his country again and again, almost as if this was what each painting was for. It was like the massacre site at Bedford Downs, how the two had made the trip out there enough times to etch it in Tony's memory as bright as day. He would often think of the station days, of how the white stockmen had ridden Gija country with their black workers, of how there had undoubtedly been times that they had been told the stories that attended the landscape around them. Perhaps like him they had felt the power of it, and realised that any claim they'd made there was tenuous at best. With all this in mind it was easy to ignore the world outside the studio and instead focus on the simple painted rhythm of the task at hand.

Like Freddie's, Paddy's work had also developed over the time he and Tony had spent working together. Most obvious were the roughly painted grounds against which his compositions found form. These had once been flat, but they were now often blurred with pigment, by drips of black or red brusquely worked into otherwise white grounds.

It had previously been easy to read Paddy's paintings in the manner that so much of the East Kimberley painting movement could be read – that they were landscapes reduced to planar form, seen from above – but the increasingly expressive backgrounds had shifted his images on their axis: the horizontal had turned vertical.

The grounds had in this way become skies.

From there, the potential readings only multiplied. They were skies stained by dry season fires, by the gathering clouds of the wet, the landforms of the country silhouetted against them.

They showed something Tony and Old Man had witnessed together often since he moved to the Kimberley: the dawn breaking over the hills, the shimmer of pink that hung there and intensified before dissipating into the bleached blue of a new day.

4.

The most discerning collectors now knew that the best place to buy Jirrawun art was Kununurra, that the unassuming house across the road from the stacked splendour of Kelly's Knob was the source of any Jirrawun art they might find at a city gallery.

Colin and Elizabeth Laverty were once again among those who embraced the opportunity to visit. They would make their way to the studio soon after settling in to their regular accommodations at the country club. It was the kind of adventure that the couple had always enjoyed, and more than once they brought others, including the South Australian collectors John and Jane Ayers, scions of the Kidman pastoral dynasty.

Tony soon made an art of these visits. At times he would explain solemnly that hosting collectors in country was an expression of Hector's notion of Two Way, which at root was true, but a far simpler fact was this: it was a great way to sell paintings. In preparation he would gather as many of the artists as he could. Part of the appeal for everyone involved was the marked informality. Plastic chairs were arranged under the dappled shade of the spreading raintree that separated the Jirrawun house from Frances's next door. Canvases were stacked against the side of the house, ready for display. The blue milk-crate that often served as Paddy's painting table was repurposed to hold a small selection of refreshments: a box of bottled water, perhaps a cold joint of cooked killer wrapped in foil, or a box of Snickers chocolate bars for visiting kids. For the most intrepid collectors it played into their sense of exclusivity: if money bought access, this was access of the rarest kind.

They would arrive immaculately dressed in fresh shirts and spotless Panama hats, the women in strappy sandals, the men in leather shoes unsuitable for the heat. Paddy would most often be there too, dressed far more simply in his faded clothes and worn Akubra. He would smoke and watch, at times chuckling as his newest works were unveiled to almost theatrical gasps of admiration. Frances would make her way from next door and settle alongside the others. Kids would mill about, half interested and playful; if Peggy dropped by she would effortlessly layer on the charm.

The works would be leant up one by one against a trestle table: a double panel by Freddie, bright red against the dull greens of the reserve behind it; a new work of Rammey's, painterly and intense; a PB with its circuits of black lines and stained blushes drifting through the white ground.

Frances would hold forth when necessary on each work's Gija name, explaining the country each referred to, and where that country was. Tony took care of the formal analysis. He would explain why a work was good, and draw on his memory of each painting's creation to impart the magic of studio practice for the collectors.

Just across Ironwood Drive, the red forms of Kelly's Knob provided an ideal backdrop. But so too did the unkempt mess of the yard around them: the drifts of dry leaves, the depleted painting materials, the folded cotton drop-cloths and the water buckets bristling with used brushes. The cement of the drive was now stained with the residue of countless paintings: smudged black pigment, an energetic over-spray of white, a spill of bright yellow mopped to a smear. At regular intervals cars idled at the nearest intersection, and then accelerated past. Bursts of Gija and Kriol broke around them.

Most of the visitors were used to seeing such paintings hung cleanly on gallery walls, professionally lit by museum-grade lighting, but on the driveway at Ironwood Drive it was the surrounding scene that made the difference: each composition was set against the very world that had carried it through the artist's mind as they committed it to canvas. Sales in that context often seemed effortless. A successful visit would see collectors part with as much as a quarter of a million dollars.

Days like this were often followed by elaborate dinners on Frances's veranda next door that added to the sense of exclusivity that now shaped the Jirrawun myth in the minds of outsiders. Rowan Page, Frances's adult son, had moved to Kununurra to live with his mother not long before. He had trained as a chef at Cafe Di Stasio in Melbourne, a white tablecloth dining institution, and was almost immediately brought into Jirrawun's orbit as 'the cook'.

Most days, this was a simple affair: if the artists were working in the studio with Tony, Page would prepare a simple lunch, perhaps scrambled eggs, toast and fried steaks. On larger occasions he would go all out: he once donned his chef's whites, complete with quilted hat, and laboured all day over a whole spit-roasted spring lamb which was served glistening to a small mob in the front yard.

Page, in his late twenties, was a large man: thoughtful beneath an initially gruff exterior. Tony soon employed him as a studio hand – someone to help mix paints and pack work for transit – in addition to his cooking duties, and he would go on to act as an informal carer for Paddy and Rammey when they travelled for exhibitions. But Page's real talent lay behind his mother's stove. The handful of more elaborate dinners that he managed to prepare in that tiny kitchen would long be remembered by those lucky enough to enjoy them. For the most part, they took place when potential benefactors and supporters were visiting, and the broader Jirrawun family would be brought together in welcome. Beyond a trickle of the luckiest collectors, this might have been a post-meeting gathering of the Jirrawun board members, or a selection of other dignitaries drawn into the artists' world. Once it was the QC Ron Merkel and his wife Beth. Another time it was the cast and crew of an ABC television documentary travel series starring the Aboriginal runner Cathy Freeman and Aboriginal actor Deborah Mailman.

Whoever it was, they would invariably leave impressed. Kununurra was hardly a famous food destination, but Page clearly embraced the opportunity to return to what had once been a passion. He would source the best local ingredients he could find, and then design a multi-part menu. *Florentine pea soup, scattered with baby watercress; tuna niçoise tartare ...* This he carefully hand-lettered on to good quality white card and placed upon a table set with equal precision.

All the artists would come too, bringing with them a scattering of grandchildren and other family members. Freddie would sit gravely at one end, Rusty would be folded into his seat nearby, rumbling away. Peggy was always a drawcard: her laugh would cut through the night at regular intervals. Since he lived on the veranda, Paddy acted like it was his domain. He often made sure everyone was sitting in their correct place:

the Gija ordered by seniority, the whites interspersed evenly among them. He would do this so quietly, employing only the faintest of hand gestures, that many would barely register what was happening.

Serious business would be discussed as the dinners progressed. Tony would use events like these to test various ideas, increasingly ambitious in scope, but in his mind entirely possible. The initiative now named Jirrawun Health was up and running under the guidance of an enthusiastic health worker called Giancarlo Mazzella who had thrown himself headlong into the Jirrawun family after first meeting them during performances of *Fire, Fire Burning Bright* in Perth. Jirrawun Health was heavily subsidised, and there were always funding issues to discuss, but there was some hope that it might become an independent entity in its own right: a tangible alternative to the haphazard patchwork of local services. The idea of a proper architect-designed studio was now at the forefront of Tony's mind; so too the vision that the range of art projects and exhibitions developing in the background could be made sustainable. All this could surely address the social vacuum of the place, or at least provide some alternative for the artists and their families. Sympathetic whites in places like the Kimberley had made an art of sitting at dinner and discussing how Aboriginal problems might be solved, but on Frances's veranda there was a simple difference: the Gija were at the table too.

If board members were present, they would confidently put forward connections to make things fall into place. Those with long-term knowledge of the Kimberley surely knew it was far from that simple, but others were largely uninitiated into the challenges of Aboriginal Australia; few of the grander initiatives hatched by the board would ever take hold. The social patterns of the Kimberley were deeply drawn, and if the board were tasked with making something lasting from the initial energies that drove Jirrawun they would fall short of the task. But simpler ideas were another matter.

An exhibition of Jirrawun paintings at Parliament House in Canberra? Ian Smith could make that one happen, and would be happy to do so. In 2005, Rusty would find himself at the show's opening, rugged up against a Canberra winter as he and Amanda Vanstone, the Liberal minister for Indigenous Affairs at the time, posed for a photo against Rusty's painting *Spirit Float Away*, a restrained and minimal work that provided a melancholy addendum to the far more complex *Waterbrain*. Paddy would be there too. He would watch official proceedings from the public gallery as 'government' played out beneath him: the previously abstract power-centre of the gardiya world made tangible for the first time.

Then there was the question of a retrospective for Paddy at the Museum of Contemporary Art in Sydney. Board member Linda Gregoriou was also a member of the director's working circle at the museum: the strings were simply dangling there waiting to be pulled. Tony would soon be on the phone to the museum's director, Liz Ann Macgregor, and the project would be in motion, the red-haired Macgregor onsite in Kununurra with her curators Keith Munro and Russell Storer, all of them hunched with Tony over a computer at Ironwood Drive, reviewing PB's archive, one luminous image at a time.

As the dinners progressed, drinks would flow freely. Bottles would usually be arranged on a side table over a lace cloth: champagne, Campari, gin and mixers; beer for the more straightforward palates; mineral water for the non-drinkers; ginger soda for the kids. Frances had fairy lights strung around the veranda's periphery and, between them and the candles arranged at intervals across the table, nights would soon take on a relaxed and friendly glow.

Overt business would eventually retreat behind the simple fact of being together. It's this that drew forth the most surprising and intimate moments. Freddie, who would move on to green cans once the dinner had finished, might pull out a harmonica, something he did only rarely, and breathe forth a burst of rough music ('I didn't know he could do that!' one of the white guests might exclaim). Frances might retreat into her cluttered lounge room and counter Freddie with an intricate passage of piano: her talent remained impressive. Rowan would join the table once dinner was clear and sit there smoking as he wryly described the challenges of producing such a meal in a tiny domestic kitchen.

As the night drew to a close, anything seemed possible. Take Paddy, sitting at one end of the table in his shirtsleeves and loosened tie, a touch dishevelled by the evening's passage but clearly happy, his eyes bleary beneath tousled grey hair. Helene Teichmann next to him, carefully made-up, draped in pearls, both her and Old Man shrouded in clouds of cigarette smoke.

Paddy loved women, and it was clear to more than one observer that it was a point of some pride to have the blonde-tressed Teichmann as the chairperson of his company board. Paddy would hold her hand tightly whenever he could. Often, when they greeted each other, or said goodbye, he would pull her close for a kiss: eventually he would, in his own way, propose to her.

'You can be my wife,' she would later recall him quietly rasping one evening on the veranda.

He had asked her to sit beside him and had then lit two cigarettes and passed one to her, a touching gesture she would always remember. He told her he knew she had a man in Melbourne, but that she didn't belong there. Her true place was with him in the Kimberley.

'I'm a rich man,' he told her. 'If I die you can get the money.'

She had to lean in to hear him, but when she did he continued in the same vein.

He told her she would be safe with him, that although he was old he wouldn't hesitate to spear anybody who disrespected her. As urbane as she was, Helene was worldly too. Little surprised her, and although she could hardly say she expected Paddy's proposal, she took it in her stride and would recount it fondly.

It was the sweetener Old Man added to the deal that shocked her.

'I promise I won't beat you,' he said with due gravity.

•

But there was a darkness too.

It was there at the edges of even the most glittering social event that Tony, Frances and the artists managed to pull together. Even at its best, the Kimberley was a rough place; as egalitarian as the dinners and the visits from collectors may have been, they still couldn't help but underscore the disparity that marked black and white relations.

Perhaps this was even their main point, as unintended as it was: once the dessert had been finished, and washed down with shots of espresso and a steady flow of decent booze, and the last of the candles extinguished, everyone went their own way.

The visitors would return to their suites in the country club, where they would ready themselves for their next-day departures, their minds fresh with Kimberley encounters they would soon rehash as stories down south.

With the exception of Paddy, who would simply return to his bed on the veranda and roll himself in his tartan blankets, the Gija would steal off into the night, the many challenges of their lives only momentarily arrested by the good meal and the enthusiastic company they had just been party to.

Tony would sit up and drink with whoever held on the longest, but eventually he would make his way next door and collapse into bed.

Overall he wasn't faring well.

It could be maddening to try and stitch together these worlds. Cracks and fissures extended between them. At times it seemed as if they patterned the edges of every interaction, and although he had somehow made his life upon that precarious ground he still felt at constant risk of slipping and falling. It gave his interactions with the white world a schizophrenic edge: trying to participate in one reality while another was clearly visible created a treacherous psychological gap.

The dreams would come later, once he'd begun pulling away from the Kimberley for good, but at that time sleep was little more than a black hole that would rise up and claim him and from which he would rouse with little or no memory at all.

Even those who came and went, like Helene, could see that he was struggling: as far as she could picture it, Tony had made a kind of pact with Paddy to look after him, to involve himself not only in Old Man's painting affairs, but in the minutiae of his day-to-day life. Helene had quickly come to understand that Tony did this because he loved Paddy. Clearly he loved the other artists as well, but when they too wanted his attention, or demanded access to the money he could seemingly make appear from the ether around them, he was put in an impossible position.

He was pulled taut, and although he'd long made a point of living beyond the edge of things, he was now straining at the seams.

5.

It was against this backdrop that the journalist Nicolas Rothwell first travelled to Kununurra. He was driven at least in part by the rumours and heightened stories that had attended Jirrawun's ascent. Rothwell was a wiry, handsome man with dark hair and eyes, and as a journalist was an immaculate observer of the social world. He revealed little of himself – preferred instead to remain on the edge, looking inwards – but he nonetheless saw everything.

Rothwell had previously published a novel, and although his travels through remote Australia were for the most part undertaken as a correspondent for *The Australian*, he was simultaneously collecting first-person impressions and fragments that applied a novelist's eye to the drama of real-world encounter. In coming years he would make this work a signature: a sole traveller, loosely himself, adrift in the freshly colonial world of remote Australia, his mind swimming with what he found there.

Rothwell's prose drew its force most obviously from the landscapes he passed through, and the observational rhapsodies he made of them, but it also found its source in the various 'characters' he encountered. These figures – black and white alike – were often cast as remote country seers, holders of hidden knowledge whose unexpected presence pushed Rothwell's narratives into their strange and urgent shapes, creating bottlenecks and eddies through which his ever-elusive narrator found some semblance of meaning. All of it was heightened, dramatic, written in an intricate and elaborate fashion out of step with the clipped directness of most journalistic prose. It was no surprise to those who had even a casual sense of Rothwell's work that he found an ideal subject in Tony and the Jirrawun artists.

Nicolas first met Tony at the annual Garma Festival in Arnhem Land, where Tony had urged him to visit Jirrawun. Nicolas knew the Kimberley well by then, had travelled its highways for years in pursuit of his stories, and in the process become familiar with the patchwork of government-funded art centres that extended from Balgo to the south, through Fitzroy Crossing, Roper River, Warmun and Kununurra. He had by then already written positively on many of them, but by the time he met Tony the inconsistencies of those strange bi-cultural organisations had clearly begun to weigh on him. In Jirrawun he recognised an alternative, and he quickly became a supporter.

In the years that followed he published a series of profiles and opinions in *The Australian* that championed the project and its chief architects. As he went, he drew close to a number of the artists, and captured each of them in deft character sketches: Freddie was *a man of few words and great silences*; Peggy, regal in the kitchen at Ironwood Drive, *on the phone and waving her hands in an agony of frustration*; Rusty, *rake thin*, staring into *a world of geometric archetypes.*

Tony also featured: he was *a Melbourne art scene enfant terrible, a captivating, drama-courting figure, the most idiosyncratic of all bush impresarios.*

Nicolas soon knew all the rumours, but where others might have blundered into the pitfall of rash judgement he held back, listening and watching. On his first visit to the studio at Ironwood Drive, Tony had casually taken up a brush as they were talking and begun underpainting a work of Freddie's as if it was nothing at all, almost as if he were testing Rothwell, tempting him to rise to the lure of scandal. Nicolas refused the bait, and the two became friends; a decade later, he would grant Tony his most comprehensive picture in a chapter of his digressive masterwork, *Belomor*. He returned to shorthand notes he'd made of their first encounter and transcribed them in detail.

Here's Tony in the front yard as Nicolas first arrives, standing there smoking as if he had been waiting for this unannounced visit all day; Tony, with his provocations ready, jumping immediately into a discussion about suicide, and only really acknowledging Nicolas's presence when Nicolas dropped the usual conventions of greeting and played along. Nicolas sensed the performed quality of Tony's darkness, but he also sensed it might be necessary, as if this were the only means by which he was holding himself together. It seemed a kind of self-imposed treatment: haphazard, at risk of failure.

Tony took his visitor to the veranda and introduced him to Freddie, Rusty and Paddy, who was sitting before an unfinished canvas. Hector was there too, visiting from Turkey Creek, resplendent in a bright yellow shirt. Evening was settling, and there was a television blaring inside.

In the studio, Tony showed Nicolas a new painting by Paddy, an Emu Dreaming that Nicolas would recall as a rectangle of darkness: *a still, hard work* that betrayed no easy access point to untutored eyes like his. Tony talked him through the iconography of it, recounting the story he now knew in fine detail: the travels of the emu and the bush turkey, the coming of night and day. By now he had his own take on it.

'It's the origins of fate,' he said.

'The emu wants to stay in a never-ending daytime. The bush turkey sleeps at sunset. So it is for us, too: we sleep; we have balance in our lives; light and dark; we know time.'

Tony took his time peeling back the painting's layers, enjoying the incremental revelations that followed.

He explained that a work like Paddy's was also a map, that this was how it would be 'read' when presented in collections of Aboriginal painting at the state art galleries. There, the painting would be accompanied by a didactic text: *this is the range, this is the plain, here is where the emu became stuck.*

But the truth of a painting like Paddy's was the history it told. This was the reveal towards which Tony had been building. He gestured towards the circle of red that innocuously adorned the composition's upper right corner.

'It's the scene of a massacre,' Tony said, referring to the story of Bedford Downs. 'That's why the painting feels so still.'

His hand moved over the work's surface as intimately as if it were his own.

'The people of that country were all killed there. Up on the side of the hill, that slight incurving is a cave: it's where the spirits of the dead sang and danced.'

•

Soon Nicolas and Tony were driving together at speed through the Kimberley landscape as Tony told the story that had by now become foundational: his and Hector's collision with the road train.

The accident was still clear in Tony's mind. He now recounted it with poetic elaborations that had become as true to him as the bare fact of the photograph of the accident's aftermath. He had secured a print of this from *The Kimberley Echo* and pinned it in his bedroom: he saw the tangled wreck of it every day, had come to understand it as a talisman, something that marked a line between one life and the next.

Hector's hand in this telling extended straight towards the oncoming monolith of the road train, in Tony's words, *like a magic wand*. The inference was clear: it was whatever power Hector wielded that day that saved them. Otherwise Tony would be dead, and Hector too.

There was an intense, intimate tone to Nicolas and Tony's exchanges, and it was perhaps unsurprising that, during this first visit, Nicolas captured the most naked account of Tony's journey to the north.

'You've heard all the stories, haven't you?' Tony asked him, referring to how he met Freddie in Melbourne, and how Freddie had soon afterwards extended the invitation to visit Gija country. It was a narrative that had already been passed with varying degrees of accuracy between a number of commentators as the mythology of Jirrawun took shape.

Nicolas had heard it many times, and assured Tony as much.

'That's all true,' Tony said.

But he wanted Nicolas to know that that version of events, however accurate, was simply the 'outside' story. The version he told himself was bound by a different kind of logic. It was the version spun through signs and wonders, the one in which his first visit to the Kimberley with Freddie had altered his life in ways he could now only characterise in oddly metaphysical terms.

He told Nicolas of his return to Wollongong after his first visit to Freddie's country in 1997, of how the experience had driven him to revisit his own practice with newfound fervour. He explained how his energies were short-lived, that although he painted one canvas after another, he burnt them all in the backyard of his rundown rental property. That narrative saw him once again lying depressed for days, driven towards suicide.

But although Tony presented his Kimberley life as a kind of salvation from the darkness that had at times overwhelmed him in Wollongong,

Nicolas was not alone in sensing that Tony remained vulnerable. In the Kimberley his depressions had returned: that's why after a draining project like *Fire, Fire Burning Bright* he might drop from contact for weeks at a time, collapsed in a Kununurra hotel room with the curtains drawn. It's also why his friendship with dealers like Dallas Gold could oscillate so suddenly between darkness and light.

During Nicolas's visit Tony unveiled ambitious plans for Jirrawun's future – his creative mind had clearly found sustenance among the Kimberley's dramatic landscapes – but it was also clear that what balance he'd found within himself was prone to collapse. At the edges there lay constant pressure points waiting to explode. Part of it was the simple fact that Tony was caught in between. On the one hand lay the world of his Kimberley friends: it swirled at speed around him, couldn't be ignored. On the other, down south, lay the art world to which he was permanently tethered by promises of exhibitions, or a commitment to facilitate interviews with Paddy, by curators and collectors clamouring for a visit, by special projects that demanded attention.

Neither world knew the other in any detail: access seemed always to thread through him.

Some days Tony could be on the phone all afternoon, talking up the latest body of work to collectors, ironing out an artist agreement for a major commission, negotiating with commercial galleries.

'The phone rings constantly,' he told Nicolas. He would answer it to voices on the other end eager to express familiarity and warmth, whether they knew him or not. Access is what they wanted, and Tony's job was at one level to transform that access into money.

'Sales,' he told Nicolas with some urgency. 'Always, sales.'

He was so far from that world that he could lie in his room at Ironwood Drive in his underwear, unwashed for days, his hair unkempt, and talk with the most powerful art-players in the country. Supine upon dirty bedsheets he cut the best deals he could for his Gija friends, sold paintings, organised new projects, drew Jirrawun into the upper echelons of Australia's art world. From the close quarters of his simple bedroom, its tiny desk covered with a drift of paper, he brought money and acclaim to the organisation hand over fist.

But no matter how many hours Tony found himself talking on the phone, conversations would only ever reach so far. With most interlocutors he could never do more than hint at the reality of the place in which he was living: how could they possibly understand the lives of the artists for whom he was now both witness and confidant? Or the way his own life had taken on the broken patterns of theirs?

From one remove he saw what his Gija friends saw: the short, sharp and brutal lives of their family members who seemed to be dying in near-constant procession; the wild-eyed kids on the street; the walking dead alcoholics stuck on their circuit between the bottle-o and the drinking camp; the black bodies crumpled drunk in the park like murder victims.

Funerals remained common. Sometimes he and Freddie's son-in-law Jeffrey Clifton would serve as gravediggers, just as they once had for Timmy Timms. The keening, quasi-symbolic mourning that the women would perform at each grave's edge would get under his skin: the rawness of it, the way it so accurately captured the tragedy unfolding around them and played it back to those gathered.

Watching the men at funerals could be just as confronting: they would most often sit in silence, the face of Elders like Paddy shaded in black under their hat brims, quiet but clearly shattered.

All that lodged in Tony's guts and stayed there. It curdled. He drank and then acted on his worst impulses. He lashed out at people, demanded fealty from old friends and new acquaintances alike.

To some extent the board of directors helped. Tony felt he could lean on his powerful supporters to ease the pressure, but that too carried its challenges: the majority of the board members were as blind as anyone to the Kimberley's stark realities. From their well-appointed city offices they could barely imagine what life there was really like.

Then there were the artists. Like many Gija they only understood the barest details of the white world. This often granted their interactions with it a circumspect and reticent air. Tony would think of Freddie, of how so few of the collectors and gallerists to whom he'd introduced his Gija friend really knew him.

At Ironwood Drive the two of them had drawn as close as they ever would: Tony knew Freddie's habits as if they were his own. The most endearing of them related to a hero of Freddie's: Horatio Hornblower, the fictional Royal Navy officer who captained his ships through CS Forester's adventure novels of the Napoleonic wars. Hornblower was now a television series that had grabbed Freddie early and not let go: by the time he and Tony settled at Ironwood Drive, Freddie had begun wearing his hair long at the back, and tying it in a rough approximation of Hornblower's dashing ponytail. Every Sunday night at eight thirty it was the same: Freddie would retreat to his room with a supply of warm green cans, close the door and switch on the television. Tony would then hear the program's rising theme as Freddie settled in for another week's adventure.

But such evenings were the exception to the rule. When he was on the grog, Freddie was an entirely different person. He could be bullish, stubbornly committed to the fulfilment of whatever desires coursed through him at any given moment. He set in motion a world of trouble near every time he drank. He would write off vehicles, chase girls, get himself locked up overnight in the drunk tank. On grog, Freddie's energy for much else was limited; in Kununurra the days he was off it were few.

But most whites never saw that.

When Freddie travelled with Tony he was a paragon of dignity: quiet and contained. 'Wow,' people would say to Tony after meeting Freddie at an opening, or sharing a table with him at a glittering post-exhibition dinner. 'What a man! What gravity!'

Many who met Freddie in those contexts were left thinking that he was like that all the time, but he wasn't. With the exception of one of Freddie's most dedicated collectors, Geoff Hassall – an old friend of Tony's who was busy amassing the largest private collection of Freddie's work and had in the early days offered Jirrawun much-needed financial support – most had no idea. Sometimes Tony would think about how horrified they would be if they knew the truth of it.

The context underscoring it all remained the same as it had at Crocodile Hole, when Tony had first come to see both sides of his Gija friends, but knowing that didn't make it any easier. Life in Kununurra was on full boil, even when the town went into shutdown at the height of the day and it seemed that nothing was happening. You couldn't live there without waiting for something terrible to unfold, without learning to live with a baseline of anxiety. It was either that, or retract entirely from the Aboriginal world. That's why there was such a divide. That's why whites most often retreated to their air-conditioned homes at night: self-preservation as much as anything.

Even the good ones did it – the health workers, schoolteachers and doctors, even, for the most part, the white employees at the Warmun Art Centre in Turkey Creek and at Waringarri Arts in Kununurra. For many it was a coping mechanism.

But Tony was in the thick of it at Ironwood Drive, just as he had been at Rugun, or Bow River. The bush telegraph was immediate and effective: it meant he heard near everything that happened almost as soon as it did. There would be news of car accidents, fatal or otherwise, of vehicles rolled at speed by drunk drivers barrelling down the Great Northern Highway between Warmun and Kununurra. It was a cemetery, that highway: a source of near-constant pain, a wellspring of trauma that did much to keep the Aboriginal community stuck in its cycle of mourning.

He'd hear other things too, a seemingly constant stream of shocking events that had by now come to define his time in country. There were suicides and assaults, deaths by violence and misadventure. There were rumours of abuse, of predatory whites patrolling the town for Gija girls, of bodies being found in the reserve, of women being beaten, even stabbed.

He could no longer ignore that this now struck him as the true heart of the place. The town presented a charming face to the stream of white travellers who passed through – *See the Argyle Dam! Stay at the country club! Cruise the Ord River at sunset!* – but the darkness was astounding.

You had to be wilfully blind to miss it. Once Tony understood that, he was rarely surprised by even the most horrific of news.

6.

Exhibition openings now came with the regularity of clockwork.

They were glamorous events held in pristine city galleries, well attended by fashionably dressed art world insiders, by wealthy collectors, even by politicians drawn to the Jirrawun vision. When Paddy first flew south with Tony for an opening the experience was new. He was held up at the security gate while a long-bladed fishing knife was removed from his carry-on luggage.

But now, Old Man was an old hand: by the time Tony flew Paddy and Rammey first class to Sydney for an art world engagement and booked them interlinked suites at the five-star Park Hyatt, Paddy had seen much of the luxury the white world had to offer. By then, it was easy. Not only was there money, but Giancarlo or Rowan would travel with the old men, acting as carers, making sure that Rammey and Paddy had everything they might need, that they were ready to meet the white world with pride.

At the Park Hyatt, they would come together at 8 am for an elaborate room service breakfast: the silver trolley laden with bacon and eggs and orange juice, Rammey and Paddy settling either side of it in their shirt-sleeves radiating contentment; beyond the double windows the harbour spreading out under the bright Sydney sun, the water traffic drawing lines of industry across its depths.

Once, earlier on, Tony had accompanied a group of the artists to meet Dame Marie Bashir, then the thirty-seventh governor of New South Wales. She welcomed the Jirrawun entourage for lunch in the harbourside gardens of Government House. That day, the artists were dressed as they then usually were: an assortment of worn clothes from the Kimberley. Bashir, graceful and achingly polite, leant over to Tony and quietly suggested that he might somehow arrange that they dress with more dignity.

He was initially taken aback by the bluntness of Bashir's remark – there was so much pressure then that clothes seemed the least of their concerns – but he soon realised she was right. If they wanted to access a world of power and influence they had to play the part. By the time 'Lunch with the Law Men' was organised in Melbourne – an event that drew together a group of Federal Court judges for lunch with Paddy, Tony and Peter Seidel – Old Man's sartorial pride was legendary. On that visit Tony took Paddy to Henry Bucks, one of Melbourne's oldest purveyors of menswear to city elites.

That's how Paddy got his immaculate pinstriped suits, his polished leather shoes, the black greatcoat that draped from his shoulders to the floor and enveloped him in his wheelchair like a cashmere blanket. That's where he found his iconic walking stick, its shaft topped with an ornately curved silver horse head. That's how Rammey received a suit of his own, purchased by way of Old Man's largesse.

At the Melbourne lunch, the guests all sat together around tables. Old Man in felt hat and woollen scarf, sitting near silent in his seat of honour, a microphone being passed around as each of the justices spoke about the law, about reconciliation, about Native Title and the importance of listening to Aboriginal Elders like Paddy.

For most who knew him it was by then near impossible to tell when Paddy's hearing aid was working. But if Old Man missed the detail of what was being said that afternoon, he surely understood the symbolism of it: one law being equated in importance to another.

When his turn came, he made his feelings on the matter clear. He held the microphone tight against his mouth, causing feedback from the speaker to crowd the room.

'My name's Paddy Bedford,' he rumbled.

'I *am* the Law!'

It was perfect.

Later, he was wheeled around the table to say goodbye; as he went, he high-fived each of the justices one after the other.

•

But as moments like that began to take on the hazy cast of memory, and the time between him and the Kimberley began to extend towards a decade, other memories would crowd Tony's recollection: dark things that took the oxygen from the light.

By then it was the funerals that he would remember with equal clarity.

One black body after another buried in the Kimberley earth.

What difference did Jirrawun make to the bare fact of that?

The urgent news; drop everything in preparation and go: someone else's son or daughter had been taken early.

The sombre trip down the highway to Warmun, or further on to Halls Creek or Fitzroy Crossing.

Standing together in treeless graveyards bleached like parchment under the Kimberley sun: the women crying, the men hidden under hat brims and shadows.

All these images threatened to blur into one, but even as Tony felt himself harden to their grim procession there would come a funeral that reached through the general trauma of the place to cut deeper.

Freddie's firstborn son Frankie, for instance.

He died in December, after the wet season clouds had built up and broken, first as dusty electrical storms and then as torrential downpours that smashed flat what long grass was left after the dry season fires and replaced it almost immediately with a wall of green.

Frankie. Softer than his father: intelligent and gentle, his young life cut short. He drank so much it would be called a suicide anywhere else.

Tony watched it happen; they all did. Frankie's habit was to drink on the veranda at a house in Kununurra that had by then replaced the Turkey Creek town drinking camp. Frankie wasn't an aggressive drunk and his mind was still sharp: he spoke with an incisive directness that Tony enjoyed, and if he were driving past he would often stop and visit.

When Frankie was diagnosed with diabetes, Tony gently asked him why he didn't give the grog away, but the question went unanswered: Frankie simply went about his business, one can of beer after the other. When he got a cut on his foot, little more than a nick, he sat and drank until it turned gangrenous.

By the time he made his way to hospital it was too late: the only option was amputation. They took his foot, but the gangrene moved to his leg: they took that too. He was dead not long afterwards.

His funeral was held in Halls Creek: the tiny church with its oversized peaked roof in corrugated tin, the spindly iron crucifix extending upwards like a skeletal finger, the priest droning from the pulpit.

It was a hot day; there were flies moving through the thick air. As always, family came from everywhere, bundled into LandCruisers and Hiluxes by the dozen. Tony drove a LandCruiser with the coffin laid out in the back, and as he slowly pulled into the graveyard he looked in the rearview mirror, out across the coffin's polished lid and through the open back doors. Behind him mourners were filing in, silent. He knew Freddie was somewhere among them, unsteady with grief alongside his two remaining sons.

It wasn't the first time Tony had been present while Freddie buried a young family member. Each time he'd think about how they'd come to know each other all those years earlier, in Melbourne, during their studio sessions in Ivanhoe. It'd been in the midst of the second of them that Tony's father had died: when he'd returned from the funeral it was as if his loss had somehow solidified their friendship. Freddie had tenderly placed his hand on Tony's shoulder and told him it would be okay.

Now, he tried to communicate something of Freddie's pain to others. The day before Frankie's funeral, he emailed the Jirrawun board, telling them the news, and asking them to observe a moment's silence when the funeral took place.

He told them in simple terms that Frankie had been an intelligent, gentle man, that he would be sorely missed. *I would like to purchase a wreath on behalf of the Jirrawun Arts board and write everyone's name on a card*, he wrote. He tried to do this whenever he could, bridge the space between worlds as much as possible, try to draw them into what he now understood as the constantly unfolding tragedy before him.

He forwarded the email to Nicolas, who was abroad, reporting on the Iraq war for *The Australian*. Nicolas had only recently visited Kununurra and his Gija friends had been worried for him: going an unimaginable distance towards a war zone, so far from the safe embrace of country. Freddie had pressed a stone into Nicolas's hand and told him to keep it with him, that if he did he would be safe.

Please send Freddie my condolences, Nicolas wrote and his mind turned immediately to the stone that was yet to leave his person. *As I am carrying a little life-enhancing stone of his around with me I am bound to him and so his loss is particularly sharp in my mind. I think of him in his silence: a terrible thing for a son to predecease a father.*

In the graveyard it was the same scene as always – the keening wail of the women rising up as one; the dull thud of the shovels hitting the dirt, the men and women dressed in their motley assortment of good funeral clothes. Freddie with a new shirt, his hat pulled low.

As the coffin was lowered Freddie knelt down and held on.

Freddie, stoic and silent. Freddie with tears running down his face. Freddie holding his son's coffin and not letting go. It seemed to Tony the most important thing in the world, the only job a father in that position could possibly perform.

'Come on mate,' Tony said quietly. 'Let go.'

And Freddie did.

Wyndham

1.

When he first moved to the block outside Wyndham in 2005, Tony would often find himself at the front of the house, waiting for Paddy to arrive for a painting session.

He would imagine Paddy on Frances's veranda in Kununurra, where he still lived, watching the steady flow of town life slip by just beyond the dark foliage of the front garden. Paddy was now there permanently, and in many ways it was ideal for him: his needs were attended to, and any time he wanted to check his money, or drive into town, someone would be on hand to assist. If it wasn't Frances, it would be Rowan or Giancarlo. Freddie still lived next door, but he now shared the Jirrawun house with Ken Watson, a quietly spoken curator from the Art Gallery of New South Wales who had recently dropped everything and moved to Kununurra with his partner Muh to work with Jirrawun.

Paddy remained lively, and still loved to paint, but as the months gathered together into his final two years, those who knew him would note that he was ever more frail. *This is the final stretch*, Tony would think sometimes when he saw Old Man after the two had been apart for a handful of days. Even that short time could cast Paddy's fragility in stark light. His eyes were watery, his hands often shook; to stand he required a strong arm to lean upon. Small things kept him happy. He liked, for instance, to have his LandCruiser parked in the driveway next door, at the Jirrawun house, so he could see the vehicle from his bed.

It won't be long now, Tony would think, *surely not.*

It was a mixed feeling to realise that the gentle intensity of their relationship would one day simply cease to be. Now, as PB's painting sessions became more stripped back, more distilled – a kind of mirror of his reduced capacity – each new painting seemed more precious than the last.

•

Tony had first purchased the Wyndham block as a permanent retreat from life in town, somewhere he could get some space for himself. He initially intended to make the hour-long drive to Kununurra as needed, but it wasn't long before he came to understand that the relative peace he was seeking would benefit the artists too: the block was soon sold on to Jirrawun. In step, Tony planned to pass as much of the organisation's work to others as he could: Ken, for instance, would be the curator, and would field the growing flood of outside contacts; Rowan would continue to cook, and pack paintings for transit. Tony now hoped he could turn the majority of his energy inward, towards the studio.

It was true that Wyndham was remote – neither in town, nor near any of the artists' home communities – but those alert to the region's history would undertake the journey from Kununurra and sense a different picture. The first suggestions of settlement (blink and you'd miss them) were the long-abandoned tin shacks at Nine Mile, just off the highway. It was there where Timmy Timms and others had been relocated from Bow River when Aboriginal involvement in the pastoral industry had collapsed in the 1970s. Earlier, when each of the artists had laboured for their white station bosses, Wyndham was the region's bustling heart: Hector, who now lived in the aged care facility in Warmun, visited Tony at the block and recalled camping there on the final leg of cross-country musters to the Wyndham port.

The turn-off to the property was easy to miss. It appeared a short distance before Wyndham itself, just before the work camp's scatter of demountables. A touch further, at Seven Mile, was the first of the town's two pubs, a dilapidated structure surrounded by mango trees; further still was the old cemetery where Afghan traders were buried with their lead camels.

The track in led through a gate and curled down to a simple fibro house. It was tucked away beside a shallow gully: a basic three-room structure, the sun-faded walls of which merged near completely with the dry wilderness beyond. It had been built in the 1980s by an ex–meat worker who had surrounded it with an elaborate garden. Low stone walls wound their way through thickets of greenery interspersed by clumps of bright green bamboo and tumbles of bougainvillea. It was decorated here and there with machinery parts from the decommissioned meat works floor: at regular intervals the strange cast-iron machinery parts broke through the undergrowth, unsettling metal points and curlicues once used to skin and de-bone carcasses, now rusted and draped in vines. It was a rough place, but after his years in the Kimberley, it felt to Tony like paradise.

Once Paddy arrived, the two of them would settle in, get comfortable. As always it was important to find a rhythm between themselves before they began to paint: a near-wordless changing of the gears that allowed each of them to mark the distance from everyday life, to access the headspace that studio sessions required. Rowan, who would soon purchase a house of his own in the Wyndham township, would prepare a simple lunch, and then dinner. It would be one night at least before PB and Tony began work.

Then it was the same as it had been since their first days together at Pindan Avenue all those years before, the routine that each of them knew so well: mixing the pigment, laying out the paper or the stretched linen, mapping out the compositions and brushing the backgrounds, sitting and watching the surrounding country as new works were propped around them to dry, waiting for Old Man to methodically adorn them with his loosely strung dots.

A cold beer, steak and eggs for lunch, a plate of kidneys for Paddy.

The work of it was almost a muscle memory that Tony's body knew as closely as Paddy's: one part after another – increments, tiny steps towards a finished work and then the image of a new painting clear against the surrounding environment. Then it was the evening meal, the cowboy film on DVD, the sleep and the next morning's dawn rise to another group of blank canvases waiting for Old Man's hand.

For years, Tony had called Paddy 'Dad', a simple and common Gija expression of the responsibility that flowed between a young man and an old. But now, as Old Man became ever more frail and dependent, that had changed. As was the Gija way it was now Paddy who called Tony 'Dad', and Tony who now had to care for him as a father might a son.

•

The moments of clarity at Wyndham were many – in the right frame of mind there was little to compare to the silence of a star-blanketed night with the black shadow of the garden pressing in – but the darkness that had threatened to overwhelm Tony in town was waiting for him there too.

When not absorbed by studio work he did what little he could to hold it at bay. He soon set in motion a simple habit: almost every day he would get up before the sun and walk to the highway and back five times – down the dirt track to the bitumen, and back again. Around him, the heat would begin to announce itself: within an hour it would be climbing towards its peak. As the remnant pockets of the night's coolness were singed away he would often think of Crocodile Hole: the smelter-like heat that at times lay over the dusty community, Old Man supine under his makeshift shelter watching from the shadows. He could still hear Paddy's soft whistle cutting through air as thick as clay, and feel the breeze that would swiftly follow.

If no one was painting, he would most often be alone. As night fell, the silence could take on a different character: peace could readily give way to loneliness. He now understood more than ever that the Kimberley's darker histories were ever present, that the frontier was a living, breathing thing. The weight of that sometimes felt insurmountable, and in an attempt to counter it he would simply sit and drink. When the silence became too much, he would put on music, open the doors onto the concrete veranda, and blast it into the darkness.

Johnny Cash's 'Sunday Morning Coming Down' was a favourite: jauntily cathartic in that sad Cash-like way. It was about waking up with a cracking hangover and drinking it away as elegiac memories crowded in. Audrey Hepburn's soft and saccharine version of 'Moon River' would get a good run, as would the instrumental 'Runaway Horses', from Philip Glass's soundtrack for *Mishima*, the Paul Schrader film from 1985. That one was urgent and fast building, layer upon layer of dense orchestral strings, until it finally fell quiet and slowly built again, this time into something bright and hopeful. Tony would turn that one up until it surged outwards into the night-time Kimberley landscape.

As the night progressed, he would sometimes shoot off desperate missives via text message, or dial a friend down south on the telephone. Some would contact him the next day, worried by the strange and urgent call they'd received the night before, or the typo-ridden message that had been waiting on their phone in the morning. Sometimes, reading over words that he himself had written only hours before, Tony would feel a not dissimilar surge of concern.

Not long after moving in he had set about painting the interior walls of his new home. For the most part he chose a red oxide mixed from the artist supplies, but he eventually painted the background of the kitchen wall black.

It was here that he began work on a rough collage: an image of Paddy's painting was stuck up, then a Philip Guston as a kind of answer. He added the photos of Dizzy Gillespie and Paddy beside them; a Colin McCahon image was soon glued to one side, and then a cover torn from an Australian Classics edition of *Capricornia*, Xavier Herbert's blistering novel of far northern race relations. It reproduced a painting of Sidney Nolan's: a rangy black cattleman leaning against a veranda post, a blasted desert landscape intense behind him. Tony had always respected Nolan's work – even loved the much-maligned late spray works – but he chose this image for a different reason. It could have depicted any one of the old men standing at the homestead's threshold on Lissadell, or Bedford Downs, or Bow River Station.

Later, he added written passages in McCahon's iconic hand: looping cursive letters, the arc of which echoed imagined sets of green hills. *Dairy country*, he thought, and returned his mind, as he so often did, to the Gippsland of his childhood, so distant now but always a source of respite among the Kimberley's chaos. He thought about the clouds there, moving in silent procession above the green pastures. He thought about the accident, about Hector's hand extended before him like a wand, the streak of pure energy he now imagined springing from Hector's outstretched fingers.

It was now nearly seven years in the past, but if he closed his eyes he could sometimes still feel the impact of the road train, could hear the screeching metal, could picture the road twisting away from beneath Hector and him as their vehicle rose up.

Perhaps most of all, he now remembered what Hector had said afterwards, deadly serious: 'That was the Jowarri devil, Ngaji, coming to get us.'

2.

In Tony's mind, Jirrawun was close to being a fully fledged organisation. As if to prove it, he'd recently commissioned a designer to create a logo, and had business cards printed for each of the employees, along with Rusty and Freddie, who still held their directorships on the board. His own card carried a simple elaboration of the role he'd always understood as his: *Tony Oliver*, it read, *Artistic Director.*

If nothing else, the title deepened the already existing line between Jirrawun and community art centres. The white workers there were most often referred to as 'coordinators' or 'advisers', impartial words that downplayed any influence, but Tony saw little reason to follow suit. The tiny painting collective that he and the artists had first established at Pindan Avenue had now morphed into something singular: if anything it resembled a theatrical production. In this light, Tony was the organisation's reigning impresario. He would readily conjure thoughts of Sergei Diaghilev, the Svengali-like director of the Ballets Russes, or of Warhol, who'd once presided with such inscrutable flair over the collaborative undertakings of his New York Factory.

The block at Wyndham brought with it a level of privacy that allowed Tony to inhabit this role as fully as ever. He was soon working closely with Peggy, Phyllis and Goody Barrett to develop new paintings that strove to articulate their individual characters, but it was with the group of sisters who had first begun gathering at the Jirrawun house in Kununurra, and who had by now named themselves the Jirrawun Chicks, that his approach as artistic director fleetingly found its most complete form.

By the time Tony welcomed them to Wyndham, and set about conceiving with them a series of paintings that attempted to capture the Kimberley's harder realities, the girls had been in the background for years. Even in the early days, when their mother Kitty had often brought them to stay at Crocodile Hole, he had recognised in them something extraordinary. She had named them with distinctive flair – Ramona, Remika, Vondean and Tennielle – that seemed to mirror the arresting courage with which they moved through the Kimberley world. In Kununurra, Jirrawun had often helped them with money or food, or invited them to join the glittering dinners on Frances's veranda. When Tony had purchased a cappuccino machine for the Jirrawun house and installed it in the front room the girls had soon begun to arrive daily for cafe lattes and conversation.

The fact they might one day take up the brush themselves was unavoidable. It wasn't just their family connections to the artists, either. Like anyone who stayed in Kununurra for even a brief period, Tony knew that the town's surfaces were regularly veiled in an oddly cohesive style of graffiti: scrawled names, swearwords and colloquial insults, all of it black or white on the town's concrete and corrugated iron surfaces. At fifteen, going on sixteen, Remika was the youngest sister, and still most firmly attached to the street world the graffiti alluded to, but all the sisters knew it well. Vondean's government house, which she'd secured after the birth of her daughter, was one attempt to leave it behind.

The sisters had quickly moved in as a group and set about making the house their own. Soon, the near-bare interior was covered with graffiti too, most of it in greylead pencil. Tony, who walked down from the Jirrawun house one day, was astonished by the effect. The girls had gone about marking the house as they did the streets: lists of names, tiny tags, unruly clusters of initials, all of it cascading down the walls and across the linoleum floors, colonising the cupboard doors and window frames. He realised that all he needed to do to spark a new project was encourage the girls to paint.

In Kununurra there had been tentative steps: stray boards were soon covered in graffiti, a pizza box with a naïve landscape; a small mismatched collection was in this way amassed. But town life was as distracting for them as it was for most of the other artists: it was only now, in Wyndham, with the cavernous interior of the machinery shed at hand, that a full-scale project seemed possible.

The sisters also had the ideal opportunity to enter the art world with a flourish. In 2005, the year before they began painting in Wyndham, Tony had engineered *Beyond the Frontier*, the first of what would be two high-profile exhibitions with a new dealer in Sydney, Sherman Galleries. It had marked one of Jirrawun's most complete productions, a kind of concentrated version of *Blood on the Spinifex*, severe and tightly curated.

Each of the artists had made singular statements. The painting Rusty had shown was a philosophically dense rumination on the different value of Gija and European approaches to material culture that he called *Gamerre – What's This Museum?* Rammey's was a painterly double panel of turbulent red-pinks that announced a new quasi-expressionist style, in no small part indebted to Tony's love for Philip Guston. Tony had worked through it with Rammey step by step, and rejoiced when the finished work turned out so beautifully. With Peggy, he had introduced the idea for a cut stencil of the boab tree at Mistake Creek, which she then traced onto each of ten gridded panels: not only an obvious riff on Andy Warhol's screen-printed repetitions, but, in Tony's mind at least, an evocation of Georgia O'Keeffe's famous painting *The Lawrence Tree*, a dramatic image of red branches set against a star-flecked sky that marked the beginning of O'Keeffe's acclaimed work in the desert of New Mexico.

Simeon Kronenberg was Sherman's long-time gallery director, and knew Tony from the days of Reconnaissance, when the two of them had moved in the same circle of art-dedicated friends. The gallery was one of the best contemporary spaces in the country, but its proprietor, Gene Sherman, had to date not shown remote-area Aboriginal art. This oversight was simply due to abiding concerns about ethics and representation, but Kronenberg clearly recalled the idiosyncratic and romantic belief in art that Tony had displayed during his career as a gallerist – Kronenberg trusted him, and was happy when collectors responded to the exhibition with enthusiasm. A run of high-profile sales were soon secured: Freddie's main work – a graceful midnight black painting called *Jack Yard* that would number among his very best – had been purchased immediately by the Art Gallery of New South Wales, where its image would go on to adorn the cover of the gallery's coffee-table book on its wide-ranging Aboriginal art collection.

But as successful as the paintings in *Beyond the Frontier* were, Tony had also turned the exhibition towards more theatrical ends. Only Freddie and Peggy attended the opening, but each of them cut a striking figure. Freddie dressed immaculately in the same suit he'd worn for *Blood on the Spinifex*; Peggy was similarly glamorous in a flowing dress. Tony himself stalked through the crowded opening in an outfit he'd recently had tailored in Melbourne for a friend's wedding. It had been based on an image of the American actor Kurt Russell in character as Wyatt Earp: pitch-black suit, floor-length trench coat, black Akubra hat, bolo tie cinched at the throat with silver fastener.

Like so much of what Tony projected from the Kimberley to the art world it was intended to illuminate and obscure in near-equal measure: if Freddie had been the very picture of urbane style, Tony had by contrast imagined himself as a tongue-in-cheek version of a white lawman fresh from the bush, the frontier sky aflame behind him. The only thing missing was the shotgun.

Beyond the Frontier was a runaway success, but it was far from clear if the exhibition's enthusiastic white audience had fully comprehended its implications. Although reviews were positive, they were characteristically muted when it came to the subject of Tony's role in its development. Only from afar did it seem the matter could be raised in any detail. An American journalist called Eric Marx visited the exhibition and, in a piece eventually published in *The New York Times*, tried to pick apart the dense knot of uniquely Australian anxieties that made the subject so taboo. Was it a problem, or not? If so, why?

Marx spoke to another long-term arts adviser, Will Stubbs, who worked in the north-east Arnhem Land community of Yirrkala; to Dallas Gold, the Darwin gallerist; to the auction house specialist Tim Klingender. Against this brief survey of the industry's archetypal players, he positioned Tony as an 'activist art advisor' at odds with those intent on maintaining a sense of Aboriginal art as something untarnished by Western influence.

The article was thin, its central questions too neatly staged, but Tony nonetheless embraced Marx's conception of his role: to his ears it sounded just about right.

Finally, he thought, *someone understands.*

Now, with the Jirrawun Chicks, he was working towards the next Sherman exhibition: it was to be another statement, once again his as much as theirs. This time, however, it would feature only the women. He consulted with Peggy, Goody and Phyllis, and they'd agreed to call it *Women's Business*, but the real focus would be the girls. It was their work that would provide the unruly energy he imagined at the exhibition's very centre.

It was a production just to set the new project in motion: the familiar feeling of anxiety and excitement readily kicked in as he tried to picture the paintings that might result, but there were new challenges too. Unlike the older painters, the girls had next to no studio experience, and brought with them a totally different social dynamic: buoyant and unpredictable. They were accompanied by a small entourage of younger family members; Leshante, Vondean's child, was still an infant. They would stay en masse at their grandfather's house in Wyndham and shuttle back and forth to the block on a daily basis.

The interior of the machinery shed was sweltering, but there were long horizontally hinged windows that could be propped up to encourage a breeze to flow through. The doors, which were huge, slid back on castors and could be left open; if work began early enough the concrete slab still held some of the night's coolness. As the first days sketched what would soon become a rhythm, the girls spread out across the space, dressed as they always were in a mismatched collage of street clothes: long basketball shorts, netted t-shirts worn over pastel halter-tops. On their wrists they wore clusters of cheap bangles; their feet were bare.

In the heat, Tony presided over the sessions in faded black boxer shorts and Crocs: the only studio attire that made the heat bearable. Michiel Dolk, an academic art historian who had first crossed paths with Jirrawun during the Darwin residencies, was on hand as an observer: in the background he was writing a long and complicated essay on Paddy's work for the retrospective, the development of which was now in its final stages.

The girls didn't know Dolk, so kept what distance they could, but a young Frenchman called Arnaud Morvan, also there as an observer, managed to get closer.

Morvan, who wore his hair in a ponytail and sported a goatee, was a graduate student of Marcia Langton's, and had already spent a number of months orbiting Jirrawun, trying to gain access through Tony to its inner sanctum. Paddy had recently been selected among a group of well-known Australian Aboriginal artists as part of a major public art commission at the redesigned Musée du Quai Branly in Paris, and Morvan was focusing his studies on this project. But any and all activity was of interest. Freddie had lost his licence following a string of alcohol-related offences, and Morvan's first months in Kununurra had seen his interviews with Paddy on Frances's veranda interspersed with an informal role as Freddie's driver. Now, as the girls made their first tentative steps as artists, Tony finally ushered Morvan closer. He wanted him on hand to record as much as he could; he hoped Morvan would co-author with Langton an essay for the exhibition catalogue.

The whole scene was at first chaotic, but Tony was encouraging.

For him, the girls were raw material: they carried only the barest of allegiances to the conventions that marked East Kimberley painting. Unlike their Elders, what they could do was wide open. Sure, he could direct them to paint country, but what country was truly theirs? If Paddy and the others had spent their childhoods walking their ancestral estates, learning as they went a complex network of intersecting stories, the girls had come of age in a radically different world. Their work, for Tony at least, needed to be urban in character if it were to succeed.

He was once again casting his mind back to New York, this time to the early 1980s vogue for neo-expressionism, a brief movement that had swiftly elevated a handful of young artists to acclaim. The tragic king among them still loomed large: Jean-Michel Basquiat, a young black Haitian-American whose scrawled canvases had led him in quick succession through fame, collaboration with Warhol, and fatal heroin addiction. He was thinking too of Colin McCahon's stark white letters on black grounds, of the way the New Zealand master had somehow transposed the pressing energies of self-doubt into exquisite and existential visual tracts.

All this he knew could be synthesised with the graffiti at which the girls were so adept.

They began their paintings on thin sheets of cardboard: unfocused scrawls that started as lists of names and quickly descended into a mess of over-painting. They moved through them quickly, yelling and laughing at the results.

As the paint dried, the sheets of cardboard curled in the heat like discarded rubbish. Tony moved among the rough works, looking. He explained to the girls how their many 'accidents' – the drips and smears, the footprints and hand marks that would invariably mark the cardboard on which they worked – could be turned in their favour. Not all of them responded well. Morvan was present for much of this: he would recall that Ramona, for one, obviously wanted to stay in Wyndham to party instead of paint. Initially she made a neat approximation of a standard East Kimberley painting, the kind of work that spilled from the art centre in Warmun by the dozen, but Tony gently steered her in the other direction. He reiterated what he found so compelling about the graffiti in the first place: the unruly energy, the rough touch, the looming sense of drama, the point of difference it presented from one generation to the next.

The others were more receptive. It wasn't just in the studio, either. At twenty-five, Morvan was only a handful of years older than the three oldest sisters and Vondean and Tennielle took him under their wing. Both were easy-going. Vondean could at times be melancholy; Tennielle was brighter: joking, flirtatious. Morvan accompanied them to house parties in Wyndham, where he listened as they recounted some of what they knew of Gija kinship and the spirit world and gossiped about the constant interfamily feuds that coursed through Kimberley life.

From cardboard they moved on to canvases, each a metre square. These could be arranged in grids against the machinery shed's walls, and shuffled. Tony painted the grounds – a rough patchwork of black and white – as arbitrarily as he could: he didn't want to impose a structure more than was strictly necessary. He intended for nothing to be fixed: the grids could be broken down and rearranged. If one canvas among the group didn't work, it could be taken out and finished as a stand-alone painting.

He spoke to each of the sisters about what they might write, encouraging them always to turn their minds back to the street, to the lists of names and the pithy one-line insults that had sparked the whole project. He encouraged them not to be fearful of rendering swearwords: if they were happy to write what they pleased on the street, they should see the canvas no differently. One work was soon dominated by the word 'CUNTS' looming over a cluster of random-seeming initials. Another screamed 'BIG HOLE', the very worst of Kimberley insults.

All the girls eventually responded to the project, but it was Remika who shone the brightest. She was whip-smart, and seemed to Tony to understand his intentions immediately. She would often stay engaged the longest, listening as he advised, and eventually put the final touch on what became his favourite painting from the series. It was a single square canvas, the truncated word 'SUX' already looming across the top. Remika simply picked up a brush and in a few finely judged strokes outlined an anamorphic cube below the scrawled text, white on a section of staggered black.

Perfect.

The paintings soon fulfilled much of what Tony had first hoped they might. He looked at them as a group in the shadowy interior of the makeshift studio, where the white of them glowed bright. He saw in them the energy that the girls had formalised as elaborate codes, sensed how such codes bound them peer to peer.

It was the same thing they expressed effortlessly in the staccato language they'd as good as invented at the intersection of Gija Kriol and English. This was a world of American hip-hop, of street brands like FUBU and Dada, of black rappers like 50 Cent blasting incongruously under Kimberley skies.

This was a world in which everyday life was governed by simple rules.

Band together for safety.

Band together for warmth at night.

Band together to share the proceeds of a day's begging 'silver' from whites outside the Coles supermarket to split whatever meal might follow: fried chicken, a hamburger, a greasy bag of hot chips.

But if all this risked drawing the girls away from their bush roots, it was clear they remained proud of where they and their kin had come from.

RONELLA
LETOYA
VONDEAN
TENNIELLE
REMIKA
RAMONA
ONLY THE RUGUN GIRLS

They scrawled this in an alliterative tumble down the side of one painting.

TOP CAMP RULE
BOTTOM CAMP RULE OKAY SLUT

Perfect, Tony thought, as he moved in and out of the shed, keeping abreast of progress.

At one point a big DON'T in block letters appeared, white on black. As in DON'T GET JEALOUS, a sentiment reiterated on one work after another. As in, stay true to your sisters; don't betray them.

Perfect again.

KNX tagged the Kununurra streets that were theirs once night fell. The session's major work – ten metre-square panels stacked two high – was eventually called *Kununurra Midnight Prowl* in honour of this invisible world that had hastened the girls to adulthood. To them 'prowling' was equal parts pastime and ideology, a rejection of both Gija and gardiya worlds in favour of something indeterminate, something in between.

The girls would soon be a hit at Sherman Galleries, their work enthusiastically received at an opening as glittering and star-studded as anything Jirrawun had yet staged, but it was *Kununurra Midnight Prowl* that would go the furthest. Their session in Wyndham was a one-off, but the success of this work would for Tony always point to what could have been, if only the Kimberley had been somewhere else entirely.

The painting was seen in Sydney by the German curator Rene Block, a senior statesman on the international stage and one-time director of *Documenta* – one of the most respected global contemporary art events – who had worked with artists as acclaimed as Joseph Beuys and Gerhard Richter. It struck a chord: Block immediately included it in his sprawling exhibition in Belgrade, *Art, Life & Confusion.*

But before this, Tony did what he always did. He simply watched as the painting drew together, subtly guiding it here and there, trying to picture the finished work in its entirety. If he sensed how fine a line he was walking, he barely hesitated.

3.

Jirrawun's board was now functioning as well as it ever would. A number of the members had grown close enough to Tony to wonder how long he could last, but the run of recent successes usually eclipsed any real concern.

Sure, Tony could at times threaten departure but he would hasten to walk back from the edge. Following the opening of *Beyond the Frontier*, he'd retreated to Melbourne and been overcome by exhaustion, drained by the months of work he'd put into the exhibition. For a moment he'd felt he wouldn't return to the Kimberley at all. He fired off a sudden resignation to the board members via text message and email, but even as he did he knew it wouldn't last. He was soon drafting a retraction: as it was wont to do periodically, the 'black dog' had emerged from its kennel, he explained. It wreaked its havoc, but he had ushered it back inside.

Each time the board now met, Tony would provide an artistic director's report. It was a relief to draw away from the harder qualities of the world around him and focus instead on the collective's spiralling list of recent achievements.

It is a time when ideas become reality, and the parts become the whole, he wrote in one report.

It was a characteristically oblique statement, but in the context of an organisation that had begun in what Tony now liked to term the 'fourth world' conditions of Crocodile Hole, it made a strange kind of sense. Long-held visions were taking shape. It wasn't simply a matter of one sell-out exhibition after another, either (although he was always careful to include a list of those in his reports too). The Jirrawun Health initiative was still running and, although it would prove unsustainable in its initial form, it was serving an admirable purpose. By having Giancarlo Mazzella drive in constant circuit across Gija country, the Jirrawun artists and their families were able to step beyond the pronounced limits of local healthcare. If they needed, they could access specialists in city centres, and not wait for treatment: in this way, Rammey was able to have an eye operation in Sydney that salvaged his faltering sight, and Paddy could travel to fix a hernia that had kept him in constant discomfort for years.

The Jirrawun artists and I are extremely proud of this organisation and the difference it makes to human beings, Tony wrote in another of his reports. *Jirrawun Health is already saving lives.*

There was talk of Jirrawun Film, a not-for-profit arm that might one day create Gija-themed content that could be screened on national television. Giancarlo, who had a background in film as well as Aboriginal health, enthusiastically took to the idea: he had been an avid photographer of Jirrawun events since his first encounters with the group, but now he was more often than not on hand with a digital camcorder, capturing near everything for what would become a vast unedited archive. Simon Georgeff, who in the years since he left the Kimberley had begun film school, had even visited for a brief and troubled period in Kununurra during which he too tried to set the film project in motion. There was also Jirrawun Editions, an idea that aimed to create an income stream around limited-edition prints by each of the artists. One run of beautiful etchings was produced in collaboration with Leon Stainer, Jirrawun's old printmaker friend from Darwin – one of the best bush printmakers there was – but like Jirrawun Film it too was never fully realised.

Other achievements were more tangible. In Kununurra, Jirrawun donated $20,000 to seed a police youth program. An oversize novelty cheque was printed, and a simple handover ceremony held at Ironwood Drive: Freddie, his face severe under his hat brim, the local constable beside him, red-faced and mustachioed in his tan uniform. They held a handshake as Giancarlo photographed the scene from every possible angle, searching for the image that would soon be printed in *The Kimberley Echo*. On-duty police would at times now visit the Jirrawun house to simply have a coffee and a chat. *The first youth camp will be taking place at Doon Doon community next month*, Tony informed the board.

Work on Paddy's commission at Musée du Quai Branly, in Paris, was moving forward too. As Tony noted to the board, the fee didn't reflect the scale and importance of the work involved, but it nonetheless came with significant international cachet. The opening of Paddy's retrospective at the Museum of Contemporary Art was also drawing near. Tony visited Sydney to confirm the final selection of work and took the opportunity to begin lobbying both the museum and the federal arts minister to tour the exhibition internationally. In his mind it was now all about the global stage. There was already talk of an exhibition in London, and although it was a commercial one – a possible show organised by the Countess Jennifer Guerrini-Maraldi at a blue-chip establishment gallery – Tony saw it as a possible stepping stone to bigger things. He was busy negotiating a key clause: the gallery had to place at least two significant Jirrawun paintings in the collection of the Tate Modern.

Although he was already unsure if the project would go ahead or not – it wouldn't – he soon proposed another proviso and diligently shared the news with the board: *I have informed her with a straight face that we will only come if Rammey and Paddy can have tea with the Queen*, he wrote. *I fully expect this to happen: of course, they will want tea at Buckingham Palace.*

There had been a run of sold-out exhibitions in Australia – in step with the successes at Sherman Galleries, William Mora had presented a series of major Jirrawun works at the Melbourne Art Fair that effortlessly grossed $700,000 – but Tony hoped the artists could achieve international prices. He underscored what was at stake

The truth is that a Paddy Bedford painting that currently retails in Australia for $60,000 (a remarkable price for a living Australian artist) will bring at least $200,000.

It won't take long, he added.

He increasingly pictured Jirrawun as an organisation that sold direct to Australian collectors, but bypassed the majority of Australian dealer galleries in favour of the best of their international counterparts.

That's where the money is, he'd tell people. Sales were by now climbing towards $3 million a year.

•

In this light, the long-gestating plan for a purpose-built studio seemed an ideal expression of Jirrawun's final consolidation. It had always been important to Tony – as much as he and the artists had made do in the most constricted of circumstances, he'd always wondered what could have been possible with a dedicated space in which to work. Now it was time to make it a reality.

He'd had an architect in mind for years: his friend Jose Alfano, whose rambling house in the tiny Victorian coastal town of Somers he had been staying at all those years earlier when news had come from the Kimberley that Timmy Timms had died. Alfano – intelligent, tightly wound and Brooklyn born – brought wide-ranging experience to a potential Jirrawun commission. His career had initially been marked by a belief that architecture provided what he characterised as a 'social anchor'. In New York he had worked on public housing developments, but more recently the tenor of his work had shifted: he was now partnered in a firm that focused on large-scale residential projects in far-flung locations like the United Arab Emirates.

'I'm the skyscraper guy,' he'd tell people in the double-time Brooklyn drawl that had never quite faded. But he was also quick to explain he was more than that, too. He had often undertaken pro-bono work in development contexts: this had taken him to the Northern Territory, to Indonesia and to South America. When Tony suggested he add the Kimberley to this list, Alfano agreed.

Initial steps were made before Jirrawun purchased the Wyndham block, and focused on replacing the house at Ironwood Drive. Alfano had flown in for consultations and spent a run of days with Tony and Freddie and Rusty, trying to get a sense of what it was they needed. He observed the same hierarchy of relations that many who worked with Jirrawun now understood: Paddy on the veranda next door, granting his approval from afar; Freddie more closely involved in the day-to-day developments; Tony at the centre, enacting the overarching vision.

At first, the commission seemed unfocused. Discussions would often be disrupted by the simplest of errands – perhaps a trip with Paddy to see the dentist – that in turn would quickly gather into a flurry of activity. Tagging along, Alfano soon became familiar with Kununurra's network of gridded streets: a short sequence of turns took them to the Tuckerbox, and then perhaps onwards for a confounding visit to an overflowing government house. There they might do little but wait for someone to emerge, sitting in the cabin of the LandCruiser as the engine struggled to cool in the heat. Then it was the same thing in reverse – a series of small engagements, each of them treated as if freighted with import – until they once again pulled up at Ironwood Drive and returned to the task of designing a studio to somehow match Jirrawun's aspirations.

A handful of late-night sessions eventually delivered a meticulous architectural model crafted from pizza boxes – a low bunker-like building in which a series of connecting passages spiralled towards an open courtyard at the centre. But although Alfano secured planning permission, the design proved prohibitively expensive: the old house would have to be demolished, and a gleaming new building erected in its place. The block at Wyndham presented a different solution: whereas the Kununurra proposal had included a studio, sleeping quarters, kitchen and gallery all in one, in Wyndham they could realise one stage at a time. It was more ambitious, but also far easier to set in motion.

Alfano immediately pictured famous forward-thinking architectural projects that had similarly been realised in stages: Paolo Soleri's experimental Arcosanti community in the Arizona desert, or Frank Lloyd Wright's acclaimed Taliesin studio complex. Closer to home he thought of a kind of Gija version of the Montsalvat artist colony in the Melbourne suburb of Eltham. He made a site visit to Wyndham with Tony, and soon had a working master plan: a studio surrounded by a proposed scatter of artists' housing clustered in turn around a mess hall. He marked sites for a future administration building and a sculpture park that would unfurl on the far side of the entry road.

But if places like Montsalvat or Arcosanti were characterised by stone and mud and stained glass – organic expressions of the landscapes in which they'd been built – Alfano's plan for the studio was like something from outer space. He'd only recently been on a site visit to the UAE, where desert temperatures were blistering. Designing for that climate was a matter of creating controlled spaces that could be hermetically sealed against the surrounding environment. With this in mind, Alfano adapted a striking prefabricated shelter constructed of an industrial skin of white PVC fabric stretched over a steel frame: the kind of thing usually employed as a semi-permanent aircraft hangar, or to cover a sports stadium or tennis centre. The fabric, pulled taut over an arcing sequence of girders that drew inward at each end, provided a hurricane-grade membrane within which they would construct what was little more than a large container. There would be a double bank of halogen lights suspended from the steel rafters, huge double glass doors at each end. To demarcate a reception and administration area from the main space, Alfano designed a triple height wooden bookshelf that almost spanned the interior's entire width. It had a built-in wheeled ladder to access the upper shelves and, along the bottom, a long desk and a run of immaculate storage cupboards.

The design was simple, but for the cost involved the space it would deliver was immense. Tony understood immediately that, if they pulled it off, it would likely be one of the best studios in the country.

•

Tony still drank at night and was most often still alone with thoughts that could darken in an instant, but watching the studio being built felt like a time of hope. The myriad doubts he now carried about his Kimberley life were easily pushed aside as the project progressed in glorious increments.

The concrete slab alone was something to marvel at.

A rough-looking team of whites from Kununurra laid it over a hectic, sweat-drenched day. Afterwards, Tony had to water it each evening in the gathering dusk so the concrete cured evenly. There was something deeply satisfying about the task: the industrial hose tracing arcs of water before him, the unadorned slab like a minimal sculpture beneath the electric blue of a darkening Kimberley sky.

Then it was the team of builders arriving by plane, meeting the truck that had made its way from Perth with the building sectioned and boxed on its trailer: the steel girders stacked in neat bundles beside the large aluminium window frames; the blocks of insulation like giant Lego. Soon there was a crane onsite, lifting girders through the sky one after the other as each was bolted into place. Freddie visited from Kununurra and Tony was touched by how proud he seemed.

The final step was the fabric exterior. Once that was done the building appeared as a blast of white against the washed-out colours of the landscape. It hunched over like an immense beast curled face-first against the earth, each end an aperture of glass to flood the interior with natural light. The finishing touches were relatively straightforward: load-bearing gallery walls, another crew of workers to polish the concrete slab. A carpenter friend of Alfano's drove from Melbourne to construct the vast bookshelf. The finished project came in under half a million dollars, but looked, even at a conservative estimate, as if it cost two times as much.

Afterwards, Tony was in a kind of awe for days: of an evening he would sit in the unadorned interior with a six-pack of beer and watch the sky through the far windows. It was like looking through the void of a James Turrell sculpture: a cleanly framed section of infinity coloured with a thousand incremental variations.

Watch a view like that for long enough, and it was easy to dream.

It was all about counterpoint, he realised. The absolute contrast between the broken, weather-blasted surrounds of Crocodile Hole – a place in which they'd been relieved to simply get a four-room demountable they could sleep in (Tony still recalled the feeling of achievement that followed the construction of the simple lean-to veranda at the front) – and the studio's carefully restrained minimalism. He readily pictured collectors making the 200-kilometre return journey from Kununurra: the barrelling heat of the highway and the almost shockingly remote ranges and plains that traced it; the indistinct dirt turn-off in what seemed the middle of nowhere, and then the studio in all its glory. They would step inside and be instantly transported to a high-end city gallery in Melbourne or Sydney. Or, better still, Chelsea or 5th Avenue.

Tony knew that sales would flood their wake, but he intended it to be about more than that too. He imagined the studio as a performance space, a site guided by culture as much as painting, a shelter that would deliver further respite and calm. The bookshelves were still mostly empty, and the gleaming silver coffee machine that Tony hastened to purchase (a top-shelf cafe-grade Rancilio) would never be wired in, but the simple fact that all of it was already real was for him enough. Those things were symbols too, much like the studio: white luxuries brought into the artists' orbit, there for them as much as anyone. It all added up to the most pronounced physical manifestation of the whole project.

The fact that Freddie was the first to paint there seemed only fitting: as central as Paddy had become, it was nonetheless Freddie who traced the narrative of Tony's Kimberley life most fully. He arrived to his first session as he often did: tired and drawn from town life. Tony set in motion the habit he'd already established at the Wyndham block, and which he now envisaged as a key part of what the studio would offer: the two of them spent a run of quiet days doing little more than eating well and relaxing before commencing work. Then Freddie started painting, and the point of building such a structure in the remote north drew into sharp focus.

Until then, every 'studio' they'd worked in had been makeshift and haphazard – the bare yard at Pindan Avenue; the concrete slab at Crocodile Hole; the driveway and front-room at Ironwood Drive. Now the difference was as simple as it was profound. Surrounded by clear white space, Freddie could do something that had never before been possible: he could work on a series of paintings and, as they were hung around him on the studio walls, see his achievement in full. He could even see the entirety of a long multi-panel painting as he led his characteristically fluid line across its surface. The resulting works were magnificent.

4.

Paddy never had a proper painting session at the studio. His 2006 retrospective in Sydney took place less than a year before the space was ready, but after his triumphant appearance at the museum opening, when he was ferried to the entrance in the chauffeur-driven Cadillac, he went downhill quickly.

Rammey made his first works there soon after Freddie, and then Phyllis, Peggy and Goody Barrett. There were steps made towards consecrating the space with a celebratory joonba. It would be based on the dreams that had come to Paddy during the development of *Fire, Fire Burning Bright*, and be threaded through with the story of Jirrawun itself, but the plan ultimately proved elusive.

Tony knew what was happening – even as the studio had taken shape before him, he had at times doubted his resolve that it would provide an answer to the impossible life he'd built himself – but he was yet to fully admit it. He had often told people that when Paddy died the whole thing would be over, that he would then leave the Kimberley for good; but now they had the studio, the thought of losing all that it promised filled him with anxiety. But so too did the idea of staying.

Those who'd closely followed the collective's steady rise had already sensed it might soon be over. Marcia Langton, who understood as well as anyone how tenuously Jirrawun hinged upon Tony's near-manic commitment, had long known that he was drinking to excess, that his mental health was suffering. That much had been clear to her when the two first met in Darwin, but now something had shifted.

'He began to get it wrong,' she would recall years later.

When Tony had asked her to co-author with Arnaud Morvan the essay for the *Women's Business* exhibition, ostensibly to introduce the turbulent street-paintings by the girls, she refused. Langton had never concerned herself with the rumours about Tony's hands-on approach in the studio. For her, the senior artists were the only correct arbiters of what was and wasn't right under Gija Law – if they were happy with Tony's practice, she was too. But with the girls it was different. They lived at a far greater distance from the Law's dictates; their paintings were darker, far more unsettling: proof, if anything, of the Kimberley's spiralling social dysfunction. Langton feared Tony had become so inured to his adopted world that he had missed what to her seemed obvious: she knew as well as he did that the girls would readily find their brief success, but she wondered how wealthy city art patrons would ever understand the reality of each girl's life. Tony had pulled these works into the world: it was the first time that Langton felt he had crossed a line.

But for Tony, staging something of the reality of the girls' lives was the point of the project: it was the so-called 'traditional' paintings – the depictions of ceremony and 'Dreamtime' narratives that flooded the art marketplace from nearly every region of Aboriginal Australia – that now seemed to him the most pernicious. Work like that made sense for Elders like Paddy, but for younger generations they risked veiling something far more urgent. He soon penned his own essay for the exhibition, a pointed indictment of what he now argued were the colonial underpinnings of the whole Aboriginal art industry.

We want the artist's 'Dreaming stories', he wrote, ... *but not their humanity, [not their] day-to-day reality* ... In relation to the girls, he made a simple point: *Their paintings are tame compared to their lives...*

He wrote this in Wyndham, hunched alone over his computer as night descended upon the overgrown garden outside and the veritable army of night insects began their raucous harmonies.

The moon was just up: heavy, an eerie red. He thought immediately of the first time he had witnessed such a sight. It was during a visit to the Bedford Downs massacre ground a handful of years earlier with Paddy and others, including Peggy. As always, they unrolled their swags at the sandy gorge, the moon appeared over the horizon, awash with a similarly unsettling hue. 'Something bad is coming,' Tony would recall Peggy saying to him, her sense of foreboding clear.

As he wrote, Tony thought of a recent visit to Kununurra on which he'd crossed paths with an Aboriginal friend not much older than himself, of how that friend had now buried each of his two sons. He thought of the station days, of how so many of the Elders he'd come to know recalled those times of hardship with an almost wistful air.

'It was better in the old days when we were working on the stations,' they would tell him. 'We had our country to walk on, and our kids were safe. We could teach them Law.'

As he wrote he received a call informing him of the latest horror: a murder, brother by brother, in the long grass directly opposite the Jirrawun house in Kununurra.

He included all this in his short essay, summarising its sequence of distilled provocations as bluntly as he could: *We do not want to see the darker realities that sit alongside the Dreaming.*

He was pointing the finger (if the city art enthusiasts wanted to continue the same myth of authenticity and tradition, then fuck them; they wouldn't last a day in this world). But he knew that he was also implicated.

How could he not be?

It was that same untenable position, trying to find traction between worlds but slipping, always slipping.

Our so-called 'lucky' country, he wrote, and would always recall the exhaustion that immediately overcame him.

•

Nicolas Rothwell, who had by now become a dependable advocate for the Jirrawun cause, visited to write about the new studio for *The Australian* not long after its completion. News of the building had spread outwards from the Kimberley with a ripple of excitement, but Nicolas couldn't help but note, once again, Tony's strange emotional turmoil: the achievement was clear, but the darkness he'd recognised in Tony when the two had first met in Kununurra seemed only to have deepened.

As always, Nicolas was working on two things at once. The first was his article for the newspaper's Weekend Review, eventually titled 'A Dream of a Studio', a glowing piece that cast the building as the kind of mad gamble that all future bush art studios would surely be measured against.

The photographer Peter Eve also soon visited, tasked with photographing the studio for Nicolas's article. Eve had worked with Jirrawun often in recent years, shooting, among other things, striking portraits of each of the artists: Peggy at Mistake Creek, proudly meeting the camera's gaze from amid the tumbled branches of the massacre boab; Rammey sitting on the veranda at Bow River surrounded by his family, the station's cattle brand clasped in his hand like a sceptre; PB posed in a calculated echo of Hans Namuth's famous portrait of Jackson Pollock at rest on the running board of his battered vehicle.

Eve documented the new building, and took pictures of Tony and Freddie too. With himself the camera's subject, Tony's intent was obvious. It was unbearably hot, but he dressed up in a dark suit and tie, lit a cigarette and stood before the studio as if he helmed a high-end New York gallery of his own. Freddie, nearby, was a perfect picture of a Kimberley stockman. It all added to the sense of theatre that had become a key part of Jirrawun's stock-in-trade, but although Rothwell played into it too (in his article he evoked the colonial anti-hero Fitzcarraldo, as immortalised by Klaus Kinski in Werner Herzog's film) it was the sense that Tony had somehow knowingly doubled down on a losing hand that ultimately stayed with him.

Much of this would be contained in Nicolas's other piece, which he'd not publish for some years. In it, he recounted his late-night arrival at the Wyndham block. He'd been delayed; by the time he finally steered off the highway and onto the dirt entrance track, Tony had turned in for the night. Nicolas cut his engine and stepped into the shadows of the garden just as the automatic watering system kicked in with a sudden hiss. He made his way into the low house and was struck by how provisional it seemed: the living room was almost bare; a pile of swags in one corner, plastic chairs arranged around a table, a couple of worn armchairs.

Tony's collection of books overloaded a set of shelves. He'd had these sent up from storage in Sydney not long after he moved to Wyndham, and counts them among his most precious possessions. There were, of course, the artist monographs (Gauguin, Picasso, McCahon), but there was also a range of tattered paperbacks: Melville's *Moby Dick*, *Capricornia* by Xavier Herbert, Malcolm Lowry's *Under the Volcano*, Conrad's *Heart of Darkness*, works by Graham Greene, Dostoyevsky, Camus and Dickens.

Nicolas found Tony asleep in one of the armchairs. There was a book open nearby, and although Tony appeared at peace, in one hand he tightly grasped a serrated kitchen knife.

The next morning Tony's complex feelings for the studio were obvious. He described what it was like when it was first finished, the feeling of hope and accomplishment that had so readily overcome him. But he also acknowledged that Paddy's death was close: that after Old Man had gone, the other artists would surely follow, one by one, and the dark rhythm of the world around him would only continue; the majority of the youth would be as adrift as ever, their lives short and hard.

As much as he'd intended the studio to be a permanent celebration of the artists' achievement – a kind of Gija temple in the heart of the far north – his thinking was now far bleaker: 'I built a mausoleum instead,' he said. As they spoke, he ushered Nicolas towards the building's striking white form, but he ultimately left him to walk through it alone.

Later, after Tony had left the Kimberley, he would tell himself and others a handful of stories that might explain his departure: how the pressures of the place grew and grew, how the demand for him to keep making money for the artists was only doubled by the unforgiving landscape of the place, by the relentless progression of the seasons. He'll blame his worst behaviour on the ruptured social world he had by then drawn so close to, on the ever-present shadow of colonial history that seemingly hung over every interaction.

In this way, he'll try and make sense of it – how he had put so much energy into building what he had, only to leave at what many observers thought to be the height of Jirrawun's achievement – but he'll struggle to make the shape of actual events conform with what his memory wants: the dramatic endpoint; the sense of dreams thwarted, of good intentions met by immovable reality.

Accurate or not, they'll only be stories: the real ending will be far more prosaic; it won't easily bend to myth. Paddy will visit him in the studio, driven from Kununurra by the male nurse, who by then was caring for him on Frances's veranda. Tony will wheel his friend around the studio's interior, looking at recent paintings by Rammey: in this way the two of them will spend their last moments together, before saying goodbye.

By then he will have sensed a means to leave. He had taken his first holiday to Vietnam a year earlier, where, in a village on the country's central coast, he'd met Le Chi, an elegant woman in her late twenties. If the relationship that followed had thrown into sharp relief the pronounced loneliness of his Kimberley life, making it more unbearable than it otherwise might have been, it had also opened an alternative. Slowly, he'd understood it could be real.

At first he'll travel back and forth, taking holidays when he can. He'll be in Vietnam when Paddy dies, but it'll only be when news reaches him, not quite a year later, that Le Chi is pregnant with their first child, a son, that he'll finally move there for good.

He will recall sitting at the Wyndham block in a green plastic lawn chair under the large tree that grew near the machinery shed, and calling Brendan Hammond to tell him it was over. He'll remember thinking that the studio couldn't have come any earlier, but that it was nonetheless far too late: he was exhausted, burnt out; Paddy was dead.

Once he'd made the decision, he'll remember the absolute relief of it.

5.

After Paddy had gone, moments would return to Tony that seemed to express something essential about their friendship. There was of course the shared activity of painting but just as often it was the simple fact of them being together, of how natural this had felt from their earliest moments. Like many gardiya, Tony's feeling for the Gija world was at best impressionistic and scattered, but with Paddy at his side a clearer picture could draw briefly into focus.

Once, early in their life together, they drove through the night to Darwin, the highway lit before them by the LandCruiser's headlights.

Silence, most of the way: just the darkness and the rhythm of their passage, the captivating thrum they both knew so well. Paddy was always the passenger, but he would stay awake as Tony drove. From time to time, Tony would ask for a cigarette, and Paddy would reach for the packet of Winfield Blues, light one, and pass it over before lighting another for himself.

Driving at night was dangerous. Vehicles barrelled at high speed through unfenced station country. Bullocks would often wander onto the highway, sometimes to simply stand there basking in the remnant heat that rose in waves from the bitumen. Hit one and you'd be lucky to survive; at the very least the vehicle would be a write-off. A driver had to stay alert, ever ready to brake or swerve.

But danger this night came in the form of a road train appearing in the distance as an oncoming flood of bright high beams. Usually, after a beat or two, this light would dim and passing would be easy, but either the driver somehow didn't notice the LandCruiser up ahead, or simply paid it no heed: the high beams stayed on, drawing closer and closer until they filled the cabin with blinding white. As far as Tony could tell, he and Paddy may have been driving straight into the road train's path; he took the only option besides trusting blind faith and steered left onto the gravel verge. As he braked, the road train flung past in an explosion of warm air.

In its wake Paddy let loose a string of invective (*Fuck'n bastard!*) and then, as Tony prepared to resume their journey, the old man cried out suddenly. He'd had a revelation.

'Jungurra,' Tony would recall him saying. 'I know why you had that crash.'

He was referring to the accident that Tony and Hector had survived, which was surely by this stage at least two years in the past.

'It was Booljoon, Jungurra,' Paddy said, using Phyllis Thomas's bush name.

'When she got angry that morning and threw that billycan of water. That's why the Jowarri came for you.'

If Tony recalled this moment – Phyllis at Crocodile Hole on the morning of the accident, losing her temper and hurling her billy into the ground – he had long pushed it from his mind.

What connection could it possibly have, he would later ask himself, *what pattern did it betray?*

But he also knew such questions were beside the point, that if Paddy identified it as the key to understanding the crash then he was probably right. From Old Man's perspective one event had gathered into another.

He would always remember that logic when he thought of Paddy, that feeling for cause and effect that was, in Tony's mind, so uniquely Cija. Everything already had its place assigned by the Ngarranggarni: there were no surprises, no mysteries. To make sense of the world, one just had to identify the web of connections that bound it.

The funeral only seemed to make this clearer still: Paddy, coming to rest at the Bow River cemetery, surrounded by the country he loved, everything in its rightful place.

•

Even so, it was a time of heightened pressure for everyone involved: the all too familiar cascade of tiny tasks that together form the unruly art of a Kimberley burial.

Who would prepare the body?

Who would drive the coffin from Kununurra?

Who would stand before the crowd and speak?

Who would organise the food?

Tony had been invested in all the funerals he'd attended, but this was different. He knew how people saw Paddy and him – the two inseparable figures – but at first struggled to fully comprehend the reality of Old Man's passing. He'd only just returned from Vietnam, and it was easier to simply focus on the little things. He wasn't sure how many people would make their way to Bow River, flying from around the country and driving from as far away as Broome and Fitzroy Crossing, but he thought again of Timmy's funeral, of how it had seemed there were a thousand people there, perhaps more.

A refrigerated truck was soon organised with a handful of partially butchered bullock carcasses in the back of it, so too were plastic troughs of coleslaw and salad. Tony asked Sir William Deane, then still Jirrawun's official patron, to travel from Canberra to deliver the eulogy; and reached out to other supporters and friends he felt would drop their commitments and fly north to attend. Finally, when all that remained to prepare was a good sleep and an early rise to drive the three hours from the Wyndham block to Bow River, he took out a huge calico drop sheet. He laid it across the studio's polished concrete floor and did what he had so often done: mixed the colours in preparation for painting.

He put on music and tried not to think of Paddy's absence.

He walked over the canvas, marking out the structure of one of Old Man's Cockatoo Dreamings. The story told of the white cockatoo ancestor, Ngayilanji, who made his way into Gija country from far to the east, of how at a place called Jawoorraban he encountered a group of men walking and blocked their path, singing them into stillness until they were stuck there forever as a tumble of stone formations.

Once the black lines were dry enough, Tony was able to fill in the background – the white enlivened by Paddy's characteristic flush of black – before adding the outline of carefully unstudied dots. He knew Paddy's hand as if it were his own, but although he could provide a near-flawless facsimile, the finished painting was little more than an approximation: without Paddy, the heart of it was absent. But this was beside the point.

For a moment the process settled Tony's mind. This would be the backdrop, hung in the Bow River machinery shed behind the coffin.

When Sir William Deane stood before it and delivered his eulogy to the gathered crowd the next day, his words were simple and heartfelt. His deep feeling for Paddy was clear. The two had first met during the performances of *Fire, Fire Burning Bright,* and had seen each other at regular intervals in the years since: Paddy was the Kimberley Lawman; Deane, in Paddy's words, his 'Canberra Brother'.

Most recently it had been the opening of Paddy's retrospective in Sydney, only the year before, that had drawn them together. That crowd had been glowing with admiration for the old Gija man who had made the paintings now deemed masterpieces and hung so carefully across the walls around them: the first boards that Tony had found in Warmun; PB's first triumphant canvas, the Emu Dreaming painted in the dust at Pindan Avenue, Hector by Paddy's side; an entire gallery of the black and white paintings that had first appeared in the art school studio in Darwin.

As he'd done for the opening of *Blood on the Spinifex,* Deane had spoken that night of reconciliation, of once and for all bringing together Aboriginal and non-Aboriginal Australia. Now, at Old Man's funeral, he spoke more simply of Paddy's character. He wished his friend safe passage, thanked him for sharing what he did with those whites like himself who were open to Paddy's view of history. He marvelled at the world that Paddy had once lived in, at the changes he'd witnessed, at the unexpected chain of events that had, in his final decade, rendered him famous.

Hector was gone now too, buried the year before at a Catholic service in Turkey Creek. Deane had known him as well – the two shared their Catholic faith with a passion – and as his eulogy drew to a close, he hastened Paddy's spirit, the white cockatoo, into the Kimberley skies to join Hector's white owl and Timmy Timms's eagle: three Lawmen spiralling above their ancestral estates, immune once more to time's passage.

•

Afterwards, most mourners drove the short distance to the cemetery, but Tony walked with Jirrawun's old friend Russell Lilford, the painter from

Darwin who'd cooked for the *Fire, Fire Burning Bright* production; both were soaked in sweat when they arrived to take their place among the other mourners.

When the time came, Tony moved to the front of the crowd and tipped a shovel of soil on the coffin, but for the most part he would remember standing at the periphery, watching in silence. Later, as the crowd thinned out, Lilford and Tony joined a handful of others, including the gallerist Dallas Gold, in carving up the partially butchered beef carcasses on trestle tables. They worked furiously to cut the ribs into sections and sever each leg at the joint as those departing before sundown lined up in the heat to receive their share. By the end of it the tables were bright with gore, and Tony's hands, cut with what seemed a thousand tiny cuts, were already throbbing with the onset of infection.

Those that stayed on spread themselves among the community's houses in groups, rolling out swags, lighting fires. The Gija had prepared a simple joonba ground in Paddy's honour and, as darkness fell, the singing started, and then the clapsticks and the dancing. An unruly group of kids were the first to perform. Peggy's familiar voice rose up as she led the singers, but although Rammey's grandson Vincent joined the children and danced with admirable skill, the joonba seemed to more than one viewer to be awkward and undisciplined.

Rammey had been quietly watching proceedings from a chair at the edge, but he soon rose up and disappeared behind the eucalypt bough screen that formed the performance's backdrop. Paddy was more than Rammey's old friend. Paddy had been almost two decades older than Rammey; Rammey often explained that Paddy had 'grown him up'. When Rammey painted, it had always been with Paddy, ever since the first boards he had made when he wandered down to the makeshift studio at Bow River and told Tony he wanted to paint.

In the months to come he and Tony will work towards one last studio session together in Wyndham that will one day count among the fondest of Tony's Kimberley memories. It'll just be the two of them. They will put on music: Rammey will choose Slim Dusty and Tony will intersperse it with the mournful trumpet-sketches of Miles Davis. They will work undisturbed for the most part, and when the paintings are done and Tony has hung them around the walls, they will sit there together as the blue light of evening floods the studio.

Each will open one can of rum and coke after another and together look at the strange, hybrid-seeming images that surround them: angular, folded compositions in yellow and black and blue, the planes of colour overlaid and twisted. Anyone familiar with Rammey's work will recognise these paintings immediately – his images have always leaned towards the geometric – but Tony will see his ideas in them too. In this way intersecting boundary lines will become swastikas, an imaginary play on the underpinning racism of the frontier world, of how this can't help but inflect the art that's made there, no matter how celebrated it becomes. More gently, Rammey's paintings will draw forth in Tony memories of Harvey Quaytman, the acclaimed New York abstractionist he once exhibited in Melbourne. As a young man he stayed at Quaytman's studio and the experience of sitting with Quaytman as the two discussed the works arranged before them had proven foundational. Painting is a serious thing, nothing to be trifled with.

It will feel the same with Rammey, sitting together and looking as the shared space of the studio momentarily holds at bay what for Tony had become the horror of the world outside.

He will look back on that moment as a kind of tribute to Paddy, engineered wordlessly with Rammey: a tribute embedded both in the paintings that result and in the time they spend making them. But as easy as memories like that will be, understanding the full arc of his Kimberley life will remain far more difficult.

It was surely true that too much of the overarching vision was his, but he'll also argue that he never believed it could have been any other way, that it was him and the artists from his very first moments in country. His life's experience had threaded into the project as much as the artists' own: what they'd built together was shared, but it was never going to last. By the time Old Man died, a fear had risen within him, irrational or not, that he too would one day be buried in the red earth at Bow River. He would even think that, for the Elders, this was the only way the story could ever end, that once he'd been truly welcomed inside, he was never meant to leave. But, except for a very few, every gardiya always did.

•

When Rammey reappeared among the other dancers at Bow River the tenor of Paddy's joonba shifted in an instant.

He had stripped to a red naga, and applied to his body a rough smattering of white ochre. He now danced as if possessed, his characteristic reticence replaced with an energy seemingly channelled from the most anarchic of ancestral spirits.

Others would recall Rammey moving across the stage among the dancing children, his sudden presence enlivening their performance until the joonba's initial looseness was tightened to perfection.

But Tony would remember it differently.

In his memory it would just be Rammey, alone on the bare earth stage, his feet kicking up drifts of red dust in the firelight, a stick held before him as if it were an anchor that fixed his sinuous movements in space.

Rammey moving in honour of his old friend Paddy Bedford, moving with an energy and focus that few, if any, would ever witness him muster again.

Epilogue: Vietnam

When Freddie died in 2017, a decade after Paddy's death, Tony had a dream in which he took off his black hat and lay his head on a dark wood counter that was somewhere like the old post office in Warmun, which had once been the police station, and later became the art centre: old colonial architecture, raised on pillars, looking out over the sun-blasted landscape.

By then Jirrawun had long shuttered its doors. The board had quickly descended into infighting after Tony's departure, and, although concerted attempts were made to continue, the remaining staff was ultimately left treading water as the whole venture faltered around them. It hadn't happened immediately, but the artists soon disengaged from the organisation they'd helped build, wary to commit to the journey to Wyndham and back; collectors began to turn their attentions elsewhere. By 2011 the once gleaming studio and the block on which it stood had been sold off to cover an avalanche of debt.

If Tony ever pictured the building, it was as he'd last seen it, during his final sessions with Rammey: clear and precise against the surrounding wilderness. But by Freddie's death the place had gone to ruin. Passed from one local owner to the next, it was by then little more than a glorified shed, its once pristine walls caked in dust, its interior stuffed full of rusting machinery. Hunting dogs stalked a perimeter crowded with broken car bodies: if any curious passerby – perhaps a traveller who'd heard of Paddy Bedford and the grand studio that had once been built in his honour – turned up the narrow dirt track from the highway to see what remained, their exit would be swift.

Freddie's last years had been brutal: spiralling alcoholism had seen him in and out of Kununurra Hospital with pancreatitis. No longer did an internet search of his name draw forth his glittering achievements as the founding artist of Jirrawun. It was now more likely to dredge images of the works he had dashed off for Kununurra carpetbaggers, accompanied by photographs of Freddie holding each painting. These were intended as proof that the works were Freddie's, but they couldn't help but double as a heart-breaking record of his physical decline. He appeared ever more pensive and jaundiced-looking as his time drew near.

In his dream, Tony entered the old post office through a series of doors, knowing somehow that Freddie's body lay there in a morgue within the building's deepest chamber. He sensed familiar presences – Peggy was there, hooded in black – but he kept moving from one door to the next until he arrived at the wooden counter. Behind it was an unfamiliar white man, waiting.

He fixed Tony with a blank gaze.

'We are just waiting on the recount,' the man said flatly, as if there had been some kind of mistake and Freddie wasn't dead at all.

•

Not long afterwards, in November 2017, the central coast of Vietnam was hit by a typhoon. It was named Damrey, a Cambodian word for 'elephant'.

As he often did, Tony was sleeping that night on the single bed in his studio: Le Chi, his wife now for almost a decade, was inside with the children, in the ground-floor room where she liked to sleep together with their two-year-old daughter in a hammock.

As the storm grew in intensity, Tony woke and crossed the courtyard to the main house. It was two storeys tall, a white-rendered monolith atop a stepped terrace that looked out across the bay, nothing between it and the sea but a rock wall and a thin stretch of beach. Usually the view was one of serenity: a scatter of simple fishing boats moored at regular intervals on a flat ocean; the dark forms of mountains on the distant peninsula. But now the bay was a churning white mass malevolently aglow in the darkness.

The family huddled together as the waves pounded against the retaining wall. The destructive power was terrifying: they listened as the wind ripped Le Chi's beautiful garden to shreds, as it stripped the decade-old frangipani trees clean of greenery, and shredded the fragile leaf-flowers of the bougainvillea to confetti. As the storm's eye passed over them, the wind dropped and left in its absence an eerie stillness.

Tony passed his eight-year-old son Jack a bicycle helmet, just in case there was falling debris, and the two of them ventured outside and down the flight of stone stairs to the lower terrace where the wall dropped to the beach below. Dawn was now rising and the scene before them was bathed in grey light. They leaned forwards, marvelling at how everything that had just been in violent motion was now still.

The fishing boats that were usually moored there had vanished without a trace. Tony looked down the beach towards the encroaching resort villas in the distance. That's when he saw it: the huge hulking shadow black against the dawn sky.

'Look,' he said to Jack.

Tony had a camera and as his son turned back to him, he snapped a photograph. The boy's face is in shadow but his expression of wonder and joy is clearly visible under the pink crown of the helmet. Behind him, just down the beach, a massive cargo freighter lies stranded in the shallow water, pushed from the harbour's depths by the storm's sheer force. Its great iron hull dominates everything around it. The crew was just visible, mere silhouettes against the sky: Tony could make out the anxious sound of them calling to each other in Vietnamese.

The next day the extent of the damage became clear. Damrey had ripped tin roofs from the surrounding houses. It had uprooted trees and felled electricity poles; rice paddies were ruined by flooding. Reports that soon gathered from across the region suggested as many as a hundred people were killed, that thousands of homes were either damaged or destroyed completely.

Tony couldn't help but think of the cyclone that once took Darwin, and the spirits that stood on Kelly's Knob above Kununurra and watched the destruction unfold. Rover Thomas's dreams had soon followed. That's how the painting movement started: the rainbow serpent unleashing the world's terrible force, and leaving in its aftermath something new. If he retained anything from the Kimberley beyond his memories, it was the sense that everything in the world was part of a greater pattern. He thought of the marooned cargo freighter and wondered what his old Gija friends would have made of it. What kind of symbol was it; what did it foretell?

By then he had returned to his own practice as a painter. He'd first begun to send images of the resulting works to a select group of friends and acquaintances five years before the storm, and had soon held a small exhibition at William Mora's Melbourne gallery. For those who were still searching for proof of Tony's influence on PB's paintings, his early works provided few concrete answers: they could be read either way.

There were the dimensions, which were the same as Old Man's smaller paintings on composition board, and also the palette of sparse dark tones offset by enveloping fields of white. One, titled *Offerings to a deceased painter*, was a clear nod to their friendship. It teetered on the edge of parody: an abandoned stockman's hat resting on a table's flat plane, a bunch of ripening bananas balancing it to one edge. The space and the roughly painted panes of colour were Bedford's, but the painting was unmistakably Tony's.

Other works betrayed different influences entirely. They were more often than not self-consciously modern in character, quasi-fauvist, more than a touch of Matisse and Gauguin. Jack sat in bright studio interiors, his face impassive and mask-like. Tony's work with Paddy had been singular, but here, once again, he was navigating the pitfalls of historical precedent and not yet emerging unscathed.

In the following years his work had grown steadily darker, its allegory heavier, more pronounced. References came with metronomic regularity: death, new beginnings, time passing. Skulls rested in caves, nearby unripe mangoes and boxes of the Vietnamese cigarettes that Tony now chain-smoked. Glass-helmed gaslights bathed stone walls in yellow; grass fires flickered on far horizons. The images spoke of regret and sadness. In step, the underlying psychology seemed always fragile, just like the emailed missives he still often bashed out to old friends.

As always Tony was playing to his darkly romantic side: in the Kimberley he'd seen signs and symbols everywhere, had often followed them with abandon; now he was painting them, one by one, carving from them a vernacular. There was the cave to which Hector had once taken him, the pipe that David Turner had performed with in *Fire, Fire Burning*

Bright, the clouds that traced the landscapes below. All this had somehow led to his new home in Vietnam, a place at first so full of promise but where he still found himself struggling.

'It's all doubt and depression,' he would say later, after the storm's memory had begun to fade, and he'd returned to the studio and completed what some suspected was his first masterpiece. The painting was long and complex. It synthesised his life's memories as narrative icons set amid a sea of angular abstraction. Those twinned emotions had always been there, driving even the most outlandish of his Kimberley dreams, pushing him, even before that, from one vision to the next. Surely that's why he reached out to others in the fashion he did, why he tried to make the uncertain space of the studio something that could be shared. Surely it's that which had drawn him so tightly to Paddy.

'I miss having him in the studio,' he'll say, referring to his Gija friend as if the sentiment alone explains everything.

And in a way, it does. Without the certainty of PB's hand, Tony's practice was traced by the kind of anxieties that mark the endeavours of all but the blindest of artists. The myriad choices that make painting so daunting had been with PB outsourced, and in the moment creation had flowed freely.

Now, as he fully committed himself to the life of a painter, that protection had peeled away: from here, everything was his.

•

At times friends travel to Vietnam.

Although Tony lives off the beaten tourist track, it's easy enough to get there: a short flight from Ho Chi Minh City to the resort town of Nha Trang. He doesn't meet them, but in keeping with local tradition instead provides a driver to take them north along the coast, past the half-finished palace-resorts on the sand's edge that so bluntly flag the country's recent economic rise.

Nha Trang is soon replaced by a series of small towns, by an endless sequence of signs in Vietnamese, by congested roundabouts that eventually open onto the new highway that links the country's north and south. Finally, the vehicle turns onto a network of ever-smaller roads until the path ahead is little more than a raised dirt track leading through a neat maze of rice paddies. If the sun is low it flickers through the water there like gold. The only resorts nearby are for Russians and Chinese; fluent English is rare.

The driver stops.

He gestures down a sandy path between unassuming tiled houses shuttered in the tropical heat. At the end of it rises Tony and Le Chi's grand residence; the walled garden, regrown since the storm, is once again an oasis of green.

Tony likes to sit on the back veranda, a far smaller space than the front, and although there's much to talk about, it won't take long for the subject of Old Man and his paintings to arise. Sometimes it will be a recent record-breaking auction result, or news about the Paddy Bedford estate, which is being managed by William Mora.

He'll point out that, of the hundreds of paintings he witnessed take shape in the Kimberley, he never kept one for himself. He did this for an obvious reason – he could never be seen to be profiting from his role – but he now wishes he had a handful on his walls: a gouache by Paddy, perhaps, or a perfect work of Freddie's.

But just as often he'll acknowledge that, as beautiful as they were, the paintings were only part of what kept him in the Kimberley. In these moments he does little more than recall the faces of his Kimberley friends. Most of them are now gone, but he nonetheless wonders what it would be like to see them again.

'I wish I could go back,' he'll say, during a lull in the conversation which has drawn briefly into silence.

'But not to paint, not this time.

'I wish I could go back there without the art, just to be there with them. Just to be there without having to do anything at all.'

He used to have a lot of fun, even in Kununurra with the alcoholics and the humbug. There was joy there amid the darkness, almost as if people had accepted the hardness of Kimberley life, and instead of fighting it were simply letting the current take them where it would.

There was a freedom to that, he now realises: it's this he misses as much as anything.

What would it be like to go back?

He will ask this out loud as the question threads its way more urgently through his thoughts. And although he'll never return, he will, from time to time, allow himself to picture what it would be like to board a plane in Ho Chi Minh City and barrel through the dark skies to northern Australia, to cross from Darwin to Kununurra, and to step once more from the tiny airport into the Kimberley's cloying heat.

He won't need to tell anyone he's coming.

Once he's there, word will spread like wildfire and he'll find himself welcomed again at the centre of that broken world he once knew so well.

Author's note

This book has largely been written through conversation. In this, it is deeply contingent upon those who spoke to me either on or off the record, along with others who corresponded via email.

Firstly, I note Tony Oliver's willing participation. Over a number of years, and countless hours, he shared his memories, good and bad, of his life in the Kimberley, and his friendships with the Jirrawun painters: without him there would be no book. Others were similarly generous; whether they committed to short or long interviews, or simply assisted in securing other contacts, they were each in their own way essential to building what picture I was able to achieve on the page. They include (in alphabetical order) Peter Adsett, Jose Alfano, Robyn Archer, Paul Boston, Jason Davidson-Hampton, Roger Foley, Simon Georgeff, Dallas Gold, Geoff Hassall, Jeffrey Harris, Peter Harrison, Robert Hirschmann, Eric Kjellgren, Simeon Kronenberg, Marcia Langton, Elizabeth Laverty, Ruark Lewis, Russell Lilford, Giancarlo Mazzella, Leon Morris, Arnaud Morvan, Rudy Panozzo, Justin Paton, Kathy Ramsey, Rammey Ramsey, Nicolas Rothwell, Andrish Saint-Clare, Tim Smith, Suzanne Spunner, Jemma Stowe, Sally Sussman, Helene Tiechmann, Imants Tillers, Kathy Watson and Ken Watson.

In addition, Giancarlo Mazzella, Suzanne Spunner, Russell Lilford and Helene Teichmann made available Jirrawun-related archives in their safekeeping; Sir William Deane generously provided copies of relevant speeches he made over the years he was drawn into the Jirrawun orbit; Simon Georgeff shared transcripts of his original recorded interviews with Hector Jandany and Freddie Timms; and Ken Watson sent me Tony Oliver's remnant archival material from Wyndham, where it somehow survived ten wet seasons in a tin shed beset by both rodents and insects. I also owe a debt to the photographers and videographers who documented aspects of the period – people, landscapes, places – I have covered here, and whose work gave me invaluable visual insight. Among them are Giancarlo Mazzella, Simon Georgeff and Peter Eve.

In writing this book I also drew on my own experiences living and working in the East Kimberley over twelve months in 2009–2010, during which I was employed by Jirrawun Arts in its final months, and on a number of subsequent visits to the region in 2012, 2014 and 2018. Specific descriptions used here in some cases reflect my own observations, as much as the recollections of others. During 2009–2010 I met and worked with, to greater and lesser extents, all the then-surviving Jirrawun artists; although I was simply one of many gardiya who crossed their paths throughout the years, the memory, for me, remains strong. In particular, along with my then-partner I gratefully received the hospitality and friendship of Rammey Ramsey and family (particularly his daughter, Kathy) at Bow River throughout this period. The recollection of watching joonba there, and of camping in the dry riverbed often returns to me.

I also respectfully acknowledge those who chose not to speak to me for this book – among them Frances Kofod, Rowan Page and Rusty Peters: I can only imagine how the resulting work would have changed had their recollections informed it.

Finally, this book was written for the most part in Melbourne and Geelong on the unceded lands of the Wurundjeri and Wadawurrung peoples; I pay my respects to their Elders past, present and future.

Acknowledgements

Many people have supported me over the time it took to write this book. Firstly, my heartfelt thanks to those friends and colleagues who have supported this endeavour both directly and indirectly throughout: you know who you are. A number of editors have offered support in recent years by publishing my work: among them are John van Tiggelen, then-editor of *The Monthly*, who published an early essay that laid out something of this narrative, and that magazine's subsequent editor, Nick Feik. Nick Tapper read two early chapter drafts, and responded with generosity. He also recommended the Roberto Bolaño novella *By Night in Chile*, from which I drew my epigraph.

In addition, special thanks to Margaret Connolly, who read the early manuscript with enthusiasm, and guided its subsequent progress. Nicolas Rothwell knew the shape of this story long before I did and offered me judicious encouragement from before I even knew I was writing a book. His reading of the early manuscript was essential, and his feedback precise. Thanks also to James Guida, a writer of admirable brevity who read a late draft and provided valuable feedback, and to Kim Mahood, who provided courage at a key moment. A big thank you to Marg Bowman at Hardie Grant, who guided this book's first edition, and to Emily Hart and Elena Callcott, who together guided the second.

I received financial support during this period from the Victorian Government, through Creative Victoria, which funded travel to the Kimberley and writing time, and through a Bundanon Trust Fellowship, which granted me valuable space to write – thanks to the relevant selection committees.

Above all, heartfelt thanks to both the Jackson family, and to my own. In particular my father, Leslie, who passed to me his twin interests in art and Aboriginal Australia; my mother, Annie, who instilled in her children a love of books; and to Virginia, Dave, Elvie and Orlando. Finally, the biggest of thank yous to Leah. She has shared her recent life not only with me, but with this book too, and has offered me boundless resources of support and belief. I owe you. Last of all, to our beautiful daughter Djuna, who arrived at exactly the right moment: if this book is anyone's, it is yours.

Notes

In addition to interviews and related material detailed in the author's note (p. 263), the following sources have been drawn upon.

Warmun / Turkey Creek

(p. 12) **These are the kinds of stories ...** Details of Freddie Timms's life are drawn from his own account in: Alex Smee (prod.), *Freddie Timms: Black Soil*, ABC Open, 2014.

(p. 13) **... how the Ngarranggarni women hunted Daiwul, the barramundi ...** This Dreaming story is published with minor variation in a number of sources. See, for example: Jennifer Joi Field, *Written in the Land: the Life of Queenie McKenzie*, Melbourne Books, Melbourne, 2008, p. 143.

(p. 15) **That's what had started it all ...** The foundation of the East Kimberley art movement is detailed in a number of sources. See, for example: 'Rover Thomas Dreams the Krill Krill' in Wally Caruana (ed.), *Roads Cross: The Paintings of Rover Thomas*, National Gallery of Australia, Canberra, 1994, p. 22; and Will Christensen, 'Paddy Jaminji and the Guirr Guirr', in Judith Ryan (ed.), *Images of Power: Aboriginal Art of the Kimberley*, National Gallery of Victoria, Melbourne, 1992, pp. 32–35. For Thomas's own account, see: 'Rover Thomas and the Getting of the Krill Krill', in Caruana (ed.), *Roads Cross*, pp. 22–24.

(p. 16) **Her spirit continued its passage ...** Following details are drawn from: 'Rover Thomas Dreams the Krill Krill' in Caruana (ed.), *Roads Cross*, p. 22.

(p. 21) **The gallery was the subject of an article ...** Martin Armiger, 'The Social Underbelly Displayed by a Young Crusader', *The National Times*, 25–31 July 1982.

(p. 25) **The way Freddie told it ...** Freddie Timms later recounted his understanding of the financial arrangement in regard to Melbourne painting trips in an interview with Simon Georgeff conducted in Kununurra in 1998. This account draws in part on an unpublished transcription of that interview.

(p. 27) **Watters would take thirty-three per cent ...** Financial details are drawn from: Watters Gallery Archive, Art Gallery of New South Wales, Sydney, MS2004.7.

(p. 27) **Compared to his experiences in Melbourne ...** Freddie Timms quoted in interview with Simon Georgeff, Kununurra, 1998.

(p. 30) **Stories of murder and massacre threaded ...** Early versions of such stories are recorded in: Helen Ross (ed.), 'Impact Stories of the East Kimberley', *East Kimberley Working Paper No. 28*, Centre for Resource and Environmental Studies, Australian National University, Canberra, 1989.

(p. 30) **Aboriginal family groups had by then gathered ...** The following details regarding the Kimberley pastoral era are drawn from: Mary Anne Jebb, *Blood, Sweat and Welfare: A History of White Bosses and Aboriginal Pastoral Workers*, University of Western Australia Press, Perth, 2002.

(p. 30) **... a period of violence and authoritarian control ...** Jebb, *Blood, Sweat and Welfare*, p. 299.

(p. 31) **Nor was welfare available ...** Jebb, *Blood, Sweat and Welfare*, pp. 285–289.

(p. 31) **The site that was chosen ...** Historical information regarding Turkey Creek is drawn from: Cathy Clement, 'Historical Notes Relevant to Impact Stories of the East Kimberley', *East Kimberley Working Paper No. 29*, Centre for Resource and Environmental Studies, Australian National University, Canberra, 1989, pp. 24–30.

(p. 31) **As the European occupation ...** The following passages draw on: Chris Owen, 'The police appear to be a useless lot up there: Law and Order in the East Kimberley 1884–1905', *Aboriginal History Journal*, ANU Press, Canberra, 2003, pp. 105–130, p. 110. See also, Clement, 'Historical Notes Relevant to Impact Stories of the East Kimberley', pp. 24–30.

(p. 32) **Francis Connor, the East Kimberley's first member ...** quoted in: Chris Owen, *Every Mother's Son is Guilty: Policing the Kimberley Frontier of Western Australia 1882–1905*, UWA Publishing, Western Australia, 2016, p. 350.

(p. 32) **In 1901 PC James Campbell Thomson ...** Owen, 'The police appear to be a useless lot up there', pp. 126–128.

(p. 32) **Prisoners from the greater region ...** Clement, 'Historical Notes Relevant to Impact Stories of the East Kimberley', p. 28.

(p. 33) **... Rhatigan was spoken of approvingly ...** Owen, *Every Mother's Son is Guilty*, p. 339.

(p. 33) **From his earliest days he was known ...** Owen, *Every Mother's Son is Guilty*, p. 294.

(p. 33) **Only two years before ...** Owen, *Every Mother's Son is Guilty*, pp. 361–363.

(p. 33) **When the postmaster departed ...** Clement, 'Historical Notes Relevant to Impact Stories of the East Kimberley', p. 27.

(p. 33) **... in 1915, Rhatigan was implicated in another massacre ...** Owen, *Every Mother's Son is Guilty*, p. 438. An account of the massacre at Mistake Creek is also offered by Bob Nyalcas and Winnie Budbaria in: Ross (ed.), 'Impact Stories of the East Kimberley', pp. 73–75. Further accounts can be found by Timmy Timms and Peggy Patrick (as told to Frances Kofod) in: Bala Starr (ed.), *Blood on the Spinifex*, The Ian Potter Museum of Art, The University of Melbourne, 2002, pp. 30–39; and Peggy Patrick, 'Statement of Peggy Patrick', in Robert Manne (ed.), *Whitewash: On Keith Windschuttle's Fabrication of Aboriginal History*, Black Inc. Agenda, Melbourne, 2003, pp. 215–216.

(p. 34) **The Gija knew where the murders and massacres had occurred.** See, for example, early oral accounts in: Ross (ed.), 'Impact Stories of the East Kimberley'.

(p. 34) **'... expended 40 rounds ...'** quoted in: Owen, 'The police appear to be a useless lot up there', p. 123.

(p. 34) **... the cave across the sandy river ...** See account of Rusty Peters (as told to Frances Kofod) in: Starr (ed.), *Blood on the Spinifex*, pp. 54–56.

(p. 34) **When award wages were enforced ...** Jebb, *Blood, Sweat and Welfare*, p. 301.

(p. 34) **The people squatting there ...** Clement, 'Historical Notes Relevant to Impact Stories of the East Kimberley', p. 30.

(p. 35) **In the late 1970s ...** The following paragraphs draw on: Jon Altman, 'The Economic Impact of Tourism on the Warmun (Turkey Creek) Community East Kimberley', *East Kimberley Working Paper No. 19*, Centre for Resource and Environmental Studies, Australian National University, Canberra, 1987.

(p. 36) **It was one of a number ...** The background of Narrangunny Art Traders, and its relationship to Kimberley Art, is drawn from volume one of Suzanne Spunner's unpublished thesis: Suzanne Spunner, *Vindicating Rover Thomas, v.1*, Centre for Cultural Materials Conservation, the School of Historical and Philosophical Studies, The Faculty of Arts, The University of Melbourne, 2012, pp. 127–130.

(p. 38) **'Who's that bugger ... '** Wally Caruana, 'Who's that bugger who paints like me?' in *World of Dreamings: Traditional and Modern Art of Australia*, National Gallery of Australia, Canberra, 2000, http://www.nga.gov.au/Dreaming/Index.cfm?Refrnc=ch5.

(p. 38) **The story was that ...** The same account was also included in an article by Simon Georgeff where it was attributed to Chocolate Thomas. Simon Georgeff, 'Kimberley Artists in a Legal Bind,' *The Australian*, 14 August 1998.

(p. 41) **... he soon began to build an understanding of Kimberley Kriol.** The following paragraphs draw in part on a short glossary of Kimberley Kriol in Catherine Massola's unpublished thesis: Catherine Anna Massola, *Living the Heritage, Not Curating the Past: a Study in Lirrgarn, Agency and Art in the Warmun Community*, School of Archaeology and Anthropology, The Australian National University, Canberra, 2016, p. xvi.

(p. 43) **In 1979, just after Warmun had come into official existence ...** Following details regarding the Ngalangangpum school are taken from: Massola, *Living the Heritage*, pp. 102–130.

(p. 43) **He once depicted himself ...** This painting is reproduced in: Massola, *Living the Heritage*, p. 146.

(p. 43) **He was known to make ready comparisons ...** Patrick Mung Mung recounted this tendency to Catherine Massola: Massola, *Living the Heritage*, p. 127.

Pindan Avenue

(p. 56) **'It doesn't matter where you go ...'** Freddie Timms quoted in: Simon Georgeff, 'Drawing the Line', *The Sunday Age*, 23 August 1998.

(p. 61) **He showed the emu ancestor untethered by frontier history ...** Michiel Dolk, 'Are We Strangers in this Place?', in Linda Michael (ed.), *Paddy Bedford*, Museum of Contemporary Art, Sydney, 2006, pp. 17–49, p. 21.

(p. 61) **Paddy would later speak in detail ...** Frances Kofod and Leon Morris, 'Neminuwarlin Performance Group History', in *Fire, Fire Burning Bright*, Theatre Program, Neminuwarlin Aboriginal Corporation/Jirrawun Aboriginal Corporation/Melbourne Arts Festival, 2002, pp. 10–13, p. 12.

(p. 62) **... a short, elegiac film ...** Simon Georgeff and Sally Law (dir.), *The Strength of Us*, 1998, unreleased.

(p. 75) **He explained the word ...** 'Jirrawun' has subsequently been defined as 'in one, all in one, at the one place', see: Frances Kofod, 'Gija Glossary', in Michael (ed.), *Paddy Bedford*, pp. 136–139, p. 137.

Rugun / Crocodile Hole

(p. 80) **Rugun was Peggy's country ...** Marcia Langton makes the same observation in: Marcia Langton, 'Goowoomji's World', in Michael (ed.), *Paddy Bedford*, pp. 51–61, p. 57.

(p. 83) **... a site called Winperrji ...** Frances Kofod, 'Places in Paddy Bedford's Country', in Michael (ed.), *Paddy Bedford*, pp. 132–135, p. 135.

(p. 83) **This was Jawoorraban ...** Kofod, 'Places in Paddy Bedford's Country', p. 134.

(p. 97) **A clear pattern had carried over from the station days ...** Marcia Langton, *Boyer Lectures 2012: The Quiet Revolution: Indigenous People and the Resources Boom*, HarperCollins Australia, 2013, p. 34.

(p. 99) **... when an image of *Untitled* ...** These works were reproduced together in: Dolk, 'Are We Strangers in this Place?', p. 42.

(p. 99) **... named for an area on his mother's and uncle's country ...** Kofod, 'Places in Paddy Bedford's Country', p. 134.

(p. 103) **Only a week before, Timmy and Paddy ...** The following paragraphs draw in part on: Kofod and Morris, 'Neminuwarlin Performance Group History'.

(p. 103) **Timmy had recounted the events ...** See account of Timmy Timms (as told to Frances Kofod) in: Starr (ed.), *Blood on the Spinifex*, pp. 18–21.

(p. 103) **When told, he'd given a simple instruction ...** Paddy Bedford quoted in: Dolk, 'Are We Strangers in this Place?', p. 53.

(p. 103) **Bedford knew the country that Timms ...** See account of Paddy Bedford (as told to Frances Kofod) in: Starr (ed.), *Blood on the Spinifex*, pp. 23–25.

(p. 106) **Rusty carried his own answers ...** The following paragraph draws on Peters' own account in: Cath Bowdler et al., *Two Laws... One Big Spirit*, 24HR Art, Darwin, 2000, unpaginated.

Juwulinypany / Bow River

(p. 112) **... the front page of *The Kimberley Echo* ...** Aaron Busch, 'Road Crash Sparks Chemical Spill Scare', *The Kimberley Echo*, 17 December 1998.

(p. 113) **The house in Gippsland was surrounded ...** The following passages draw on unpublished writing by Tony Oliver: '... the surface of his winter flesh' is his phrasing.

(p. 115) **At face value, Curnow, an ex-lawyer ...** Details of Kevin Curnow's role in Balangarri's collapse are drawn from: Sally Neighbour and Morag Ramsay, 'Catch Me if You Can', *Four Corners*, ABC Television, broadcast 20 March 2001.

(p. 117) **That had been the home of ...** Ann Marie Ingham, *Pioneers of the Kimberley: The Maggie Lilly Story*, Halstead Press, Sydney, 2000, pp. 87–89.

(p. 120) **In one work ...** Details of Timms's two paintings are drawn from: Sotheby's, *Important Aboriginal Art*, auction catalogue, Sotheby's Australia, Melbourne, July 2007, Lot 36 & 37, pp. 48–49.

(p. 122) **Timmy was no stranger ...** Following details drawn from: Leon Morris, 'Obituary: Kamaliny Palmentarri (Timmy Timms)', *The Sydney Morning Herald*, 16 January 2001.

(p. 126) **She had been a little girl ...** Kofod and Morris, 'Neminuwarlin Performance Group History', p. 10.

(p. 127) **When they spoke in Kriol or English ...** The following details are in part drawn from: Kofod and Morris, 'Neminuwarlin Performance Group History', p. 11.

(p. 128) **The icon of this was a dance object called the woorrangoo ...** The following paragraphs, including details regarding the woorrangoo, draw in part from: Arnaud Morvan, 'The East Kimberley Painting Movement: Performing Colonial History', in *Australian Aboriginal Anthropology Today: Critical Perspectives from Europe*, Symposium proceedings of the Musée du Quai Branly Jacques Chirac, 2014, http://actesbranly.revues.org/579; and Arnaud Morvan, 'Performing Landscape and Memory: Kija Local and Global Art in Circulation', in Jaynie Anderson (ed.), *Crossing Cultures: Conflict Migration and Convergence*, Miegunyah/University of Melbourne Press, Melbourne, 2009, pp. 797–892.

(p. 129) **The mine, which would soon negotiate ...** These further developments, including the role of the manthe ceremony at the mine, are detailed in: Kim Doohan, *Making Things Come Good: Relations Between Aborigines and Miners at Argyle*, Backroom Press, Broome, 2008, pp. 115–139.

(p. 132) **Peggy spoke with a striking theatricality ...** The following paragraph draws in part from: Cath Bowdler, 'Looking Forward, Looking Back: In the East Kimberley', *Artlink*, June 2005, pp. 44–47. The observation that Peggy Patrick was in tears as she spoke is Bowdler's.

(p. 134) **If the whole scene appeared unwieldy ...** The following paragraph draws in part from: Debra Jopson, 'A Big Boss is Buried In the Land He Loved', *The Sydney Morning Herald*, 5 February 2001.

(p. 135) **In the coming days he would publish ...** Morris, 'Obituary: Kamaliny Palmentarri (Timmy Timms)'.

Bedford Downs

(p. 140) **In its first years Bedford Downs had been a wild place ...** Historical details concerning Bedford Downs Station are drawn from: Clement, 'Historical Notes Relevant to Impact Stories of the East Kimberley', pp. 3–4. Frances Kofod also recounts historical aspects of Bedford Downs and the broader pastoral history of the East Kimberley in: Frances Kofod, 'Paddy Bedford and Kimberley History', in Georges Petitjean & Akkie Groen (eds.), *Paddy Bedford: Crossing Frontiers*, AAMU–Museum of Contemporary Aboriginal Art, Utrecht, 2009, pp. 49–55.

(p. 141) **He was one of six children ...** The following passages draw biographical details of Paddy Quilty from: Cathie Clement, 'Quilty, Thomas John (1887 – 1979)', *Australian Dictionary of Biography*, National Centre of Biography, Australian National University, http://adb.anu.edu.au/biography/quilty-thomas-john-11471/text20453, published first in hardcopy 2002.

(p. 141) **The pastoralists pushed westward ...** For an in-depth account of the violent settlement of the Queensland Gulf see: Tony Roberts, *Frontier Justice: A History of the Gulf Country to 1900*, University of Queensland Press, Brisbane, 2005.

(p. 141) **The women worked at the homestead ...** The following passages draw on the oral history account of Gija man Charlie McAdam, who was born on Springvale Station in the mid-1930s. He describes station life in detail, including wet season 'holidays', and related practices described here. See: Charlie McAdam and family (as told to Elizabeth Tregenza), *Boundary Lines*, McPhee Gribble/Penguin Books, Ringwood, Victoria, 1995, pp. 6–13. The cultural aspects of wet season 'holidays' are also detailed in: Jebb, *Blood, Sweat and Welfare*, pp. 172–178.

(p. 142) **To the south-west, for instance, lay Barlooban ...** Frances Kofod, 'Barlooban–Motor Car Yard', in Michael (ed.), *Paddy Bedford*, p. 94.

(p. 142) **To look up at night was to recall Kunjin ...** Story recounted in: McAdam, *Boundary Lines*, pp. 4–5.

(p. 145) **... although songs associated with someone ...** Peggy Patrick quoted in: Kofod and Morris, 'Neminuwarlin Performance Group History', p. 12.

(p. 147) **... on one trip Tony and Paddy accompanied him ...** The following paragraphs draw additional detail from: Kofod and Morris, 'Neminuwarlin Performance Group History', p. 12.

(p. 148) **... Quilty was 'only a little bit bad' ...** Paddy Bedford quoted in: Dolk, 'Are We Strangers in this Place?', p. 18.

(p. 151) **... the cast had in large part been identified ...** Cast details in the following paragraphs draw in part from: 'The Cast: Actors and Dancers', *Fire, Fire Burning Bright*, Theatre Program, pp. 16–17.

(p. 154) **... according to Rover Thomas's *Guirr-Guirr* ...** See: Kim Ackerman, 'Rover Thomas: Tribute', *Artlink*, March 2000, pp. 22–23.

(p. 155) **Rusty painted a work that detailed ...** See account of Rusty Peters (as told to Frances Kofod) in: Starr (ed.), *Blood on the Spinifex*, pp. 54–56.

(p. 155) **Kofod would later recount ...** Starr (ed.), *Blood on the Spinifex*, pp. 54–56.

(p. 155) **Phyllis painted a work that was ...** Starr (ed.), *Blood on the Spinifex*, pp. 52–53.

(p. 156) **As with Phyllis's painting, Goody's also depicted two narratives ...** Starr (ed.), *Blood on the Spinifex*, pp. 46–48.

(p. 157) **Nyadbi knew the same story ...** Starr (ed.), *Blood on the Spinifex*, pp. 50–51.

(p. 157) **She painted a story that Timmy had first covered ...** Starr (ed.), *Blood on the Spinifex*, pp. 36–39.

(p. 166) **Major's story, a kind of Kimberley legend ...** Details of Major's story are drawn from: Bruce Shaw, 'Heroism Against White Rule: The "Rebel" Major', in Eric Fry (ed.), *Rebels and Radicals*, Allen & Unwin, Sydney, pp. 8–26; and Bruce Shaw, *Banggaiyerri: the Story of Jack Sullivan, as told to Bruce Shaw*, Australian Institute of Aboriginal Studies, Canberra, 1983, pp. 70–74 and pp. 215–219.

(p. 168) **The official police account ...** PC Fanning quoted in: Shaw, *Banggaiyerri*, p. 216.

(p. 169) **Jandamarra's skull was sent ...** Howard Pedersen and Banjo Woorunmurra, *Jandamarra and the Bunuba Resistance*, Magabala Books, Broome, p. 194; see also June Oscar, address to Centre for Australian Studies, Kings College London, 29 April 2015, https://aiatsis.gov.au/explore/articles/encountering-truth-real-life-stories-objects-empires-frontier-and-beyond

(p. 169) **Across the top of the left-hand panels ...** Painting details are drawn from: Starr (ed.), *Blood on the Spinifex*, p. 44.

(p. 170) **That visit had drawn the ire of Keith Windschuttle ...** A detailed account of this episode is found in: Cathie Clement, 'Mistake Creek', in Manne (ed.), *Whitewash*, pp. 119–214.

Ironwood Drive

(p. 192) **... a run of high-profile authorship-centred scandals.** See, for example: Fred Myers, *Painting Culture: The Making of an Aboriginal High Art*, Duke University Press, Durham and London, 2002, pp. 323–330; and Vivien Johnson, 'The "Aboriginal Art Scandals" Scandal', *Artlink*, December 1999, pp. 32–35.

(p. 192) **There were more recent reports of paintings made to order ...** See, for example: Nicolas Rothwell, 'Scams in the Desert', *The Australian*, 4–5 March 2006.

(p. 196) **... the horizontal had turned vertical.** I owe this reading to Peter Adsett.

(p. 200) **In 2005, Rusty would find himself at the show's opening ...** This photograph was printed in: Matt Price, 'Black's Art "our greatest cultural gift"', *The Australian*, 29 November 2005.

(p. 205) ***... a man of few words and great silences ...*** Nicolas Rothwell, *Belomor*, Text Publishing, Melbourne, 2013, p. 120.

(p. 205) ***... on the phone and waving her hands ...*** Nicolas Rothwell, *Another Country*, Black Inc., Melbourne, 2007, p. 229.

(p. 205) **...** ***rake thin,*** **staring into a** ***world of geometric archetypes.*** Rothwell, *Another Country*, p. 230.

(p. 205) **... a** ***Melbourne art scene enfant terrible*** **...** Rothwell, *Another Country*, p. 225.

(p. 205) **... a** ***captivating, drama-courting figure*** **...** Rothwell, *Belomor*, p. 119.

(p. 205) **...** ***the most idiosyncratic of all bush impresarios*** **...** Nicolas Rothwell, 'A Bridge Between Worlds', *The Weekend Australian Review*, 18–19 April 2009.

(p. 215) **In the graveyard it was the same scene ...** The following passages draw on unpublished writing by Tony Oliver.

Wyndham

(p. 225) **The fact they might one day take up the brush ...** Additional details are drawn from: Nicolas Rothwell, 'The Writing's on the Wall', *The Weekend Australian Review*, 19–20 January 2013.

(p. 227) **... a piece eventually published in** ***The New York Times.*** Eric Marx, 'For Aboriginal Artists, Western Ideas and Techniques From a City Maverick', *The New York Times*, 1 June 2005.

(p. 231) **This was a world in which everyday life ...** The following passage draws on: Rothwell, *Another Country*, pp. 111–114.

(p. 241) **He soon penned his own essay ...** The following details and quotes are drawn from: Tony Oliver, 'Women's Business', in *Women's Business*, Sherman Galleries, Sydney, 2006, unpaginated.

(p. 243) **The first was his article ...** Nicolas Rothwell, 'A Dream of a Studio', *The Weekend Australian Review*, 21–22 July 2007, p. 9.

(p. 244) **In it, he recounted his late-night arrival ...** Rothwell, *Belomor*, pp. 150–151.

(p. 244) **The next morning Tony's complex feelings ...** The following passage draws on: Rothwell, *Belomor*, pp. 158–160.

(p. 248) **The story told of the white cockatoo ancestor ...** Frances Kofod, 'Cockatoo Dreaming', in Michael (ed.), *Paddy Bedford.*, p. 84.

Epilogue: Vietnam

(p. 257) **Reports that soon gathered ...** Rebecca Ratcliffe, 'Vietnam Braced for Second Storm After Devastating Impact of Typhoon Damrey', *The Guardian*, 11 November 2017.

Image credits

p. 1 Paddy Bedford painting at Ironwood Drive, Kununurra, 2005, photographer Tony Oliver

p. 9 Kimberley landscape, photographer Simon Georgeff

p. 49 Paddy Bedford painting at Pindan Avenue, Kununurra, 1998, photographer Simon Georgeff

p. 77 Rugun community sign, 1998, photographer Martin Browne

p. 109 Paddy Bedford in Darwin, holding a brochure from his recent Sydney solo exhibition at Martin Browne Fine Art, 2001, photographer Dallas Gold

p. 137 Rammey Ramsey dancing in *Fire, Fire Burning Bright*, Melbourne, 2002, photographer Giancarlo Mazzella

p. 171 Tony Oliver with works by Freddie Timms, Ironwood Drive, Kununurra, 2002, photographer Giancarlo Mazzella

p. 217 Tony Oliver at the Jirrawun studio, Wyndham, 2007, photographer Peter Eve

p. 253 Kimberley landscape, photographer Simon Georgeff